Xiaochun Yun · Weiping Wen
Bo Lang · Hanbing Yan · Li Ding
Jia Li · Yu Zhou (Eds.)

Cyber Security

15th International Annual Conference, CNCERT 2018
Beijing, China, August 14–16, 2018
Revised Selected Papers

Editors
Xiaochun Yun
CNCERT
Beijing, China

Weiping Wen
Peking University
Beijing, China

Bo Lang
Beihang University
Beijing, China

Hanbing Yan
CNCERT
Beijing, China

Li Ding
CNCERT
Beijing, China

Jia Li
CNCERT
Beijing, China

Yu Zhou
CNCERT
Beijing, China

https://doi.org/10.1007/978-981-13-6621-5

Preface

The China Cyber Security Annual Conference is the annual event of the National Computer Network Emergency Response Technical Team/Coordination Center of China (hereinafter referred to as CNCERT/CC). Since 2004, CNCERT/CC has successfully held 14 China Cyber Security Annual Conferences. As an important bridge for technical and service exchange on cyber security affairs among industry and academics, as well as research and application, the conference has played an active role in safeguarding cyber security and raising social awareness.

This year, the China Cyber Security Annual Conference 2018 was held in Beijing, China, during August 14–16, 2018, as the 15th event in the series. The theme of the conference was "Leveraging Smarter Technologies for a More Secure Ecosystem." The mission was to present and share a new emerging focus and concerns on cybersecurity, and to discuss new countermeasures or approaches to deal with them. There were over 2,500 attendees at the conference. Please refer to the following URL for more information about the event: http://conf.cert.org.cn.

The papers contained in these proceedings of CNCERT 2018 address a series of cyber-related issues ranging from negative logic system, privacy protection-based access control schemes, mobile devices security management, malware detection with neural networks, malicious website identification, blockchain security, Android malware detection, APT attack defense, and vulnerability leak detection, to name just a few.

We announced our call for papers (in Chinese) on the conference website, after which 53 submissions were received by the deadline from authors at a wide range of affiliations, including research institutions, NGOs, universities, and companies. After receiving all submissions, we randomly assigned five papers to every reviewer, and every paper was reviewed by three reviewers. All submissions were judged on their credibility of innovation, contribution, reference value, significance of research, language quality, and originality. We adopted a thorough and competitive reviewing and selection process that took place in two rounds. We first invited the reviewers to provide an initial review. Based on the comments received, 27 papers passed and the authors of these 27 pre-accepted papers made modifications accordingly. In the second round, their modified papers were reviewed again. Finally, 15 out of the 53 submissions stood out and were accepted. The acceptance rate was 28.3%. However, at the last minute, one of the 15 dropped out and thus finally 14 papers were published.

We sincerely thank all authors for their interest in participating, and our thanks also go to the Program Committee chair and members for their considerable efforts and dedication to this program in helping us solicit and select papers of quality and creativity.

We hope these proceedings of CNCERT 2018 will serve not only as a snapshot of the current cyber landscape and developments, but also as a catalyst and inspiring work for your own research toward a securely shaped cyber world.

November 2018

Xiaochun Yun
Weiping Wen
Bo Lang
Hanbing Yan
Li Ding
Jia Li
Yu Zhou

Organization

Program Committee

Program Chair

Xiaochun Yun	CNCERT, China

Program Committee Members

Weiping Wen	Peking University, China
Xinhui Han	Institute of Computer Science and Technology, Peking University, China
Kangjie Lu	University of Minnesota, USA
Haixin Duan	Tsinghua University, China
Chao Zhang	Tsinghua University, China
Dawn Song	University of California, Berkeley, USA
Xinguang Xiao	Antiy Corporation, China
Bo Lang	Beihang University, China
Stevens Le Blond	Max Planck Institute for Software Systems, Germany
Senlin Luo	Beijing University of Technology, China
Baoxu Liu	Institute of Information Engineering, China Academy of Sciences, China
Guoai Xu	Beijing University of Posts and Telecommunications, China
Xueying Li	Topsec Corporation, China
Yongzheng Zhang	Institute of Information Engineering, China Academy of Sciences, China
Yuanzhuo Wang	Institute of Computing Technology, China Academy of Sciences, China
Min Yang	Fudan University, China
Purui Su	Institute of Software, China Academy of Sciences, China
Guojun Peng	Wuhan University, China
Hua Zhang	Beijing University of Posts and Telecommunications, China
Siri Bromander	University of Oslo, Norway
Xu Meng	Georgia Institute of Technology, USA
Daniel Scofield	Assured Information Security, USA
Khundrakpam Johnson Singh	National Institute of Technology, India
Bryan Perozzi	Stony Brook University, USA
M. E. J. Newman	University of Michigan, USA
Yaniv David	Technion, Israel

Zoubin Ghahramani	University of Cambridge, UK
Andrew Ng	Stanford University, USA
Michael Backesa	Saarland University and CISPA-Stanford Center, Germany and USA
Christopher Kruegel	University of California, USA
Hanbing Yan	CNCERT, China
Li Ding	CNCERT, China
Jia Li	CNCERT, China
Yu Zhou	CNCERT, China
Teng Zhang	CNCERT, China

Contents

Identity Authentication

Research on Identity Authentication Method Based on Negative Logic System

Yexia Cheng[1,2,3(✉)], Yuejin Du[1,2,4(✉)], Jin Peng[3(✉)], Jun Fu[3], and Baoxu Liu[1,2]

[1] Institute of Information Engineering, Chinese Academy of Sciences, Beijing, China
chengyexia@iie.ac.cn
[2] School of Cyber Security, University of Chinese Academy of Sciences, Beijing, China
[3] Department of Security Technology, China Mobile Research Institute, Beijing, China
pengjin@chinamobile.com
[4] Security Department, Alibaba Group, Beijing, China
yuejin.dyj@alibaba-inc.com

Abstract. With the rapid development of computer and network, new technologies and services such as mobile Internet, Internet of Things, cloud and artificial intelligence have arisen and changed people's life. The identity authentication is a must for these services. To solve the problem, identity authentication system and method based on negative logic system (NLS) is proposed in the paper. NLS is introduced to improve security in the essence of attack and defense. Security mechanisms based on NLS are proved effective to increase attack cost and strengthen defense ability. So NLS-based identity authentication system and method in the cloud environment are designed. Meanwhile, the corresponding converters, distributed storage, distributed detectors and authentication are proposed. The proposed method can improve security and provide identity authentication for cloud, IoT, etc. The theoretical performance analysis proves that it is feasible and effective.

Keywords: Negative Logic System · Attack and defense · Identity authentication · Cloud security · Secure accessing · Internet of Things

1 Introduction

With the rapid development of computer and network, new technologies and services are being generated, evolved and promoted constantly, bringing great convenience and changes to people's life. Of which, mobile Internet, Internet of Things, cloud and artificial intelligence are all becoming the rising topics. Concerning to these technologies and services, the identity authentication is the precondition to guarantee secure accessing. Taking cloud environment as an example, it has some features and advantages such as broadband interconnection, resource pool sharing, flexible configuration, on-demand services, etc. However, while providing services and sharing resources in an open cloud environment, how to ensure the confidentiality, integrity, and availability

X. Yun et al. (Eds.): CNCERT 2018, CCIS 970, pp. 3–15, 2019.
https://doi.org/10.1007/978-981-13-6621-5_1

of system resources and user's data in the cloud is an important issue, and identity authentication is a premise guarantee to achieve this goal.

The researchers have already taken some studies on identity authentication. At present, Ghosh et al. focus on NFC and biometric algorithms [1]. Chien proposes video recognition technology [2]. Hu et al. point out the privacy protection using images and identity information [3]. And some other researchers propose the identity based encryption [4–10]. Of which, the identity based encryption is a new tendency for identity authentication. Urbi et al. propose PUF+IBE scheme, which contains the identity authentication algorithm for Internet of Things devices and its connection and protocol process based on elliptic curve [4]. In the field of aviation aircraft, a layered identity-based authentication IBV scheme is proposed. Wu et al. talk about the mobile device authentication and key agreement protocol based on elliptic curve [5]. Yuan et al. propose identity-based identification, mobile identity identification solutions based on IBI [6].

Although the research on identity authentication are more and more, there is a common problem on it, that is all the researches are based on positive logic system. It means that the user account authentication and other information are all stored in the identity authentication system based on positive logic system. Once the user's account is leaked or stolen, the attacker can make use of the acquired user information to access to the system and resources. Even worse, the attacker uses it as a springboard for taking deep cyber attack and penetration, which is a great security risk for the whole system. In addition, the security bottleneck of identity authentication lies in the selection of the authentication algorithm, which is the attacker's focused attack goal. If the authentication algorithm is attacked, the security of the entire cloud environment is hard to guarantee. Furthermore, the existing identity authentication technology does not involve the elements of a distributed cluster in the cloud environment, which has certain limitations in adaptability and scalability.

In order to solve the above problems, we propose the negative logic system (NLS) and take research on the method of identity authentication based on negative logic system in this paper. The identity authentication system and method based on negative logic system is proposed in the paper. NLS is introduced to improve security in the essence of attack and defense. Security mechanisms based on NLS are proved effective to increase attack cost and strengthen defense ability. So NLS-based identity authentication system and method in the cloud environment are designed. Meanwhile, the corresponding converters, distributed storage, distributed detectors and authentication are proposed. The proposed method can improve security and provide identity authentication for cloud, IoT, etc. The theoretical performance analysis proves that it is feasible and effective.

Our Innovations and Contributions. In this paper, there are some innovations and contributions. One of which is the negative logic system. The other is the security attack and defense mechanisms based on negative logic system. The third is the identity authentication method based on negative logic system. And the last is the method of converters and distributed storage based on NLS as well as the method of distributed detectors and authentication based on NLS.

The rest of this paper is organized as follows. Section 2 introduces the motivation. Section 3 proposes negative logic system. Section 4 presents security attack and defense mechanisms based on negative logic system. Section 5 proposes the identity authentication system and method based on NLS. Finally, in Sect. 6 we draw the conclusion of this paper.

2 Motivation

The existing security attack and defense mechanisms are based on the security attack and defense mechanisms of the positive logic system (PLS), that is to say, the state description of the security attack and defense is positive to the logic description of the security attack and defense. Hence, in the PLS-based security attack and defense mechanisms, the information is same and equal for both offensive and defensive sides. The essence of security attack and defense is the cost and expense of both offensive and defensive sides taken while attacking and defending. On the basis of information equivalence, the degree of confrontation, the superiority and inferiority status and the active and passive situation of both offensive and defensive sides can only rely on the cost and expense of cyber attack and defense tactics.

Therefore, the disadvantage of the existing PLS-based security attack and defense mechanisms is the limitation of offensive and defensive information equivalence. Firstly, on the basis of PLS, information is a one-to-one correspondence. Relatively speaking, the attacker can use a large number of attack groups to achieve an attack. The attack group here is a broad group that includes both the actual attacker population and any host, device, or computer network system that can be used in the network. Secondly, the existing attack and defense mechanisms increase the cost of information network defense side relatively. When it comes to the network or system of defensive side, it can be protected and defended by the defensive side only. For the decentralized or centralized attack methods and attack groups, only by strengthening the protection system of the defense side, can it be possible to defend against the attacker's attack, so that the defense cost and expense is much greater.

In order to solve the disadvantage of the existing mechanisms, the security attack and defense mechanisms based on negative logic system are innovatively proposed in the paper. That's the motivation of this paper. The NLS-based security attack and defense mechanisms can break the situation of information equivalence between offensive and defensive sides, so as to achieve that the information for both offensive and defensive sides is not equal, and then increase the cost and expense of cyber attacks, and meanwhile reduce the cost and expense of cyber defense.

What's more, the method of using the negative logic system for identity authentication is also proposed innovatively. And this NLS-based identity authentication method can be applied not only in the cloud environment but also in the Internet of Things (IoT) environment, which is of great significance to secure accessing.

3 Negative Logic System

We innovatively propose the negative logic system in the cyber security area together with the security attack and defense mechanisms based on negative logic system as well as the principle and method of our negative logic system.

Principle and Method of Negative Logic System. The principle and method of our negative logic system is described as follows.

The negative logic system is the opposite logic to the positive logic [11–17], and the corresponding relationship is 1:N mode, i.e. a one-to-many relationship. As for the formal language description, it can adopt the normal binary, octal, decimal, or hexadecimal formats, and it can also use the state number of the practical applications as well, for example, the state number of the application is N, then it can use N bases. Therefore, its formal language description method is flexible and can be selected according to the requirements.

We take the actual state number as an example to give the formal language description and definition of negative logic system. Assuming that there are n kinds of states in a system, which are defined as $S_1, S_2, S_3, \ldots\ldots, S_n$. Let $S = \{S_1, S_2, S_3, \ldots\ldots, S_n\}$, so that for any state $S_i \in S$, in which $i \in \{1, 2, 3, \ldots\ldots, n\}$, the negative logic value of S_i is any one of the states in S except S_i. That is to say, $NLS(S_i) \stackrel{def}{=} \{S_j | S_j \in S, S_j \neq S_i, j \in \{1, 2, 3, \ldots\ldots, n\}\}$.

The method of NLS is illustrated in following Fig. 1.

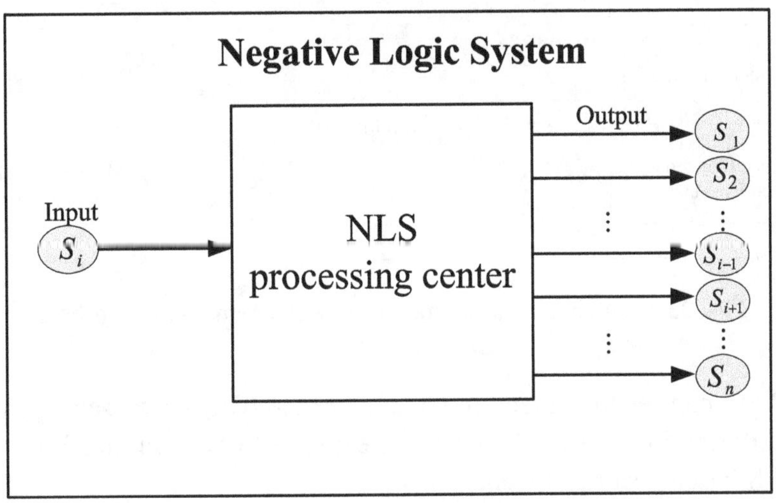

Fig. 1. Method of NLS

According to the above Fig. 1, the method of NLS is combined with input, NLS processing center and output.

As for input item, it is the value for inputting, which is transferred to the NLS processing center. The input value can be data information formatted in binary base, data information formatted in decimal base, data information or text information formatted in hexadecimal base, etc.

As for NLS processing center, it includes NLS processing mechanisms, the choosing and the transforming of number bases, selecting algorithm, calculation method, etc. Its main function is to determine the negative logic values according to the input and give result to the output part. For example, when the input is S_i, the negative logic values are in the following sets $\{S_1\}, \{S_2\}, \cdots, \{S_{i-1}\}, \{S_{i+1}\}, \cdots, \{S_n\}$.

As for output item, one of the negative logic values will be output randomly according to the selecting method and the calculation method set in the NLS processing center and even the time the input value being inputted into the NLS processing center. Taking the above example, one of $\{S_1\}, \{S_2\}, \cdots, \{S_{i-1}\}, \{S_{i+1}\}, \cdots, \{S_n\}$ may be outputted as the actual output value, such as S_2 at this moment. So the negative logic system result for S_i at the moment is S_2.

4 Security Attack and Defense Mechanisms Based on Negative Logic System

The structure of security attack and defense mechanisms based on negative logic system is shown in Fig. 2 below. It is comprised of the attack module, NLS module and defense module.

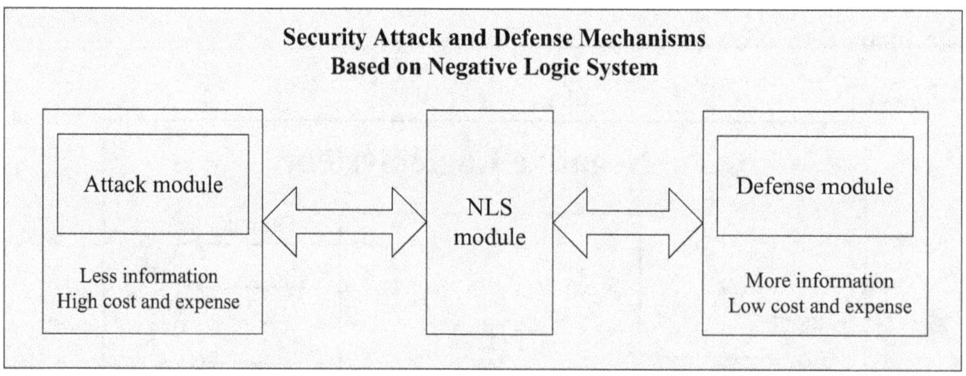

Fig. 2. Security attack and defense mechanisms based on NLS

In Fig. 2, we can see that attack module under the NLS-based security mechanisms is with less information so that the cost and expense to take an attack is much higher than ever PLS-based security mechanisms.

NLS module is the negative logic system and it is implemented according to the principle described in Fig. 1.

Defense module is under the NLS-based security mechanisms and its information is much more so that the cost and expense to take defense is much lower than ever PLS-based security mechanisms.

The performance analysis of security attack and defense mechanisms based on NLS is presented as follows.

According to the NLS principle and method, and combing with the security attack and defense mechanisms based on NLS, it is assumed that the number of states of a system is n, which are defined as $S_1, S_2, S_3, \ldots\ldots, S_n$. Let $S = \{S_1, S_2, S_3, \ldots\ldots, S_n\}$, so based on NLS, there are $n - 1$ possible kinds of negative logic value for any state $S_i \in S$, such as $\{S_1\}, \{S_2\}, \cdots, \{S_{i-1}\}, \{S_{i+1}\}, \cdots, \{S_n\}$. Therefore, in order to get the value of S_i, at least $n - 1$ different values after data de-duplicating must be given. And by combing and analyzing, the value of S_i can be computed. Compared to the PLS, to get the value of S_i requiring only 1 value, the space of NLS is much greater than PLS. As for the entire system space, the space of PLS is n, while the space of NLS is $n(n-1)$. When a logic value is given, the probability of a successful PLS judgment is $\frac{1}{n}$, while the probability of a successful NLS judgment is $\frac{1}{n(n-1)}$.

In the security attack and defense mechanisms based on NLS, the defense side knows the number of all the states as well as the scope of the whole system space. It is therefore that the information for the defense side is much more than the attack side, and the cost and expense that needed to take is much lower.

However, as for the attack side in the security attack and defense mechanisms based on NLS, objectively speaking, the whole system security space is greatly expanded at first. It is expanded to the second power relationship for NLS from the linear relationship for PLS. Secondly, in the actual attack and defense, the attack side doesn't know or cannot get known of the number of all states such as n, so that, even if the attacker obtains k kinds of different logical values, the attacker cannot know how many times it still needs to get the correct information he wants when he doesn't know n. Thus, the complexity and difficulty of the attack is greatly increased. It is therefore that the information for the attack side is less than the defense side, and the cost and expense required for the attack side is much higher and more.

From the viewpoint of the essence of security attack and defense, the essence of the attack lies in the cost and expense of taking attack, while the essence of the defense lies in the cost and expense of taking defense. From the above performance analysis, we can know that the security attack and defense mechanisms based on NLS can essentially increase the cost and expense required for the attack and reduce the cost and expense required for the defense. The security attack and defense mechanisms based on NLS are of important practical value and significance in the field of security.

5 Identity Authentication System and Method Based on Negative Logic System

Based on the proposed negative logic system, we propose NLS-based identity authentication. The NLS-based identity authentication system and method can be applied not only in the cloud environment but also in the Internet of Things environment, which is of great significance to secure accessing. Here we take cloud environment as a specific application scene. And we will give out the identity authentication system and method based on NLS in the cloud environment as well as the method of converters and distributed storage based on NLS, and the method of distributed detectors and authentication based on NLS.

Firstly, we compare our NLS-based identity authentication system and method with the existing identity authentication system and method.

The existing identity authentication system and method are all based on positive logic system. It means that the user account authentication and other information are all stored in the identity authentication system based on positive logic system. Once the user's account is leaked or stolen, the attacker can make use of the acquired user information to access to the system and resources. Even worse, the attacker uses it as a springboard for taking deep cyber attack and penetration, which is a great security risk for the whole system. In addition, the security bottleneck of identity authentication lies in the selection of the authentication algorithm, which is the attacker's focused attack goal. If the authentication algorithm is attacked, the security of the entire cloud environment is hard to guarantee. Furthermore, the existing identity authentication method and system does not involve the elements of a distributed cluster in the cloud environment, which has certain limitations in adaptability and scalability.

The identity authentication system and method based on negative logic system can break the situation of information equivalence between offensive and defensive sides from the essence. The information for both offensive and defensive sides of identity authentication system is not equal. It can increase the cost and expense of cyber attacks of the system, and meanwhile reduce the cost and expense of cyber defense of the system. Besides, this NLS-based identity authentication method can be applied not only in the cloud environment but also in the Internet of Things (IoT) environment, etc., which is of great significance to secure accessing. And according to the theoretical performance analysis in Sect. 4, it proves that it is feasible and effective.

5.1 Identity Authentication System Based on NLS in the Cloud Environment

The system structure of identity authentication system based on NLS in cloud environment is shown as follows, in Fig. 3.

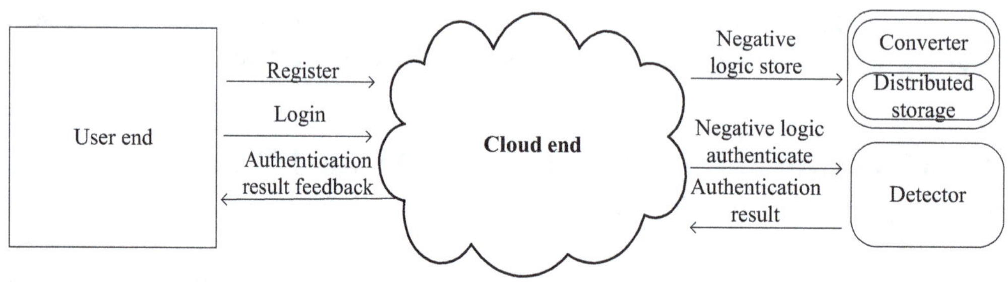

Fig. 3. System structure of identity authentication system based on NLS in the cloud environment

As is illustrated in Fig. 3, the system structure is comprised of user end, cloud end, converter, distributed storage and detector. The procedure of the system mainly contains two periods, one of which is the period of user registering, the other of which is the period of login authenticating.

(1) **User Registering Period**

In user registering period, at first, the user end is used to send register information to the cloud end.

The cloud end receives the register information from the user end and obtains the set of user identity information based on the negative logic system through the negative logic converter, and then distributes the negative logic-based identity information set by the distributed storage.

The converter is used to receive the information from cloud end and transform the information to the negative logic presentation and then obtain the set of NLS-based identity information.

The distributed storage is used for receiving identity information from the converter and distributing them to storage.

(2) **Login Authenticating Period**

In the login authenticating period, the user end is used for sending user's login information to the cloud end and receiving the authentication result from the cloud end.

The cloud end can receive the login information set sent from user end and then transport the login information set to the detector so as to take distributed detection and then get the authentication result. Besides, the cloud end receives the authentication result and then feedbacks the identity authentication result to the user end.

The detector is used to receive the login information from the cloud end and take distributed detection. The authentication result can be concluded according to the comparison of the number of matched detector with the maximum number of tolerances. After that, the authentication result is outputted to the cloud end.

5.2 Identity Authentication Method Based on NLS in the Cloud Environment

The following Fig. 4 describes the method of identity authentication based on NLS in the cloud environment.

According to the above Fig. 4, the method of identity authentication based on NLS in the cloud environment includes the following steps.

Step 1: User's registration requesting. The user end sends request to the cloud end with the user's registration information.

Step 2: User's registration information obtaining. The cloud end obtains user's registration information.

Step 3: Identity information transforming. Extract corresponding information from registration information, and transform identity information based on NLS to obtain the corresponding NLS-based identity information set. For example, there are n kinds of NLS-based identity information. Concerning with the information, only when not less than m kinds of different identity information are obtained at the same time, then the identity information of the user can be authenticated. Here, m is the maximum number of tolerances to authenticate.

Step 4: Distributed storing. Distribute the n kinds of NLS-based identity information to distributed storage.

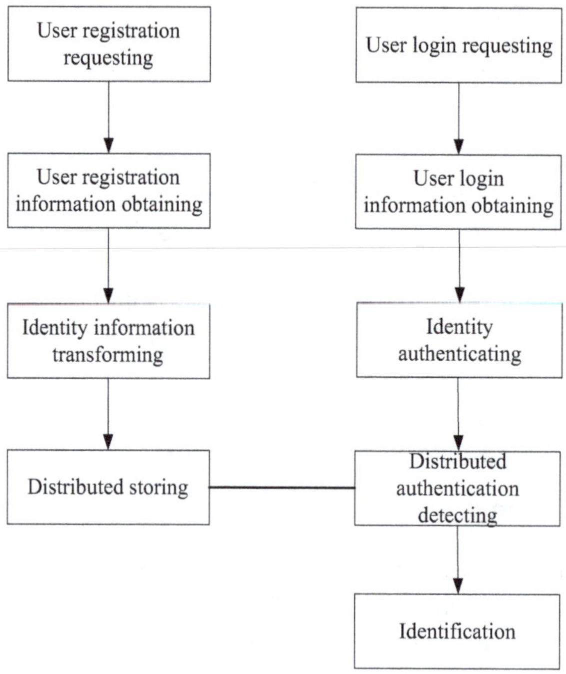

Fig. 4. Method of identity authentication based on NLS in the cloud environment

Step 5: User login requesting. The user end sends request to the cloud end with the user login information set.
Step 6: User login information obtaining. The cloud end obtains user login information set.
Step 7: Identity authenticating. The cloud end begins identity authenticating procedure.
Step 8: Distributed authentication detecting. Distributed detect the user login information set. Assuming that user login information set contains t kinds of different identity information. By detecting based on NLS, the number of matched detectors will be figured out, e.g. the number is k. Then compare k with the maximum number of tolerances m. Only when $k \geq m$, the user information can be gotten, otherwise the user information cannot be gotten.
Step 9: Identification. According to the result of Step 8, the identification is taken out.

5.3 Method of Converters and Distributed Storage Based on NLS

As in the above, we can know that, the method of converters and distributed storage is of great importance to the identity authentication based on NLS. So Fig. 5 shows the specific method of converters and distributed storage based on NLS.

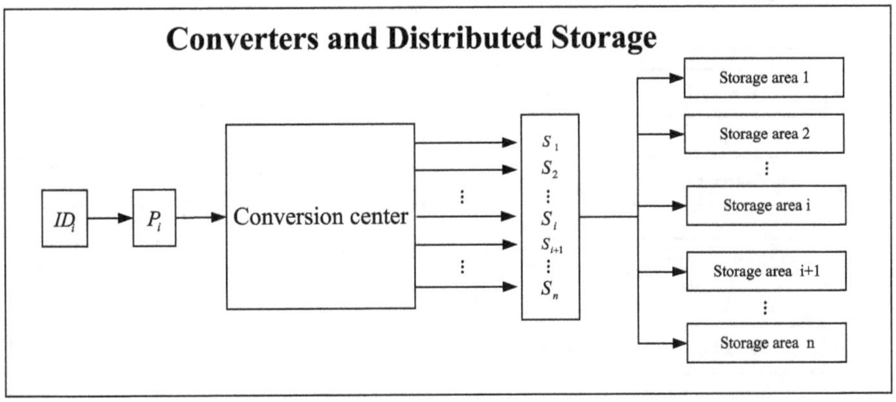

Fig. 5. Method of converters and distributed storage based on NLS

We can see from Fig. 5 that the method procedure of converters and distributed storage based on NLS includes five components. For the first thing, input the user's registration information, for example the user's registration information is written as ID_i. For the second thing, obtain the user's original identity information, which is written as P_i.

For the third thing, the conversion center, which is based on NLS, is the main function and component. Assuming that the user's registration information is ID_i and the related original real identity information is 1 kind, denoted as P_i, the corresponding non-real identity information is n kinds, written as $S_1, S_2, S_3, \ldots\ldots, S_n$. Let $T = \{P_i, S_1, S_2, S_3, \ldots\ldots, S_n\}$, then as for user's registration information ID_i, the corresponding NLS-based identity information set is $T' = T - \{P_i\}$, i.e. $T' = \{S_1, S_2, S_3, \ldots\ldots, S_n\}$. The conversion result will be outputted to the next component, receiving the identity information set T' based on NLS of ID_i, that is $\{S_1, S_2, S_3, \ldots\ldots, S_n\}$.

And for the last thing, the identity information set T' based on NLS of ID_i is distributed to different storage area, such as storage area 1, 2, $\cdots$, i, i + 1, $\cdots$, n.

5.4 Method of Distributed Detectors and Authentication Based on NLS

The procedure of distributed detectors and authentication based on NLS is shown in Fig. 6. It is the distributed detecting and authenticating based on negative logic system, in which, the maximum number of tolerances is m, that is to say, the identity information of the user can be authenticated with at least m kinds of different identity information.

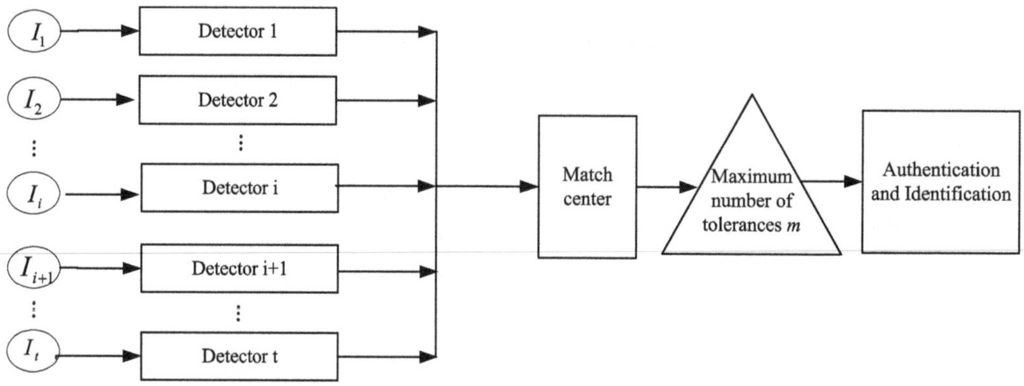

Fig. 6. Method of distributed detectors and authentication based on NLS

In Fig. 6, we get the user's login information set and extract different elements as $I_1, I_2, \cdots, I_i, I_{i+1}, \cdots, I_t$. Then we transfer them to distributed detectors.

In the detectors, let the obtained value and elements correspond to different distributed detectors, such as detector $1, 2, \cdots$, i, $\mathrm{i}+1, \cdots$, n. Meanwhile, take the detection of the t kinds of different identity information $I_1, I_2, \cdots, I_i, I_{i+1}, \cdots, I_t$ based on NLS and judge whether it belongs to the corresponding NLS-based identity information set T' of user's registration information ID_i, for which $T' = T - \{P_i\}$, and at the same time, $T' = \{S_1, S_2, S_3, \ldots\ldots, S_n\}$. Simply speaking, judge whether it belongs to the element of set T'. After that, feedback the result to the mach center. Then the match center calculates the number of matched detectors, denoted as k. And compare k with the maximum number of tolerances m. Finally, according to the result of the comparison, we take identity authentication, judging whether the user is a legal user. Only when $k \geq m$, the user's real original information can be gotten and the user begins to access to the resource in the cloud and use the resource, otherwise the user's real original information cannot be gotten, hence the user can't login and can't access to the resource in the cloud.

6 Conclusion

In this paper, identity authentication system and method based on negative logic system is proposed to solve the problem of identity authentication, NLS is introduced to improve security in the essence of attack and defense. Security mechanisms based on NLS are proved effective to increase attack cost and strengthen defense ability. So NLS-based identity authentication system and method in the cloud environment are designed. Meanwhile, the corresponding converters, distributed storage, distributed detectors and authentication are proposed. The proposed method can improve security and provide identity authentication for cloud, IoT, etc. The theoretical performance analysis proves that it is feasible and effective.

Acknowledgement. This work is supported by the National Natural Science Foundation of China (No. 61702508 and No. 61602470) and Strategic Priority Research Program of Chinese Academy of Sciences. This work is also supported by Key Laboratory of Network Assessment Technology at Chinese Academy of Sciences and Beijing Key Laboratory of Network Security and Protection Technology.

References

1. Ghosh, S., Majumder, A., Goswami, J., Kumar, A., Mohanty, S.P., Bhattacharyya, B.K.: Swing-Pay: one card meets all user payment and identity needs: a digital card module using NFC and biometric authentication for peer-to-peer payment. IEEE Consum. Electron. Mag. **6**(1), 82–93 (2017)
2. Chien, H.-Y.: Efficient authentication scheme with tag-identity protection for EPC Class 2 Generation 2 version 2 standards. IJDSN **13**(3) (2017)
3. Hu, G., Xiao, D., Xiang, T., Bai, S., Zhang, Y.: A compressive sensing based privacy preserving outsourcing of image storage and identity authentication service in cloud. Inf. Sci. **387**, 132–145 (2017)
4. Urbi, C., et al.: PUF+IBE: blending physically unclonable functions with identity based encryption for authentication and key exchange in IoTs. IACR Cryptology ePrint Archive 2017, 422 (2017)
5. Wu, L., Zhang, Y., Xie, Y., Alelaiw, A., Shen, J.: An efficient and secure identity-based authentication and key agreement protocol with user anonymity for mobile devices. Wirel. Pers. Commun. **94**(4), 3371–3387 (2017)
6. Yuan, Y., Zhao, J., Xi, W., Qian, C., Zhang, X., Wang, Z.: SALM: smartphone-based identity authentication using lip motion characteristics. In: SMARTCOMP 2017, pp. 1–8 (2017)
7. Wu, L., Zhang, Y., Choo, K.K.R., He, D.: Efficient and secure identity-based encryption scheme with equality test in cloud computing. Future Gener. Comput. Syst. **73**, 22–31 (2017)
8. Xie, Y., Wu, L., Shen, J., Alelaiwi, A.: EIAS-CP: new efficient identity-based authentication scheme with conditional privacy-preserving for VANETs. Telecommun. Syst. **65**(2), 229–240 (2017)
9. Yang, A., Tan, X., Baek, J., Wong, D.S.: A new ADS-B authentication framework based on efficient hierarchical identity-based signature with batch verification. IEEE Trans. Serv. Comput. **10**(2), 165–175 (2017)
10. Teh, T.-Y., Lee, Y.-S., Cheah, Z.-Y., Chin, J.-J.: IBI-Mobile Authentication: a prototype to facilitate access control using identity-based identification on mobile smart devices. Wirel. Pers. Commun. **94**(1), 127–144 (2017)
11. Buchman, D., Poole, D.: Negative probabilities in probabilistic logic programs. Int. J. Approx. Reason. **83**, 43–59 (2017)
12. Ori, L., João, M., Yoni, Z.: Sequent systems for negative modalities. Log. Univ. **11**(3), 345–382 (2017)
13. Thomas, S.: Decidability for some justification logics with negative introspection. J. Symb. Log. **78**(2), 388–402 (2013)
14. Norbert, G.: A sequent calculus for a negative free logic. Stud. Logica. **96**(3), 331–348 (2010)

15. Nikodem, M., Bawiec, M.A., Surmacz, T.R.: Negative difference resistance and its application to construct boolean logic circuits. In: Kwiecień, A., Gaj, P., Stera, P. (eds.) CN 2010. CCIS, vol. 79, pp. 39–48. Springer, Heidelberg (2010). https://doi.org/10.1007/978-3-642-13861-4_4
16. Lee, D.-W., Sim, K.-B.: Negative selection algorithm for DNA sequence classification. Int. J. Fuzzy Logic Intell. Syst. **4**(2), 231–235 (2004)
17. Duccio, L., Franco, M.: An operational logic of proofs with positive and negative information. Stud. Logica. **63**(1), 7–25 (1999)

Design of Multi-dimensional Electronic Channel Unified Identity Authentication Method for Power Information System

Baoxian Guo[1(✉)], Ying Xu[2], Renjie Li[1], and Xingxiong Zhu[3]

[1] State Grid Electronic Commerce Co. Ltd., Beijing, China
winzyy@163.com
[2] State Grid Zhejiang Electric Power Company, Hangzhou, China
[3] State Grid Huitongjincai (Beijing) Information Technology Co. Ltd., Beijing, China

Abstract. At present, State Grid Corporation has established a wealth of electronic service channels, including 95598 website, electric E-power, hand-held power, national network mall, E-charging, WeChat, with the rich application of various electronic channels, while gradually facilitating user use. There has been a problem of poor user experience such as registration and query service sharing, lack of unified management of multiple electronic service channels, and lack of service supervision for various electronic channels. Therefore, it is urgent to start from the source to conduct specific research on unified identity authentication system among various electronic channels. So in this paper, we proposed a multi-dimensional electronic channel unified authentication method based PKI certificate for power information system. By the proposed method, users can directly access each application system and perform fast and secure switching between application systems without multiple authentication process, providing users with the convenience and security of engaging in complex business management activities.

Keywords: Certificate · Unified authentication · Ticket

1 Introduction

In recent years, China's "Internet+" and mobile Internet technologies have been vigorously developed and widely used. All industries continue to be driven by "Internet+", making full use of Internet platforms and other electronic channels to provide convenient services to customers. The construction of a high-efficiency three-dimensional service marketing channel system presents new marketing business ecology [1]. In order to adapt to the new form of "Internet+" marketing service, State Grid Corporation put forward the "Opinions on Marketing Automation Construction Work in 2014", comprehensively deepen the construction of "big marketing" system, and guide and promote the third industrial revolution. Smart grid and the Internet, further deepen the application of marketing business systems, realize high-end applications of marketing automation based on big data and cloud computing, promote the comprehensive improvement of intelligent interaction level of power supply services. It's important to

X. Yun et al. (Eds.): CNCERT 2018, CCIS 970, pp. 16–23, 2019.
https://doi.org/10.1007/978-981-13-6621-5_2

build marketing intelligent interactive service access management to meet the unified access and services of interactive websites, Weibo, WeChat, video, mobile terminals, SMS and other service channels [2]. At present, State Grid Corporation has established a wealth of electronic service channels, including 95598 website, electric E-power, hand-held power, national network mall, E-charging, WeChat, with the rich application of various electronic channels, while gradually facilitating user use. There has been a problem of poor user experience such as registration and query service sharing, lack of unified management of multiple electronic service channels, and lack of service supervision for various electronic channels. Therefore, it is urgent to start from the source to conduct specific research on unified identity authentication among various electronic channels.

With the continuous development of information technology of State Grid Corporation and the continuous pursuit of service level and quality by State Grid Corporation, various departments and subordinate units of the company have built a wealth of electronic service channels, including 95598 website, electric E-power, hand-held power and electricity, business, E-charging, WeChat, etc. Since each business application system is independent of each other, the user cannot obtain the services provided by the multi-system service application through one login. Although the 95598 smart interactive website and the national network mall have made hyperlinks to each other, they need to log in again to enjoy the next business system. The application service is cumbersome and has a poor experience. In addition, because each electronic service channel is independent and operates independently, the State Grid Corporation cannot integrate the customer resource advantages of each electronic service channel and implement targeted marketing operations [3]. Meanwhile, State Grid Corporation is lack of a unified management and monitoring platform for each electronic channel, the current management is more dispersed for lack of support means [4]. Therefore, this article starts from the source, establish a unified identity authentication management system for users, in order to optimize the user experience of each Internet electronic channel, enhance the country Grid company's Internet service competitiveness.

2 Related Works

The development of identity authentication technology has gone through the process from software authentication to hardware authentication, from single-factor authentication to dual (multiple) factor authentication, from static authentication to dynamic authentication. Common authentication methods includes password-based authentication method, smart card, token-based authentication method, PKI digital certificate-based authentication method [4], biometric-based identification method (fingerprint, palm print, iris, retina, face, voice, Signature, etc.), identification method based on combination factor. At present, domestic identity authentication technology is mainly based on weak identity authentication, including user name/password authentication technology and dynamic password authentication technology. The username/password authentication method is one of the simplest and most commonly used authentication technologies. Dynamic password authentication is developed on the basis of traditional username/password, so that the user's password is dynamically changed according to time or usage. Achieve one-time identity authentication technology [5].

The development of future domestic identity authentication technology will be based on quantum cryptography-based authentication technology as the main development trend. Because quantum cryptography is the product of the combination of cryptography and quantum mechanics, quantum states are used as information carriers to pass keys between legitimate users via quantum channels [6]. Quantum cryptography can achieve the two ultimate goals that classical cryptography can't achieve: First, legitimate communication parties can detect potential eavesdroppers and take corresponding measures. Secondly, the eavesdropper can't crack quantum ciphers, no matter who tries to crack them. The use of the non-stealing and non-replicability of quantum cryptography in authentication technology can be used to authenticate the identity of both communicating parties. In principle, it provides an unbreakable, non-stealing and large-capacity secure communication system, which truly guarantees the absolute security of communication.

Traditional single sign-on (SSO) solutions can be divided into two categories based on the way the application is logged in. One is a script-based SSO solution, the other is an access-based ticket (AccessTicket)-based SSO solution [7]. The main goal of a script-based SSO solution is to automate the login process through scripting. The advantage of this solution is that it is easy to implement, and can add a target system to the SSO solution without modifying the code of the target system. And the disadvantage is that the client software needs to be installed, and the security needs to be improved, because the target system does not need to be used. Modifications, implementation of some other functions besides login (such as Single Log-out, secure exchange of user data between target systems, centralized management of user identity, etc.) are also difficult to solve. SSO is not the same as automatic login, but other security functions need to be considered. For the SSO solution based on access ticket, the main goal is to implement SSO by requiring the target system to transform and accept the access ticket. The verification of the user is the responsibility of the SSO server. The responsibility of the target system is only to verify the validity of the access ticket to the SSO server [8]. This solution tends to form an SSO standard (including representation of access tickets, communication between users and SSO servers, communication between target systems and SSO servers, etc.), and each target system that requires SSO must follow this standard. The advantage of this scheme is that it can realize a full-featured SSO. But the disadvantage is that the target system needs to be modified, and the original user authentication part is changed to the verification of the access ticket. It is also important that the SSO standard must be widely accepted by the software vendor.

3 Proposed Unified Identity Authentication System

This paper designs a unified identity authentication system based on PKI certificate, including certificate application, certificate verification, certificate issuance and certificate issuing mechanism for various application systems of the network [9]. The identity authentication system is divided into an authentication client, an authentication server, a ticket server, and an LDAP directory server as shown in Fig. 1. The user only needs to actively perform one identity authentication process in the network, and then can access all the resources on the network that he is authorized to use without actively participating in the subsequent identity authentication process. By enabling users to log in once, they can traverse all the systems running on the network, that is, realize the so-called "one-point login, multi-point roaming" [10].

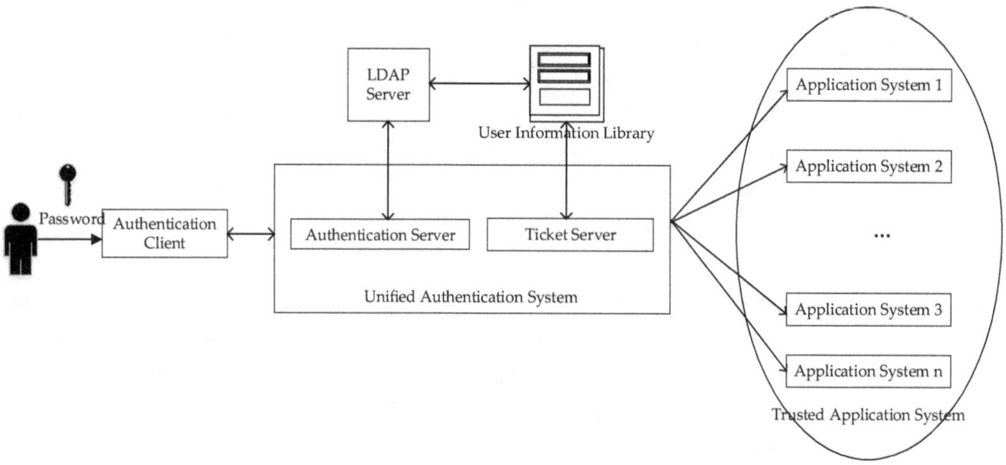

Fig. 1. Logic structure of proposed unified authentication system

In the system design, the user uses the password to log in to the authentication client, and the authentication client submits the user information to the identity authentication server. The identity authentication server connects the PKI and the LDAP server to complete mutual authentication with the user. Ticket server will applied after the authentication process.

3.1 Description of Unified Proposed Authentication System

The main notations used are described in Table 1.

Table 1. Notation used

Attribute	Content
$E_X(M)$	Encryption of message M using the public key of principal X
$Sig_X(M)$	Signature with appendix of message M by principal X
N_X	64 bit random nonce value generated by principal X
$\{M\}_K$	Symmetric encryption of message M with key K
C_X	X's certificate

The authentication client mainly realizes the management of the system and the customer, and provides a simple and operable interactive interface for the end user.

The authentication server is used to receive the information of the client and verify the certificate chain, certificate validity period, certificate blacklist and certificate holder when verifying the validity of the client certificate (Verify the private key signature). The Certificate Revocation List (CRL) and certificate chain are stored locally and periodically download new CRLs to LDAP [11]. After the authentication is successful, the system is transferred to the ticket server, and if it fails, it returns to the user login interface. The message exchanged in the proposed authentication method is as shown in Table 2.

Table 2. Message exchanged in the proposed authentication method

Process	Message
Authentication Request	$U \rightarrow AS : Cert(U), N_U, Capabilities, Sig_U(N_U)$
Authentication Response	$AS \rightarrow U : Cert(AS), N_U, N_{AS}, E_U(AK), Lifetime, SID, Sig_{AS}(N_U, E_U(AK))$
Key Confirmation	$U \rightarrow AS : N_{AS}, ID_U, \{N_{AS}, ID_U\}_{AK}$

The process of proposed authentication system is shown at Fig. 2. At the first step, the user sends an Authentication Request message to its AS, which includes the user's certificate, security capabilities, a random number generated by the user, Rivest, Shamir and Adleman (RSA) signature over the random number to assure the authenticity of the authentication request message.

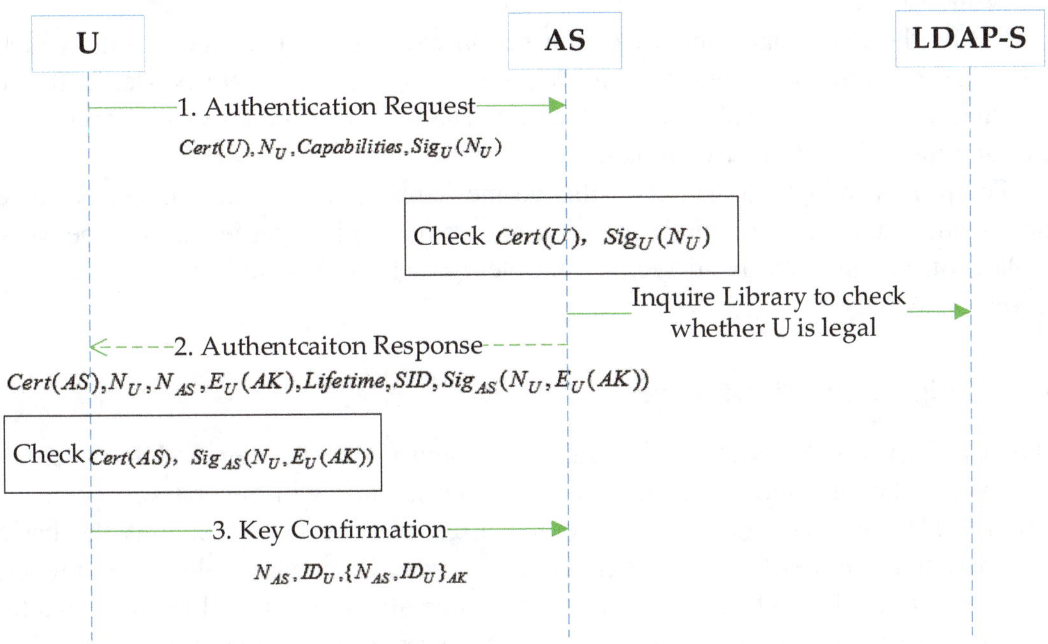

Fig. 2. The process of proposed authentication system

After receiving the information, the server first verifies the legality of the user certificate, which contains the following four steps:

(1) Verify the certificate whether is issued by a trusted Certificate Authority (CA) which involves authentication of the entire certificate chain. If the certificate cannot be directly trusted, it will always look up until it finds its trusted or root CA.
(2) If the certificate is a certificate issued by a trusted CA, then the certificate must be parsed to obtain the content of the certificate;
(3) Verify the serial number of the certificate whether is valid. Check the CRL to see if the certificate is invalid.
(4) Verify that the certificate whether has expired. After the user certificate is verified, the AS use the user public key to verify that the signature is correct.

If the verification fails, the user is denied to login. After the verification is passed, the server extracts identity information, such as user name or certificate serial number, from the client certificate. Then the server inquires the user list of the LDAP server to determine whether the user is a registered legal user. If it is not a legitimate user, then refuse the client log in. If it is a legitimate user, the authentication server determines the encryption algorithm and protocol support it will share with the user, activates an authentication key (AK) for the user, encrypts it with the user's public key, and sends it back to the user in an Authentication Response message. The Authentication Response Message includes the AS's certificate to verify its identity, a AK encrypted with the user's public key, an AK sequence number to distinguish between successive generations of AKs, AK lifetime, a random number generated by the AS along with the user's random number used to ensure the key liveliness, RSA signature over all the attributes in the Authentication Response message to assure the authenticity of the Reply messages.

Lastly, the User sends the Key Confirmation which consists of the identity of the user, the random value received in Message Authentication Response, and the encryption with the two values under the AK. The AK is the new session key for the user and the AS for further communication.

The process adopts the nonce-challenge mechanism, which can completely solve the identity authentication problem of the communication parties in the network application system, and avoid security problems such as fake websites or malicious server camouflage.

3.2 Design of the Ticket Server

The ticket server includes a ticket issuing module and a ticket parsing module. After the user passes the authentication, the ticket issuance module will generate an authentication credential ticket (i.e., a ticket) of the user, and the ticket contains the basic information of the user (name, gender, document type, ID number, telephone number, email, etc. for the individual user), some information about the user's login required by the system, as well as information about the list of systems that the user can access. The user's login ticket is respectively digitally signed for the specific application system and using the public key corresponding to the digital certificate of the application system, so that only the application system can decrypt it, and the user information is prevented from leaking to the unrelated application system.

The system stores the user's ticket information in the session of the authentication platform. When the user logs out of the system, the authentication platform destroys the session by itself and clears all the ticket information about the user. When the user switches between different systems, the application system uses the Web Service technology to apply to the unified identity authentication system to verify whether the current ticket of the user is legal. If it is a legitimate user, then the user can log in to the system. The system uses the root digital certificate to decrypt to obtain the specific information of the user. Otherwise, it returns to the login interface.

4 Conclusion

The PKI-based unified identity authentication system effectively solves the trust problem in the information network space, and determines the uniqueness, authenticity and legitimacy of the various economic and management actors (including organizations and individuals) in the information network space. Thereby protecting the security interests of various subjects in the information network space. Users can directly access each application system and perform fast and secure switching between application systems without multiple authentications, providing users with the convenience and security of engaging in complex business management activities.

Acknowledgment. This work is supported by the science and technology project of State Grid Corporation of China under the Grants No. 52110417001D.

References

1. Bedi, G., Venayagamoorthy, G.K., Singh, R., et al.: Review of Internet of Things (IoT) in electric power and energy systems. IEEE Internet Things J. **5**(2), 847–870 (2018)
2. Katsikogiannis, G., Mitropoulos, S., Douligeris, C.: UACS: towards unified access control services. In: IEEE International Symposium on Signal Processing and Information Technology, pp. 127–132. IEEE (2016)
3. Liu, Z., Zhang, P., Guan, X., et al.: Joint subchannel and power allocation in secure transmission design for femtocell networks. IEEE Syst. J. **12**(3), 2688–2698 (2018)
4. Chen, C.L., Tu, Z.-W., Guo, L.: Practice of network and information security situation awareness in SGCC. Electric Power Inf. Commun. Technol. (2017)
5. Ahmavaara, K.I., Palanigounder, A.: Certificate-based authentication (2017)
6. Yu, Z., Wu, X., Fang, D.: A dynamic vulnerability evaluation model to smart grid for the emergency response (2018). 052028
7. Nagy, M., Nagy, N.: Quantum-based secure communications with no prior key distribution. Soft. Comput. **20**(1), 87–101 (2016)
8. Mainka, C., Mladenov, V., Schwenk, J.: Do not trust me: using malicious IdPs for analyzing and attacking single sign-on. In: IEEE European Symposium on Security and Privacy, pp. 321–336. IEEE (2016)

9. Lee, H.Y.: The implementation and investigation of securing web applications upon multi-platform for a single sign-on functionality. Int. J. Adv. Res. Comput. Sci. **6**(23), 39–46 (2016)
10. Luo, Y.G., Zhang, H.X., Zhu, H.Y.: Design of unified identity authentication system based on URL single sign on. Electron. Des. Eng. (2017)
11. Davydov, A., Morozov, G., Sergeyev, V., et al.: Methods, apparatuses, and systems for multi-point, multi-cell single-user based multiple input and multiple output transmissions (2018)
12. Priyadharshini, M.D., Ananth, C.: A secure hash message authentication code to avoid certificate revocation list checking in vehicular adhoc networks. Int. J. Appl. Eng. Res. (IJAER) **10**(2), 1250–1254 (2017)

Mobile Security

Extension of ISO/IEC27001 to Mobile Devices Security Management

Xiaobo Zhu and Yunqian Zhu(✉)

National Computer Network Emergency Response Technical Team/Coordination Center of China, Beijing, China
{zhu, zyq}@cert.org.cn

Abstract. Mobile security is more and more important with the fast growth of mobile devices, and people are becoming more dependent on mobile devices in their daily life. Malicious samples in mobile devices are growing in double times each year from 2011 to 2017 in China. ISO/IEC 27000 family of standards helps organizations keep information assets secure, such as financial information, intellectual property, employee details or information entrusted to you by third parties. ISO/IEC 27001 is the best-known standard in the family providing requirements for an information security management system (ISMS). However, ISO/IEC 27001 is not quite adaptable for mobile devices, because these developing mobile information devices lead to new challenges and security risks. This paper analyzes mobile devices security issues, and gives the drawback for 27001 in mobile security. Finally, this paper gives a consideration to these issues under ISO/IEC 27001 information security management system framework.

Keywords: Mobile security · Information security · ISO/IEC 27001 · ISMS

1 Introduction

Mobile devices are growing fast with more and more functions and good performance, such as laptops, personal digital assistants (PDAs) and handheld digital devices. Smartphones exceeded 55% of the mobile phone market [1]. Mobile devices are becoming a center of bank transaction, entertainment, communication, shopping and even work. However, mobile security is becoming more severe than ever, as shown in Fig. 1 [2]. These mobile devices provide significant value add to organizations but risks associated with their use need to be managed. Smart phones can be infected with malicious software, and sensitive data can be stolen. Phishing attacks work just as effectively with smartphones as with any other device.

Using a smart phone without security software has become unthinkable. With mobile phones, this sense of responsibility has not yet reached the majority of users, even though important personal data, personal photos and even company data can be stored on smartphones. Therefore, for an organization, mobile devices security management is much more important than ever before. ISO/IEC 27001 is the best-known standard providing requirements for an information security management system (ISMS).

X. Yun et al. (Eds.): CNCERT 2018, CCIS 970, pp. 27–35, 2019.
https://doi.org/10.1007/978-981-13-6621-5_3

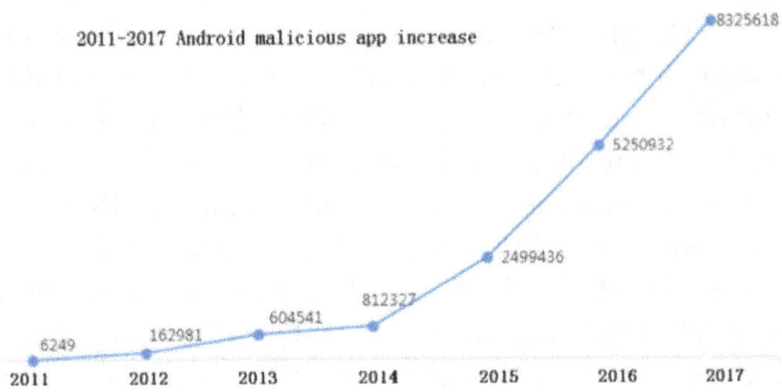

Fig. 1. 2011–2017 Android malicious app increase

2 ISO/IEC 27000 Family

2.1 Overview of ISO/IEC 27000 Family

ISO/IEC 27000 family of standards helps organizations keep information assets secure. Using this family of standards will help your organization manage the security of assets such as financial information, intellectual property, employee details or information entrusted to you by third parties. ISO/IEC 27001 is the best-known standard in the family providing requirements for an information security management system (ISMS) [3]. Its new version is ISO/IEC 27000:2018. ISO/IEC 27000 family includes multiple standards for building Information Security Management System (ISMS), as show in Fig. 2.

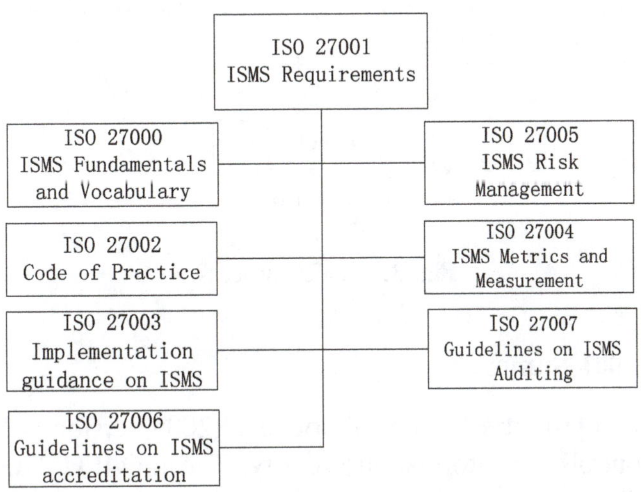

Fig. 2. ISO/IEC 27000 family

ISO/IEC 27001 is the only standard in this family that is used to providing certification for an organization. It outlines the ISMS framework by which an organization can build its own ISMS based on PDCA (Plan-Do-Check-Action) model. The other standards in this family provide profound support for an organization to build its own

ISMS. ISO/IEC 27002 provides choice from 133 concrete controls based on risk assessment. Though mobile devices covered, but it is not enough due to the ongoing technique limitations. ISO/IEC 27003 is ISMS Implementation guidance which implements PDCA in more detail, including identification of assets, threat identification, risk assessment, analysis and improvement of controls. ISO/IEC 27004 is ISMS Metrics and measurement which evaluates effectiveness of information security controls and objectives. ISO/IEC 27005 is ISMS Risk Management which is a new standard that is mainly concerned with risks. ISO/IEC 27006 is Guidelines on ISMS accreditation. ISO/IEC 27007 is Guidelines on ISMS Auditing.

2.2 Plan-Do-Check-Action Process

According to 27001, ISMS is built via a 4-phase process called PDCA (Plan-Do-Check-Action) process, as shown in Fig. 3. In each phase, there are different activities. In phase PLAN, there is only one activity called "establish ISMS". In phase DO, there exist two activities, called "Implement and operate the ISMS". In phase CHECK, there are two activities called "monitor and review ISMS". In ACT phase, two activities called "maintain and improve" are involved.

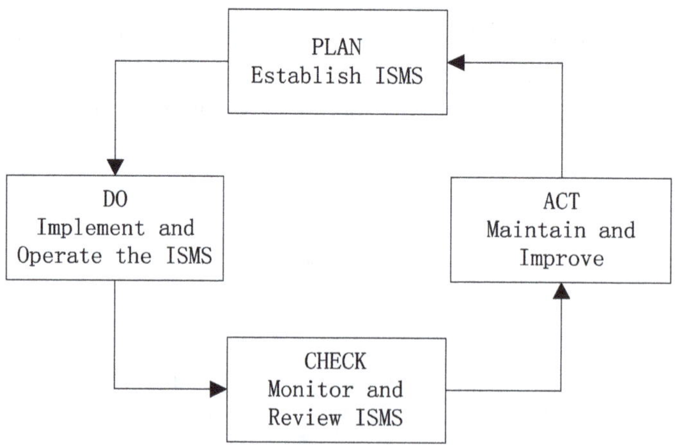

Fig. 3. PDCA process.

2.3 ISO/IEC 27001 Summary

ISO/IEC 27001:2013 provides 14 control domains (2005 version is 11) and 113(2005 version is 133) controls for information security. The ISO/IEC 27001 categories are shown in Fig. 4. The form is as shown in Fig. 5.

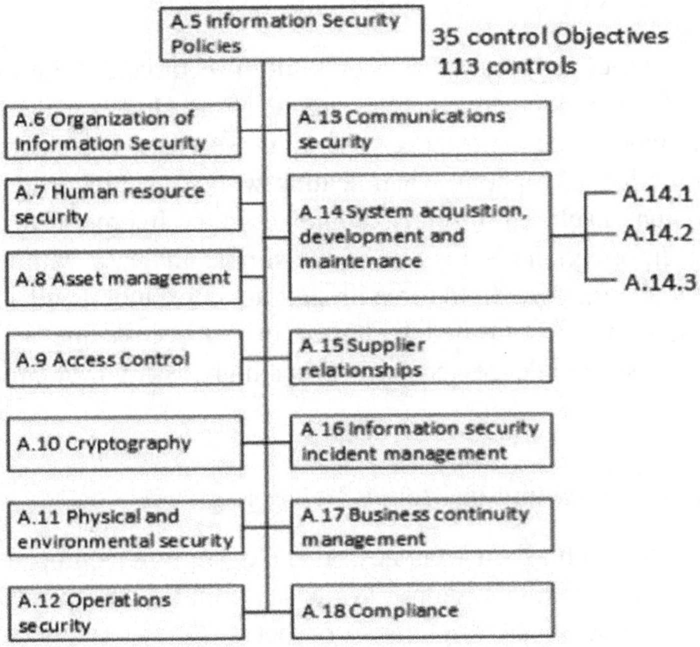

Fig. 4. ISO/IEC 27001 categories.

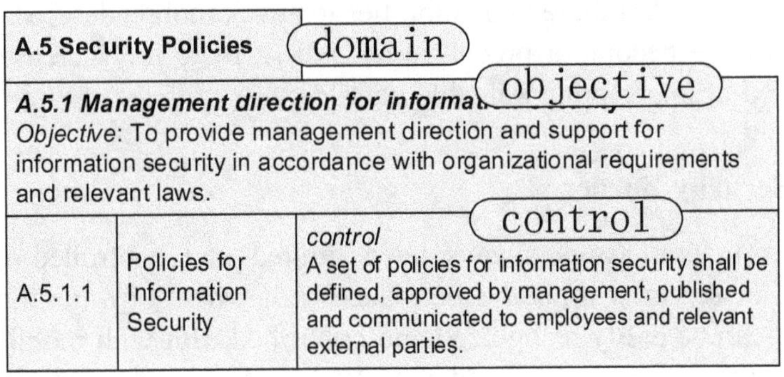

Fig. 5. Form of ISO/IEC 27001 domain, objective and control.

However, these control objectives and controls are mostly too general, and for mobile devices information security it is not quite adaptable.

3 Analysis of Mobile Devices Security Management

Mobile Devices are widely used in any organization, and also the mobile device security management is every important. Therefore, issues and risks of mobile devices security management must be recognized. Due to the rapid development of mobile device technique, numerous new problems arise from the absence of management to the specific consideration of mobile devices.

3.1 Easy Information Disclosure via Mobile Devices

Even though a strict security system has been built in accordance with ISO/IEC 27001, and firewalls or IDS/IPS is deployed in an organization. However the organization is still in great risk under the circumstances of mobile services. For example, a user can photo the screen with a smartphone when dealing with something important, and then the important content displayed in screen is already in the Internet if the mobile phone is in the Internet. Information disclosure is quite simple and easy with mobile devices. It is not proper for an organization to force its staff no to use mobile devices. Meantime, mobile devices are easily controlled by unauthorized access due to the users low security awareness, so mobile devices will bring high risk if they are controlled by malicious app.

3.2 High Computing Ability of Mobile Devices

Many mobile devices such as smartphones or PDAs are now equipped with fast processor and embedded operating system (OS). Many applications specific to embedded OS are developed and deployed. As a matter of fact, such mobile devices are powerful computers. Meantime, these devices are usually installed with multiple communication measures, such as Bluetooth, TCP/IP protocols, etc.

With these rich and powerful features, vulnerabilities are also exposed to potential adversary, who can exploit these vulnerabilities to attack mobile devices. Therefore, the mobile devices have become a prized target, where there are increased numbers of malware targeted at intercepting valuable data [5].

3.3 Vague Security Border

End-to-end information assets always have limited and controlled boundary. For example, a PC or server will always be placed somewhere of a building, and so the security border can be easily recognized and controlled. But with mobile devices, it is hard to control the range or border of mobile devices. So, the security boundary is becoming vague under the existence of mobile devices. It seems in anywhere.

3.4 Versatile Function of Mobile Devices

USB drives can now store much more software, and so it is quite easy to make a USB drive as a booting disk which can easily go into a PC disks but avoid the protection software of that PC. A smart phone can have 128 G storage space with versatile functions such as recording, photograph, GPS, etc. Therefore, mobile devices can play more functions, such as storing data, booting system, mp3 player, etc. It is convenient for people to use mobile devices, but it is in high risk when using these versatile functions of mobile devices.

3.5 Cross-border Information Theft

Mobile devices can be anywhere, as the inherent mobility (beginning from laptops) has always made it impossible to rely on a strong perimeter for adequate protection. The cloud computing revolution and the myriad of hosted application services that are not geographically fixed has made it easier for data to cross national borders [6]. With the increased use of mobile network, the applications and data stored in mobile devices lost locally and globally, may put critical infrastructure at risk. In addition, data travelling on the mobile devices is typically subject to laws and regulations that will vary from one jurisdiction to another.

3.6 Data Disposal

The amount of data that can be stored and processed in mobile devices has been growing dramatically. Inappropriate device disposal procedures may bring the risk of sensitive information being retained on the device and unauthorized access. Organizational computing assets should be subject to company asset management procedures which should include secure disposal for assets containing sensitive data. However, the execution of these procedures can often be a grey area when dealing with personal devices in the workplace. This requires clear organizational policies in order to safeguard sensitive, confidential and highly valued information (including commercial intelligence).

4 Mobile Devices Security Under ISO/IEC 27001 Framework

4.1 Information Security Policy Consideration

As ISO/IEC 27001 says, the objective of information security policy is to set up management direction and support for information security. Information Security Policy is a directive and strategic file which includes the goal and strategy of information security. As the mobile devices security is particularly important and weak, so it must be particularly shown and considered in Information Security Policy and Information Security Policy should include the following aspects: information security view, objective, strategy, range, organizational structure, responsibility, assets, etc. Especially, policy relating to mobile devices should be effective, definite and complete. However, concrete and detail process should not covered in policy.

Developing information security policy should obey to a flow: (1) determine the range of information security policy, (2) assess and analyze risk, and (3) check, approve and implement information security policy. While developing information security policy, advanced information security technique on mobile devices is the basic assurance. All related techniques should be collected and updated in time.

4.2 Organization of Information Security

Information security will be managed within an organization. Management will approve information security policies, assign security roles, and coordinate and review the implementation of security across the organization. Information assets and information technology regarding to mobile devices must be recognized and updated in time.

4.3 Human Resources Security

Mobile devices are always used by people, so human resources security is important. Everyone in an organization must understand his or her responsibilities and will know the manners to reduce the risk of theft, fraud or misuse of mobile devices. Thus, responsibilities should be divided into different layers. The top layer usually monitors and audits the information security activities of an organization. The second layer manages the routine information security activities. The third layer is mobile device owner who operates mobile devices according the policy, and is subject to upper layer's management.

4.4 Physical and Environmental Security

Though mobile devices have not limited boundary, physical and environmental security must be considered in order to prevent unauthorized physical access, damage, theft, compromise, and interference to mobile information and facilities. Locations housing mobile devices will be secured with appropriate security barriers and entry controls. They will be physically protected from unauthorized access, damage and interference. Secure areas will be protected by appropriate security entry controls to ensure that only authorized personnel are allowed access. Security will be applied to off-site equipment. All equipment containing storage media will be checked to ensure that any sensitive data and licensed software has been removed or securely overwritten prior to disposal in compliance with statewide policies.

4.5 Communications and Operations Management

There are much more communications and operations for mobile devices than for other devices. Responsibilities and procedures for administrating mobile devices must be established according to information security policy. Virus and malicious code for mobile devices should be detected protect the integrity of software and information in mobile devices. Exchange of sensitive data with other organizations must be done based on a formal exchange policy. Mobile devices containing sensitive data will be protected against unauthorized access, misuse.

4.6 Access Control

For an organization with mobile devices, access control includes two aspects: one is access to organizational information systems from mobile devices, the other is access to outer information facilities from mobile devices. Both these two aspects of access control for mobile devices should be controlled on the basis of business and security requirements. Formal procedures should be established for the mobile devices to control access rights to both inner and outer information facilities, to prevent unauthorized access.

5 Conclusion

Extension of ISO/IEC 27001 Information security management with mobile devices always meets new challenges with the rapid development of mobile technique. This paper analyses the issues of information security with mobile devices. It is a good practice with ISO/IEC 27000 information security series standards. The design, operation, use, and management of mobile information assets are subject to statutory, regulatory, and contractual security requirements in order to avoid breaches of any law.

The following controls are a good reference for Information Security Management system under ISO/IEC 27001 framework.

- Never set the login dialog box to remember the password;
- Keep antivirus protection up-to-date, as well as the operating system and application security patches;
- Password-protect all devices, such as removable drives and compact disks (CDs);
- Do not store unencrypted sensitive information on mobile devices;
- Incorporate a time-out function that requires re-authentication after 30 min of inactivity;
- Back up your data to a location separately from the device;
- Include both hardware/device-based authorization and application-based authorization for access control mechanisms;
- Do not keep mobile devices online when not in use. Either shut them off or physically disconnect them from the Internet connection;
- Lost or misplaced government-issued devices must be immediately reported to management.

References

1. Conti, M.: Body, Personal and local ad hoc wireless networks. In: Ilyas, M. (ed.) The Handbook of Ad Hoc Wireless Networks. CRC Press LLC, Boca Raton (2003)
2. http://www.aqniu.com/industry/32319.html
3. https://www.iso.org/isoiec-27001-information-security.html
4. http://www.comscore.com/ger/Insights/Presentations_and_Whitepapers/2013/The_Mobile_Shift

5. Kao, I.: Securing Mobile Devices in The Business Environment. IBM Global Technology Services – Thought Leadership White Paper, October 2011
6. Ernst & Young: Data Loss Prevention: Keeping Your Sensitive Data Out of The Public Domain, Insights on IT Risk Business Briefing (2012)
7. ISO/IEC 27000:2009: Information Technology—Security Techniques—Information Security Management Systems—Overview and Vocabulary. ISO/IEC, Geneva (2009)
8. ISO/IEC 27001:2005: Information Technology—Security Techniques—Information Security Management Systems—Requirements. ISO/IEC, Geneva (2005)
9. ISO/IEC 27002:2005: Information Technology—Security Techniques—Information Security Management Systems—Code of Practice for Information Security Management. ISO/IEC, Geneva (2005)
10. ISO/IEC 27003:2010: Information Technology—Security Techniques—Information Security Management System Implementation Guidance. ISO/IEC, Geneva (2010)
11. ISO/IEC 27004:2009: Information Technology—Security Techniques—Information Security Management—Measurement. ISO/IEC, Geneva (2009)
12. ISO/IEC 27005:2008: Information Technology—Security Techniques—Information Security Risk Management. ISO/IEC, Geneva (2008)

Android Malware Detection Method Based on Frequent Pattern and Weighted Naive Bayes

Jingwei Li, Bozhi Wu, and Weiping Wen(✉)

School of Software and Microelectronics, Peking University, 24th Jinyuan Road, Daxing Industrial District, Beijing 102600, China
weipingwen@ss.pku.edu.cn

Abstract. With the market share of Android system becoming the first in the world, the security problem of Android system is becoming more and more serious. How to effectively detect Android malware has become a significant problem. Permissions and API calls in Android applications can effectively reflect the behavior patterns of an Android application. Most researchers have only considered a single permission or API feature, and did not consider associations and patterns inside the permission or API features. Some scholars have also tried to find the combination modes inside the permission features in malwares, but the detection of maliciousness according to this combination mode is too absolute. This paper proposes a malware detection method, which combines the advantages of frequent pattern mining and Naive Bayes to effectively identify Android malwares.

Keywords: Android OS · Malware detection · Frequent pattern mining · Naive Bayes

1 Introduction

The Android operating system is based on Linux and is an open source operating system developed by Google. From the official release of Android 1.0 in 2008 to the first quarter of 2011, Android market share reached 48% in just three years, and surpassed Symbian to become the world's first. As of August 2017, only the Android system has a market share of over 80% in China. According to the first Smart Phone Market Report [1] published by market research firm Gartner in 2018, Android's market share has reached 85.9%, far exceeding the IOS market share of 14.1%. Android, which maintains such a huge advantage, benefited from the outstanding performance of Chinese brands such as Huawei, Xiaomi and OPPO in the worldwide mobile phone market. However, the rapid development of Android system not only brought about a rapid expansion of market share, but also made the security problem of Android system become more serious. The 2017 CVE Details report shows that the Android system ranked first in the number of product vulnerabilities with 842 vulnerabilities, an increase of 61.0% compared with 523 in 2016 [2]. According to a research report released by China's largest Internet security company 360 in the first

X. Yun et al. (Eds.): CNCERT 2018, CCIS 970, pp. 36–51, 2019.
https://doi.org/10.1007/978-981-13-6621-5_4

half of 2018 [3], as of December 2017, up to 93.94% of Android phones have security vulnerabilities, and 360 Internet Security Center has intercepted 7.573 million new malware samples on the Android platform, monitoring 214 million Android users infected with malware.

On the one hand, because Android is an open source operating system, major mobile phone manufacturers have deeply customized it, resulting in frequent loopholes; on the other hand, the security of a large number of third-party software cannot be effectively guaranteed. Android is based on the Linux kernel, but Android's third-party software is quite different from Linux. Linux runs open source software that has been reviewed by the open source community, and security can be guaranteed. Android runs third-party closed source software, and because the Android system is too fragmented and free. In addition to Google Play, there is no authoritative audit platform for Android third-party software, especially in China. The software is closed source and there is no effective and reasonable auditing mechanism, that allows malware to run on Android. As the Android operating system quickly became the smartest operating system with the highest market share, the number of Android software has also grown rapidly. A recent report showed [4] that by September 2017, the number of Android software on Google Play has reached 3.3 million, and in addition to Google Play, there are many third-party app stores that also offer downloads of Android software. Due to the openness, open source and relatively simple checking mechanism of Android system, Android system has attracted many malicious application developers. So Android has become a main platform for malicious applications.

In order to help identify Android malicious applications effectively, this paper introduces a android malicious application detection method based on frequent pattern and weighted Naive Bayes, which performs frequent pattern mining on the extracted privilege features and API features of Android applications, and then use the frequent pattern as feature to identify and distinguish Android malicious applications through a weighted Naive Bayes algorithm. Frequent pattern mining [5] is an effective classification method in the field of data mining and machine. It searches for frequently occurring patterns (item sets, sub-sequences, sub-structures) in the data set, and then identifies and classifies the samples to be tested based on the frequent patterns of such in-line associations. But identifying and classifying the malware directly through the frequent patterns found in the rights and API features tends to have a high false positive rate. This is because a large number of normal Android applications often have frequent patterns of malicious Android applications. It is generally and irresponsible to classify malicious applications directly based on frequent patterns. Naive Bayes algorithm [6] is also an important classification method in the field of supervised learning, and it is also one of the few classification algorithms based on probability theory. The Naive Bayes principle is simple and easy to implement, and is mostly used for text categorization. But it is based on a simple assumption: the attributes are independent of each other. However, the permissions of the Android application and the API features are not independent of each other. They cooperate with each other to make the whole software run normally and have certain correlation. Therefore, it is not appropriate to simply use the Naive Bayes algorithm for the identification of Android malicious applications. Therefore, the detection method in the paper combines frequent pattern mining with Naive Bayes, and uses the characteristics of frequent pattern connotation to compensate for the unreasonable assumptions of Naive Bayes, and compensates for frequent pattern recognition with the probability of Naive Bayes. Through such improvement on Naïve Bayes, frequent patterns and Naive Bayes can be well coordinated.

The main contributions of this paper are as follows:

We introduce the approach that performs Android malicious application detection based on frequent patterns and weighted Naive Bayes. Firstly, filtering the feature feature and API call feature by the feature differentiation degree defined in the text, and then mine frequent pattern of malicious application and Benign App based on the filtered feature. Finally, combine the frequent permission & API call feature and weighted Naive Bayes method to classify Android apps.

Based on this Android malicious application detection method, we implement a detection tool that can effectively classify and identify whether an Android application is a malicious application or not.

2 Related Work

Many scholars have done a lot of work on the identification and detection of Android malicious applications. The current mainstream detection technologies are static detection technology, dynamic detection technology and hybrid detection technology. The static detection mainly analyzes the source code, and identifies the malicious application by extracting the relevant features of the analysis source code. Although this method is fast, it has a high false positive rate; the dynamic detection technology is generally executed in a sandbox environment. The program identifies the malicious application by extracting the running behavior of the analysis application. This method can effectively detect the known and unknown malware, but the detection time is slow. The hybrid detection technology combines the static detection technology and the dynamic detection technology to identify the malicious application, and use machine learning methods for classification.

A common method for static detection is to detect malicious applications based on signature features. Liang et al. [7] proposed to declare the order of permissions in the Android Manifest file to find out the permissions frequently requested by the malware but not by the normal software, thus automatically generating a set of rules, using for malware identification. Yang et al. [8] proposed the detection of malicious applications based on frequent pattern algorithms. This method relys on finding the combination modes of the permission features in malicious applications to detect malicious applications, but this method is too absolute, and combinations or patterns of these permissions often appear in normal applications, resulting in a lower accuracy rate-79.6%, sometimes only 73.8%. There is also a component-based detection method [9, 10], which decomposes the application and extracts important contents such as permissions, resources, and byte codes to evaluate the program security. Another mainstream static detection method, Apposcopy [11], uses static stain tracking, combined with internal component calls, to generate signatures through semantic extraction. However, their method is only effective for the detection of several malware families, and it is difficult to detect malware with new signatures.

Dynamic monitoring generally detects the behavior characteristics of the application during its operation, and has certain requirements for real-time and operating environment. The more mainstream dynamic monitoring methods are generally based on behavioral characteristics. TaintDroid [12] combines analysis to track malicious information by detecting the source of information and sensitive data, but many normal software also need to access sensitive data. Crowdroid [13] distinguishes between normal and malicious applications by collecting real-time system calls for individual applications in conjunction with machine learning. TaitDroid [14] captures malicious advertisements through sandbox detection attacks. Riskranker [15] studied malicious code in multiple markets, using risky behavior features such as attack signatures, code encryption, and sending and receiving data for identification.

Hybrid detection combines static detection and dynamic monitoring to combine the advantages of both to compensate for the shortcomings of both. AMDetector [16] applies the attack tree model to organize and develop behavior rules, and uses static analysis to mark attack tree nodes, filtering out most normal applications, and retaining them for application. In the dynamic analysis phase, the ability of the application and the ability to detect the selected behavior are analyzed for maliciousness, and a high detection accuracy is achieved. Mobile-Sandbox [17] uses static analysis results to guide dynamic analysis to extend the execution code coverage through the mobile phone sandbox, record API calls and combine machine learning methods for malicious application detection.

Since the static features of normal applications and malicious applications have many similarities, static detection based on the combination mode features such as permissions, API calls, and components often has a high false positive rate, while dynamic detection and hybrid detection not only are time-sensitive, but have high requirements for the operating environment. Therefore, the method proposed in this paper is based on static detection technology, using Naive Bayes algorithm to make up for the shortcomings of pattern matching in static detection, and using frequent pattern mining authority and API correlation to make up for Naive Bayes "features are independent" The preconditions of idealization. It has not only the advantages of timeliness of static detection technology, but also low false positive rate and high accuracy.

3 Our Approach

This paper proposes an Android malware detection method based on frequent patterns and weighted Naive Bayes, Fig. 1 shows the overall process of our approach, it works in the following step:

Permission and API extraction, extracting the permission features and API call features in Android applications, and filtering according to the degree of discrimination of these features, and selecting the top 40 features with the best discrimination.

Permission & API call frequent pattern mining, based on the top 40 features, perform frequent pattern mining on the Android application dataset to find the permission & API call modes that frequently appear in malicious samples.

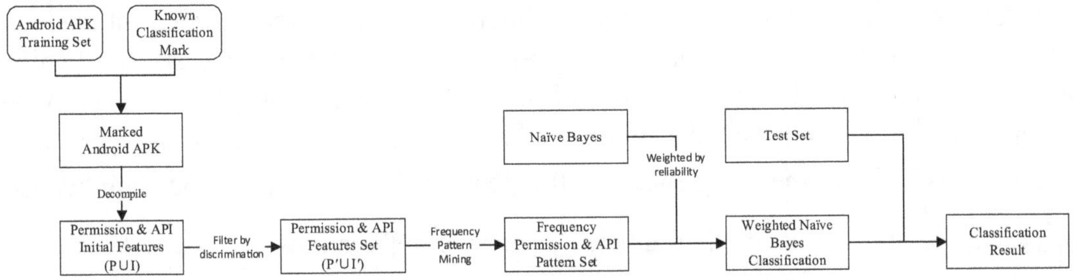

Fig. 1. Overview of the Android malware detection method based on frequent pattern and weighted Naive Bayes

The weighted Naive Bayes classification is characterized by the frequent permission & API call mode, and weighted the naïve Bayes by the reliability of the frequent pattern to establish a detection model.

3.1 Permission and API Extraction

The features used in the detection method of this paper mainly come from the permission information and API call information of Android application, then mining the frequent pattern based on the permission and API features, and further combines the weighted Naive Bayes algorithm to classify the Android application. So first step is extracting the initial features from the permission features and the API call features. Each Android application is mapped to a set consisting of the permission features and the API call features. The permission of Android is mainly used to control specific operations executable by the application. During the developing, all the permissions should be applied in the file named *Manifest.xml*. Android has 134 permissions, and also allowing users to customize permissions. However, among these 134 permissions, *INTERNET, ACCESS_NETWORK_STATE, ACCESS_WIFI_STATE* and other permissions are widely used in both benign applications and malware. Such features are often not good for detect malwares. But the frequency of permissions being requested in normal and malicious programs is quite different, such as *WRITE_EXTERNAL_-STORAGE, READ_SMS, WRITE_SMS, etc.* These features tend to have a better effect on classification. The API call has the same situation. *Runtime; -> exec, DataOutputStream; -> writeBytes, ActivityManager; -> getProcessMemoryInfo* occur more frequently in malicious applications.

In this case, all the permissions of Android are represented using a set *P*. All the API call sets are represented using a set *I*, and the set *A* represents the Android application data set. Considering that many permissions and API calls do not have an obviously distinction in frequency between benign applications and malwares. Representatively, we do not directly map the Android application dataset *A* to the collection $P \cup I$ composed by permissions and API calls. Because it not only has a bad classification effect, but also causes huge waste of computing resources. so we simplify the set $P \cup I$ to $P' \cup I'$ by discrimination, $P' \cup I' \subseteq P \cup I$.

The elements in the set $P' \cup I'$ should be frequent occurrences in malwares and have a less frequency in non-malicious applications, or have a less frequency in malicious applications and frequently occurring in non-malicious applications. Represent the total number of malicious application samples to $|A_{mal}|$, the total sample size of benign applications is $|A_{ben}|$, the total number of all the malicious application samples with feature f_i is $|f_{i,mal}|$, and the total number of all the benign application samples with feature f_i is $|f_{i,ben}|$, the frequency of the feature f_i in the malicious application $F_{i,mal} = \frac{|f_{i,mal}|}{|A_{mal}|}$, the frequency that appears in normal applications is $F_{i,ben} = \frac{|f_{i,ben}|}{|A_{ben}|}$.

Definition 1. Measuring a feature's discrimination for malicious applications and normal application by $dis(f_i) \in [0, 1)$.

$$dis(f_i) = 1 - \frac{\min\{F_{i,mal}, F_{i,ben}\}}{\max\{F_{i,mal}, F_{i,ben}\}} \tag{1}$$

When $dis(f_i)$ is 0, it means that the frequency of the feature f_i in the normal application is equal to the malicious application, and has no discriminating; When $dis(f_i)$ is close to 0, which means that the discrimination in the feature f_i is worse; When $dis(f_i)$ approaches 1 means that the feature fi has a best discrimination.

Calculate the distinguishing degree of each feature in the permissions & API calls which belong to the set $P \cup I$. We collected 1,000 malicious apps from VirusShare [18] and 1000 benign apps from Google Store, averaging them into training set and test set. We calculated the discrimination of the permission and API call features in 500 malwares and 500 benign applications in the training set and sorted these features by discrimination from big to small. Then added the top 20 permissions with the highest degree of discrimination in the permission feature to the set P', and the top 20 with the highest degree of discrimination in the API calls set I to set I', which together form the reduced permissions & API call set $P' \cup I'$. Some elements in set $P' \cup I'$ are shown in Table 1.

Table 1. Partial high discriminating permission & API

Permission	API
WRITE_EXTERNAL_STORAGE	Timer;->schedule
READ_SMS	NetworkInfo;->toString
WRITE_SMS	DataOutputStream;->writeBytes
SEND_SMS	Socket;->getSoLinger
RECEIVE_SMS	Runtime;->exec
READ_CONTACTS	System;->setErr
WRITE_APN_SETTING	DexClassLoader;->LoadClass
CALL_PHONE	ContextImpl;->getSystemService
READ_PHONE_STATE	Intent;->setAction
INSTALL_PACKAGES	CoontextWrapper;->registerReceiver
...	...

3.2 Permission and API Call Frequent Pattern Mining

In the previous step, 40 permissions and API calls features were extracted to form a new feature set $P' \cup I'$ But Naive Bayes classifier is directly applied this feature set for classification is not appropriate, because the permissions and the API calls requested by an Android application have a strong correlation, but the significant premise of Naïve Bayes is that *all features are independent of each other*. But the situation that using the permissions and the API calls as the features to recognition Android malicious application obviously does not meet this precondition. To deal with this problem, we further perform frequent pattern mining on the feature set $P' \cup I'$. Android's permissions and API calls reflect the behavior pattern of the application in a certain extent. Mining the recognition between permissions and API calls can effectively identify Android malicious applications. Moreover, the permissions and API call frequent pattern, rather than directly using the privilege and API calls as features of the Naive Bayes classifier, can compensate for the problem of non-independence between each permission and API call. It also overcomes the issue that Naive Bayes' conditions conflict with classifying Android malwares.

Definition 2. Feature itemset. The set of features for an Android application represented by $F = \{f_1, f_2, \ldots f_n\}, f_i \in P' \cup I'$.

Definition 3. Transaction database. A collection of transactions, each transaction formed by an Android application's feature items set and an identifier (APKID).

Definition 4. Support degree. The availability of the permission & API call pattern mined by the frequency pattern mining, represents the percentage of Android APK transactions in the transaction database that contain a feature itemset, expressed by $P(Items_i)$.

Definition 5. Minimum support degree threshold, if the support degree of the feature items set is bigger than the minimum support degree threshold, it is called a frequent feature itemset.

Definition 6. Maximal frequent feature itemset, if the feature itemset $Items_i$ is frequent in the transaction database, and there is no frequent item set $Items_i'$ belongs to the transaction database that $Items_i'$ *is* a superset of $Items_i'$.

Based on the above definition, we can use the Apriori algorithm [19] to perform frequent pattern discovery for the Android application transaction database. The feature set of each application constitutes the transaction of the application, and all application transactions constitute the transaction database, and the minimum support degree threshold is *MIN_SUP*. Find all frequent permission item sets that satisfy the support degree not less than *MIN_SUP*, and finally gets the maximal frequent feature itemsets. As shown in the Table 2, we use an example to explain how to use the Apriori algorithm mining the Permission & API call frequent pattern. For easy to understand, this example assumes that minimum support degree threshold is 2/9, and there are 5 permissions & API call features and 9 transactions in the Android application transaction database.

Table 2. Example of frequency permission & API pattern mining

ItemID	Permission & API item	APKID	Permission & API feature itemset	APKID	Permission & API feature itemset
F1	WRITE_EXTERNAL_STORAGE	APK001	F1, F2, F5	APK006	F2, F3
F2	RECEIVE_BOOT_COMPLETED	APK002	F2, F4	APK007	F1, F3
F3	NetworkInfo;->toString	APK003	F2, F3	APK008	F1, F2, F3, F5
F4	ActivityManager;-> getProcessMemoryInfo	APK004	F1, F2, F4	APK009	F1, F2, F3
F5	DataOutputStream;->writeBytes	APK005	F1, F3		

Then use the Apriori algorithm to find the frequent itemsets in the transaction database as follows:

(1) Finding all the itemsets in the transaction database formed by only one item to constitute a set C_1, and counting the number of occurrences in the transaction database that each element belongs to C_1;
(2) Determining the set of the frequent 1-items set L_1 by the minimum support degree threshold MIN_SUP equals to 2/9;
(3) Combining the elements in L_1 with each other to itemsets formed by two items. And adding these 2-items itemsets into a set C_2. Counting the number of times each element in C_2 appears in the transaction database;
(4) Determining the set L_2 of frequent 2-item itemsets L_2 by the minimum support degree threshold;
(5) Combine the elements in L_2 into a set C_3 of the 3-items itemsets, and simplify C_3 according to the Apriori rule: "If the subset of an element in C_3 does not belong to L_1 or L_2, then remove the element". For each element in C_3, count the number of occurrences in the transaction database;
(6) Determining the set L_3 of frequent 3-item itemsets by the minimum support degree threshold;
(7) Recursively generating the set $L_4, L_5, \ldots, L_n$ of frequent n-item itemsets until $L_{n+1} = \varnothing$ (Fig. 2).

Then, according to the above method, all valuable frequent patterns $Items_i$ in the Android malicious application are acquired based on the permission & API calling feature to form the frequent pattern set D as the naïve Bayes' features set.

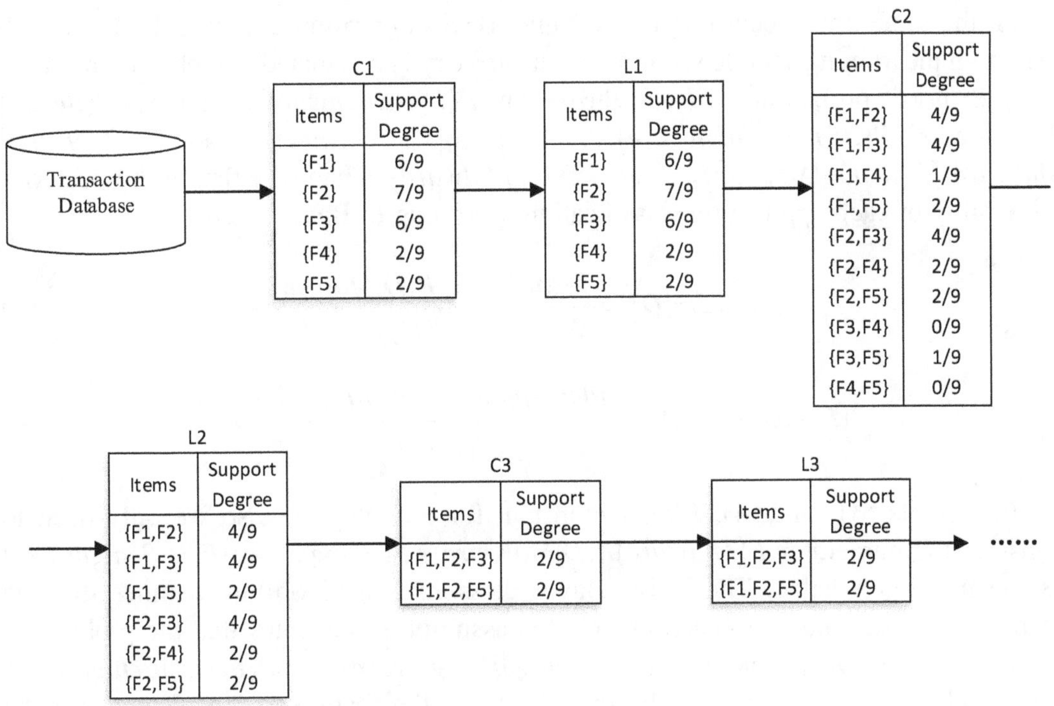

Fig. 2. Process of frequency permission & API pattern mining

3.3 The Weighted Naive Bayes Classification

Next step, we use the frequent permission & API call feature pattern $Items_i$ as the Naive Bayes feature to classify malwares. Bayes classification is very suitable for filtering a large number of application data sets, because it can be trained to perform fast classification, the computational cost is low. It can be known from the mining process of frequent patterns that the support degree $P(Items_i)$ of a frequent feature pattern $Items_i$ is the prior probability of the frequent feature pattern, which can be directly applied to the Naive Bayes algorithm. Thus frequent pattern mining has a good adaptability to Naive Bayes. However, in the process of frequent pattern mining, we find that the more the number of items in a frequent pattern $Items_i$, the lower its support degree will be, so as to its class likelihood $P(Items_i|Malware)$ or class likelihood $P(Items_i|Normalware)$. But the more the number of items in a frequent pattern $Items_i$, the more accurate and reliable the judgment which based on it, so we have a weighted improvement on Naïve Bayes.

For the reliability of frequent itemsets, the more items in a frequent itemset $Items_i$, which belongs to the frequent feature item set D, the more reliable the classification is.

Definition 7. The reliability is represented by $reli(Items_i)$, and are concentrated. The number of items in a frequent pattern is represented by $|Items_i|$, then:

$$reli(items_i) = \frac{|Items_i|}{\max\{|Items_k|\}}, Items_k \in D \tag{2}$$

At the same time, according to the Naive Bayes algorithm, the probability of each feature in the training sample set under each category is calculated, which is represented by the prior probability $P(D|Malware)$ and $P(D|Benignware)$, that is $P(Items_1|Benignware), P(Items_2|Benignware), \ldots, P(Items_n|Benignware)$ and $P(Items_1|Malware), P(Items_2|Malware), \ldots, P(Items_n|Malware)$. Then calculating the posterior probability of each application classification according to Bayes' theorem:

$$P(Malware|D) = \frac{P(Malware)P(D|Malware)}{P(D)} \tag{3}$$

$$P(Benignware|D) = \frac{P(Benignware)P(D|Benignware)}{P(D)} \tag{4}$$

In formula (3) and (4), *P(D)* is constant for all categories, so we only need to consider the numerator $P(Malware)P(D|Malware)$, $P(Benignware)P(D|Benignware)$ as the maximum value. The Naive Bayes classification algorithm assumes that the features are independent to each other. This assumption indicates that the probability product of $P(Items_1|Benignware), P(Items_2|Benignware), \ldots, P(Items_n|Benignware)$ for the classification is exactly the probability of the feature $P(D|Malware)$ for the category, so there are:

$$P(D|Malware) = \prod\nolimits_{k=1}^{n} P(Items_i|Malware) \tag{5}$$

$$P(D|Benignware) = \prod\nolimits_{k=1}^{n} P(Items_i|Benignware) \tag{6}$$

Therefore, we substitute formula (5) & (6) into formula (3) & (4) to get formula (7) & (8):

$$P(Malware|D) = \frac{P(Malware)\prod_{k=1}^{n} P(Items_i|Malware)}{P(D)} \tag{7}$$

$$P(Benignware|D) = \frac{P(Benignware)\prod_{k=1}^{n} P(Items_i|Benignware)}{P(D)} \tag{8}$$

Since different frequent patterns have different reliability for classification, the weighted Naive Bayes formula is considered of the reliability in each frequent pattern, formula (7) & (8) are further changed to formula (9) & (10):

$$P(Malware|D) = \frac{P(Malware)\prod_{k=1}^{n} [P(Items_i|Malware) \cdot reli(items_i)]}{P(D)} \tag{9}$$

$$P(Benignware|D) = \frac{P(Benignware)\prod_{k=1}^{n} [P(Items_i|Benignware) \cdot reli(items_i)]}{P(D)} \tag{10}$$

Finally, it is classified by comparing the probability that an application is classified as a malware $P(Malware|D)$ with the probability of a benign application $P(Benignware|D)$.

4 Implementation

In this section, we present the implementation details that readers may be interested in. The malicious application detection tool is mainly divided into two modules, namely the permission and API call feature extraction module and the Bayes classification module. The permission and API call feature module decompiles the Android application and extracts frequent permission & API call mode information, and the Bayes classification module classifies the Android application according to the information acquired by the feature extraction module (Fig. 3).

In this paper, the application's permission information and sensitive API call information in the application are used as feature attributes to maliciously detect and identify the application. The feature extraction module mainly prepare the pre-model of the tool design, including the extraction of the authority and the sensitive API, and the feature processing after the extraction. Permission information in the static configuration file (AndroidManifest.xml), in the extracted content after decompressing the application package, see AndroidManifest.xml contains the name of the Android application package, Linux user ID, permissions, and the minimum API version required for this application. Sensitive API calls exist in the application source code. This article uses androguard, a powerful static analysis tool, which uses the DED decompile reverse tool to decompile by default. It uses get_permissions and get_apis in androguard to extract permission lists and sensitive API calls. For the Bayes classification module, we call the Naive Bayes algorithm in the scikit-learn library to see if there is some kind of frequent permission & API invocation pattern as the feature, and the characteristic attributes of Naive Bayes are attributed to the reliability of the frequent pattern. After weighting, the feature weighted Naive Bayes algorithm is finally obtained, and the detection model is established.

5 Evaluation

We systematically evaluated the approach and tool in this article to answer the following questions:

What is the effect of screening the initial permissions and API features based on the degree of discrimination?

After frequent pattern mining, using Naive Bayes for classification, is there any improvement compared with the direct application of separate permissions and API features?

Under the premise of applying the frequent permission & API calling mode, does the weighted Naive Bayes classification effect improve compared to the unweighted Naive Bayes classification?

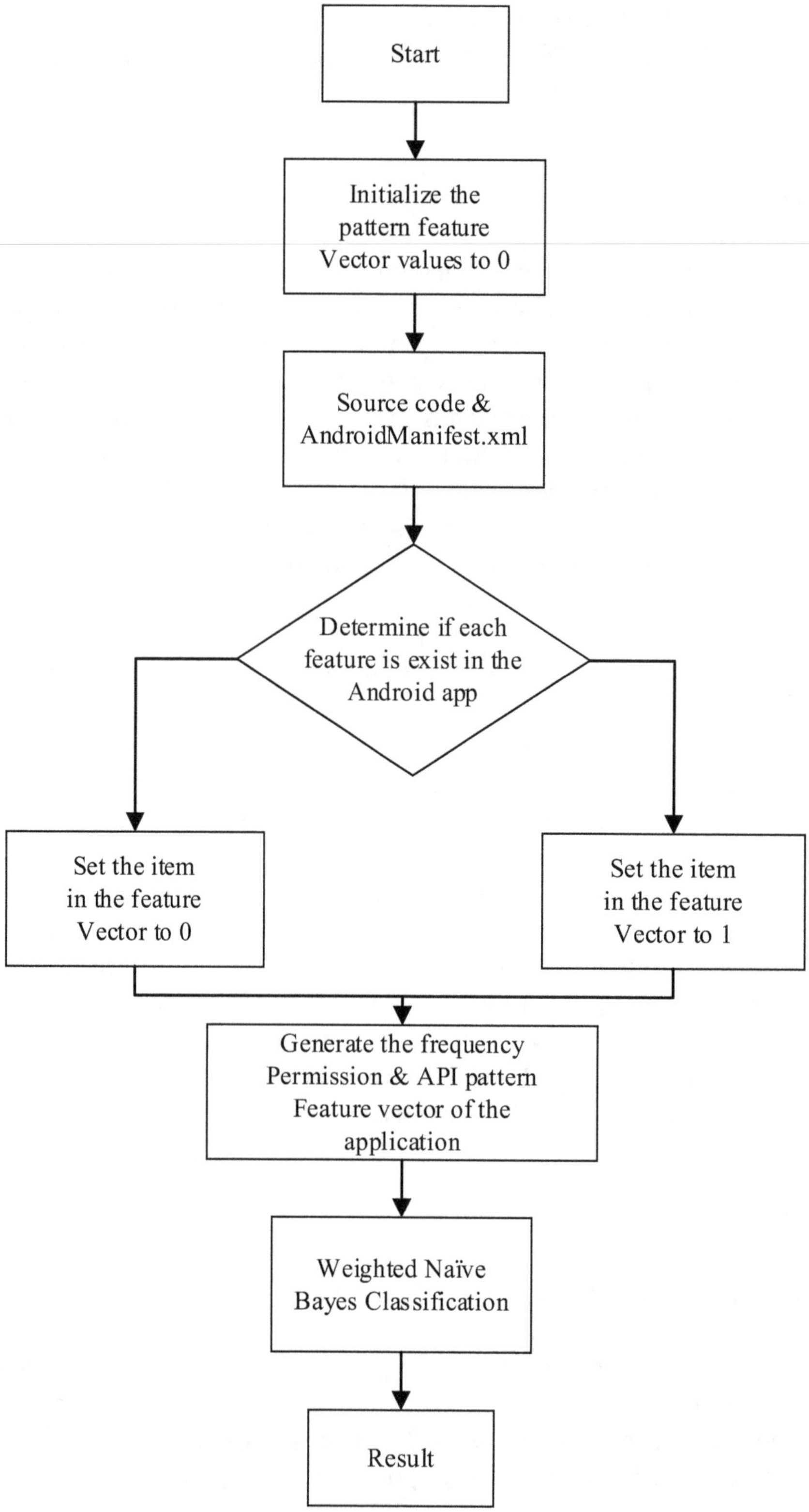

Fig. 3. Process of detection tool

Based on the above three questions, we conducted relevant experiments and evaluated them based on evaluation criteria such as accuracy, false positive rate, and running time. We collected 1,000 malicious apps from VirusShare and 1000 benign apps from Google Store, averaging them into training set and test set, and used the test set for method test evaluation.

First, for feature attributes, we use the degree of discrimination to filter, remove the feature attributes with poor discrimination, and reduce the impact of some feature attributes on the classification results. Therefore, Experiment 1 was used to test the performance of the feature processing method we used. We first compare the performance of the Naive Bayes algorithm without feature filtering and the performance of the Naive Bayes algorithm after feature filtering (Table 3).

Table 3. Evaluation index table-1

Algorithm	Evaluation index	Pre-filter	Post-filter
Naïve Bayes	ACC (%)	72.75	82.34
	FP (%)	20.41	16.53
	Runtime (s)	143.18	72.83
Random forest	ACC (%)	70.59	81.96
	FP (%)	23.63	14.23
	Runtime (s)	203.69	79.38
SVM	ACC (%)	73.02	81.96
	FP (%)	18.63	14.23
	Runtime (s)	194.18	86.06

From the above chart, we can see that the detection accuracy of Naive Bayes algorithm without feature screening is lower than that of feature screening, indicating that our feature processing method improves the detection performance of Naive Bayes algorithm to some extent. At the same time, we also deal with the random forest algorithm and the support vector machine algorithm, and compare the obtained detection results with the results of the random forest algorithm and the support vector machine algorithm without feature processing. Through the above vertical and horizontal comparisons of Naïve Bayes algorithm, random forest algorithm and support vector machine algorithm, it can be seen that the detection accuracy of feature screening is significantly lower than that of feature screening, and also shows our feature screening method has nothing to do with the type of algorithm applied, and it can generally improve the detection performance of the algorithm.

Second, in order to evaluate the performance of the weighted Bayes method based on frequent patterns, the second experiment is to compare the test results of Naïve Bayes based on pre-filtering permission & API features, Naïve Bayes based on post-filtering permission & API features, and Weighted Naive Bayes based on frequent permission & API patterns.

As can be seen from the Table 4, the accuracy of the method in this paper (88.69%) is better than the method's mentioned in Chapter 2 (up to 79.6%), which is based on the

Table 4. Evaluation index table-2

Evaluation index	Naïve Bayes based on pre-filtering permission & API features	Naïve Bayes based on post-filtering permission & API features	Weighted Naive Bayes based on frequent permission & API patterns
ACC (%)	72.75	82.34	88.69047619047618
FP (%)	20.41	16.53	12.3
Runtime (s)	143.18	72.83	80.65

combination mode of the permission features in malicious applications. And the detection accuracy of Naïve Bayes based on pre-filtering permission & API features and Naïve Bayes based on post-filtering permission & API features are both lower than that of weighted Naive Bayes based on frequent permission & API patterns. It shows that both the frequent pattern feature and the weighted Naive Bayes algorithm have further improved the detection performance.

6 Conclusion and Future Work

Android-based systems are becoming more and more exclusive in mobile phone systems, and malicious acts that use malicious applications to illegally obtain users' information and interests are also increasing. The mainstream technologies for malicious application detection include static analysis detection technology and dynamic analysis detection technology. However, dynamic analysis detection is more technically demanding, consumes more resources, and is more demanding in real time. In this paper, the characteristics of static analysis are applied. The features are classified based on the degree of discrimination and the frequent feature patterns. The Naive Bayes algorithm is also used to improve the weighted attributes of frequent pattern reliability. Finally, this feature processing method and the improved Naive Bayes algorithm design is combined to implement a Android malicious application detection tool. The experimental results show that the feature screening method and the frequent feature pattern mining method can improve the detection performance of the algorithm to a certain extent. At the same time, for the Naive Bayes algorithm, the weighted property can be improved after reliability to achieve better results.

There are also some limitations and unfinished work in the approach of this paper. First of all, although the method considers the association between each permission and API call, it does not consider the correlation between frequent patterns. Since this method is still based on static detection technology, the detection effect on unknown malicious applications may not be ideal for detection of packed malicious applications: Because the author of malware uses obfuscation and encryption to make the code difficult to understand, some applications often cannot use this method to check for maliciousness. The method of this paper will be further developed and improved based on the above three points in the future.

References

1. Gartner Says Worldwide Sales of Smartphones Returned to Growth in First Quarter of 2018. https://www.gartner.com/newsroom/id/3876865. Accessed 29 May 2018
2. Android's annual malware report (2017). (in Chinese) http://bbs.360.cn/thread-15355463-1-1.html
3. Android Security Environmental Research (2017). (in Chinese) http://zt.360.cn/1101061855.php?dtid=1101061451&did=210555695
4. Google Play. Number of available applications in the Google Play Store from December 2009 to September 2017. https://www.statista.com/statistics/266210/number-of-available-applications-in-the-google-play-store/
5. Park, J.S., Chen, M.S., Yu, P.S.: An effective hash-based algorithm for mining association rules. ACM (1995)
6. Domingos, P., Pazzani, M.: On the optimality of the simple Bayesian classifier under zero-one loss. Mach. Learn. **29**(2–3), 103–130 (1997)
7. Liang, S., Du, X.: Permission-combination-based scheme for android mobile malware detection. In: IEEE International Conference on Communications (ICC), Sydney, Australia, New Jersey, 10–14 June 2014, pp. 2301–2306. IEEE (2014)
8. Yang, H., Zhang, Y., Hu, Y., et al.: Android malware detection method based on permission sequential pattern mining algorithm. J. Commun. **34**(Z1), 106–115 (2013). (in Chinese)
9. Fuchs, A.P., Chaudhuri, A., Foster, J.S.: SCanDroid: Automated Security Certification of Android Applications. University of Maryland, Technical report CS-TR-4991 (2009)
10. Lu, L., Li, Z., Wu, Z., et al.: CHEX: statically vetting android apps for component hijacking vulnerabilities. In: Proceedings of the 2012 ACM Conference on Computer and Communications Security, Raleigh, NC, USA, 16–18 October 2012, pp. 229–240. ACM, New York (2012)
11. Feng, Y., Anand, S., Dillig, I., et al.: Apposcopy: semantics-based detection of android malware through static analysis. In: Proceedings of the 22nd ACM SIGSOFT International Symposium on Foundations of Software Engineering, (FSE-22), Hong Kong, China, 16–22 November 2014, pp. 576–587. ACM, New York (2014)
12. Enck, W., Gilbert, P., Han, S., et al.: TaintDroid: an information-flow tracking system for realtime privacy monitoring on smartphones. ACM Trans. Comput. Syst. (TOCS) **32**, 1–5 (2014). (5)
13. Burguera, I., Zurutuza, U., Nadjm-Tehrani, S.: Crowdroid: behavior-based malware detection system for android. In: Proceedings of the 1st ACM Workshop Security and Privacy in Smartphones and Mobile Devices, Co-located with CCS 2011, Chicago, USA, 17 October 2011, pp. 15–26. ACM, New York (2011)
14. Wang, D., Dai, S., Ding, Y., et al.: POSTER: AdHoneyDroid – capture malicious android advertisements. In: Proceedings of ACM Conference on Computer and Communications Security, 2014, Scottsdale, Arizona, USA, pp. 1514–1516. ACM, New York (2014)
15. Michael, G., Zhou, Y., Zhang, Q., et al.: Riskranker: scalable and accurate zero-day android malware detection. In: The 10th International Conference on Mobile Systems, Applications and Services, Ambleside, United Kingdom, 25–29 June 2014, pp. 281–294. ACM, New York (2012)
16. Zhao, S., Li, X., Xu, G., et al.: Attack tree based android malware detection with hybrid analysis. In: The 13th IEEE International Conference on Trust, Security and Privacy in Computing and Communications (TrustCom), Beijing, China, 24–26 September 2014, pp. 380–387. IEEE, New Jersey (2014)

17. Spreitzenbarth, M., Schreck, T., Echtler, F., et al.: Mobile-Sandbox: combining static and dynamic analysis with machine-learning techniques. Int. J. Inf. Secur. **14**(2), 141–153 (2015)
18. Virus Share Homepage. https://virusshare.com/
19. Agrawal, R., Imielinski, T., Swami, A.N.: Ming association rules between sets of items in large databases. In: Proceedings of the 1993 ACM SIGMOD the International Conference on Management of Data, Washington DC, USA, pp. 207–216 (1993)

Emerging Technologies

An Overview of Blockchain Security Analysis

Hai Wang[1,2], Yong Wang[3], Zigang Cao[1,2], Zhen Li[1,2], and Gang Xiong[1,2](✉)

[1] Institute of Information Engineering, Chinese Academy of Sciences, Beijing, China
xionggang@iie.ac.cn

[2] University of Chinese Academy of Sciences, Beijing, China

[3] National Computer Network Emergency Response Technical Team/Coordination Center, Beijing, China

Abstract. The blockchain, with its own characteristics, has received much attention at the beginning of its birth and been applied in many fields. At the same time, however, its security issues are exposed constantly and cyber attacks have caused significant losses in it. At present, there is little concern and research in the field of network security of the blockchain. This paper introduces the applications of blockchain in various fields, systematically analyzes the security of each layer of the blockchain and possible cyber attacks, expounds the challenges brought by the blockchain to network supervision, and summarizes research progress in the protection technology. This paper is a review of the current security of the blockchain and will effectively help the development and improvement of security technologies of the blockchain.

Keywords: Blockchain · Network security · Cyber attacks · Network supervision

1 Background

1.1 Origin and Development of the Blockchain

The first blockchain was conceptualized by a person (or group of people) known as Satoshi Nakamoto in 2008 [1]. It was implemented the following year by Nakamoto as a core component of the cryptocurrency bitcoin, where it serves as the public ledger for all transactions on the network.

Comparing to the rapid development of blockchain technology, relevant norms and standards on it are still incomplete. The first descriptive document on the blockchain is the "Bitcoin: A Peer-to-Peer Electronic Cash System" written by Nakamoto, in which blocks and chains are described as a data structure recording the historical data of the bitcoin transaction accounts. "A timestamp server works by taking a hash of a block of items to be timestamped and widely publishing the hash, such as in a newspaper or Usenet post. The timestamp proves that the data must have existed at the time, obviously, in order to get

X. Yun et al. (Eds.): CNCERT 2018, CCIS 970, pp. 55–72, 2019.
https://doi.org/10.1007/978-981-13-6621-5_5

into the hash. Each timestamp includes the previous timestamp in its hash, forming a chain, with each additional timestamp reinforcing the ones before it (Fig. 1)." The blockchain is also called the Internet of value [2], which is a distributed ledger database for a peer-to-peer network.

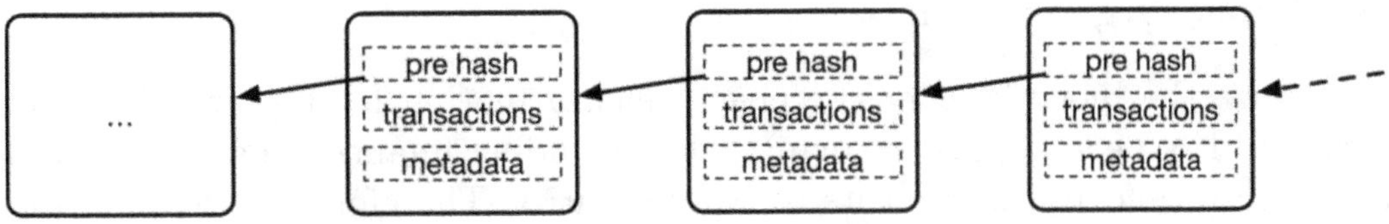

Fig. 1. The structure of blockchain.

As a rule, most innovations do not appear out of nowhere, nor does the blockchain. The blockchain is actually a natural result of that the ledger technology developed into distributed scenarios. Ledger technology has evolved from single entry bookkeeping, double-entry bookkeeping, digital bookkeeping to distributed bookkeeping. The blockchain structure (Fig. 1) naturally solves the problem of multiparty trust in distributed bookkeeping [3].

Due to its decentralization, tamper-resistance, safety and reliability, the block-chain technology has received extensive attention since its birth. After nearly 10 years developing, the blockchain technology has experienced the period of v1.0-bitcoin, v2.0-Ethernet and v3.0-EOS. Not only has the technology itself been greatly expanded and developed, but it has also been applied in many fields.

1.2 Blockchain Classification

According to the way users participate, blockchains can be classified into Public Blockchain, Consortium Blockchain and Private Blockchain, and also can be classified into main chains and side chains based on the relationship of chains. In addition, several blockchains can form a network. The chains in the network are interconnected in order to generate the Interchain [4].

Public Blockchain: a consensus blockchain that everyone can get an access to. He or she in the blockchain topology can send transactions and validated. Everyone can compete for billing rights. These blockchains are generally considered to be "completely decentralized", typical use like the bitcoin blockchain, in which the information is completely disclosing.

Private Blockchain: a blockchain in which the permission to write remain in one organization. The permission to read can be public or limited to some extent. Within a company, there are additional options, such as database management, audit, and so on. In most cases, public access is not necessary.

Consortium Blockchain: in between Public Chain and Private Chain, it refers to the blockchain whose consensus process is controlled by pre-selected nodes. For example, there is a system of 15 financial institutions, each of which manages one node, and at least 10 of which must confirm each block to be recognized as valid and added to the chain. The right to read the blockchain can be open to the public, or limited by participants, or "hybrid". Such chains can be called "partially decentralized".

1.3 Paper Organization

At present, the blockchain has received much attention for its own characteristics, and has been applied in many fields including finance. However, there is little concern and research on its network security. Therefore, this paper introduces the birth, development and application of blockchain technology in detail, comprehensively searches and investigates various documents targeted on the security needs of blockchains, and systematically analyzes the security threats and defense technologies of blockchains.

The Sect. 2 of this paper introduces applications of the blockchain in different fields. The Sect. 3 focuses on the security threats in different layers of blockchains and summarizes common attacks. The Sect. 4 summarizes the research progress of blockchain security protection technologies. At the end of this paper, we summarize the work of the full paper.

2 Blockchain Applications

The large-scale digital currency system represented by the Bitcoin network runs autonomously for a long time, through which it supports the global real-time reliable transactions that are difficult to achieve in the traditional financial system. This has caused infinite imagination for the potential applications of the blockchain. If the business value network based on the blockchain gets real in the future, all transactions will be completed efficiently and reliably, and all signed contracts can strictly follow the agreement. This will greatly reduce the cost of running the entire business system, while sharply improving the efficiency of social communication and collaboration. In this sense, the blockchain might trigger another industrial revolution as the Internet did.

In fact, to find the right application scenario, we should proceed from the characteristics of the blockchain itself. In addition, you need to consider the reasonable boundaries of the blockchain solution. For example, blockchain applications for mass consumers need to be open, transparent, and auditable, which can be deployed on a borderless public chain or on a blockchain that is commonly maintained by multicenter nodes.

The application of blockchain in the financial services is the most concerned currently, and many banks and financial institutions around the world are the main promoters. At present, the processing after global securities trading is very complicated. The cost of liquidation is about 5–10 billion dollars. The post-trade analysis, reconciliation and processing costs exceed 20 billion dollars. According to a report by the European Central Bank [5], the blockchain, as a distributed ledger technology, can make a good deal with the cost of reconciliation and simplify the transaction process. Relative to the original transaction process, the ownership of the securities can be changed in near real time.

Blockchain can be used for ownership and copyright management and tracking. It includes transactions of valuables such as cars, houses and artworks, as well as including digital publications and digital resources that can be tagged. For example, Factom tried to use blockchain to revolutionize data management and logging in business societies and government departments. Similarly, in response to the problem of food fraud, IBM, Wal-Mart and Tsinghua University jointly announced at the end of 2016 that blockchain will be used to build a transparent and traceable cross-border food supply chain [6]. This new supply chain will improve the traceability and logistics of food and create a safer global food market.

While enjoying the convenience of cloud storage, we will inevitably mention privacy concerns. This concern comes from two aspects. One is that the storage center may be attacked by hackers, causing their own data outflow, and the second is that the company wants to get more profits to abuse the privacy of users. Blockchain solves these problems perfectly. At present, there are many distributed cloud storage projects, such as Sia, Storj, MadeSafe, and IPFS in foreign countries, and FIGTOO and GNX in China. InterPlanetary File System (IPFS) is a global, peer-to-peer distributed file system, which aims to supplement (or even replace) Hypertext Transfer Protocol (HTTP), seeks to connect all computing devices with the same file system. Replacing domain-based addresses with content-based addresses to get a faster, safer, more robust, and more durable web [7].

The relationship between FIGTOO and IPFS: IPFS is a peer-to-peer hypermedia protocol and a distributed web and FIGTOO is developed on the basis of its open source. It is a branch of IPFS, which is equivalent to bitcoin and Ethereum in the blockchain. The infrastructures are all based on the blockchain. FIGTOO creates a shared trading market for free storage space and shares global storage resources through the shared economy model. It uses red chain technology to store files in slices, builds decentralized cloud storage and becomes the infrastructure of global red chain distributed file storage [8].

User Generated Content (UGC) is one of the important aspect of blockchain application. In the era of information explosion, how to quickly find the most important content from the overloaded information has become a core issue of the Internet. UGC Network is the world's first content value forecasting platform, a fair and value-driven content-incentive network with the mission of creating a content-driven blockchain value community that differentiates truly valuable content and achieves a reasonable return [9]. It committed to solving problems such as excellent content discovery and pricing on the UGC platform, unreasonable distribution of benefits, and centralized content storage.

Other UGC applications include YOYOW (You Own Your Own Word) - a blockchain-based UGC platform that all processes rely on interest-based implementation. It solves the problems in current content platform like lacking of high-quality content incentives, community pollution (piracy and Advertising) serious [10]. BiHu - a token investor vertical community. In the BiHu, the user's contribution will be rewarded with the token (KEY) representing the BiHu and its surrounding ecological use rights [11].

Due to its decentralization, eliminating trust, tamper-resistance, safety and reliability characteristics, the blockchain technology has been used in lots of fields including financial services, credit and ownership management, trade management, cloud storage, user-generated content, copyright protection, advertising and games. In these cases, blockchain either solves the problems of multiparty trust in the transaction, or reduces the costs and risks of traditional industries.

3 Blockchain Security Analysis

3.1 Security Situation

With the blockchain technology has been widely used, various types of attacks have emerged. Such as from the more and more digital currencies have been stolen to the exchanges have been attacked and other events. According to the statistics of the BCSEC on the blockchain attack events, about 2.1 billion dollars of economic losses due to blockchain security incidents in 2018 [12]. These are only a part of the currently exposed, and as the value of blockchain increases, the number of attacks will continue to increase (Fig. 2).

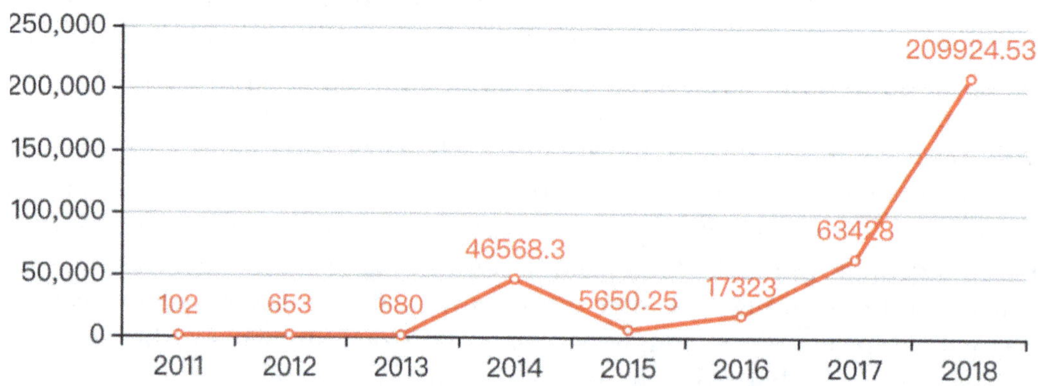

Fig. 2. Economic losses caused by blockchain security incidents (ten thousand dollars).

Blockchain technology itself is still in the initial stage of rapid development, and its security is far behind the needs of development. The risks may come from attacks by external entities or internal participants. The popularity of blockchain makes new demands on security and privacy protection on data storage, transmission and applications, and puts forward new challenges to existing security solutions, authentication mechanisms, data protection, privacy protection and Information regulation.

With the current recurrence of a series of digital currency theft, hacking of exchanges, and theft of user accounts, it is urgent to establish one or more collaborative security solutions to improve the security performance of the blockchain system.

3.2 Security Analysis of Each Layer of Blockchain

The current blockchain structure can be roughly divided into application layer, smart contract layer, incentive layer, consensus layer, network layer and data layer from top to bottom. The security analysis of each layer will be performed separately below.

Application Layer. Application layer security mainly covers the security issues of centralized nodes such as the exchanges which involve digital currency transactions and manage large amounts of funds. These nodes are at any point of failure of the entire blockchain network, and the attack yield is high and the cost is low, which is the preferred target of the attackers [13].

Unauthorized Access to An Exchange Server. Exchanges often deposit large amounts of money and are easily targeted. Once the exchange server authority is obtained and the key information is modified, the attacker can steal the funds key, tamper with the transaction amount or leak sensitive information, causing economic and reputational devastating blows to the exchange.

For example, the Youbit (formerly Yapizon) stolen event. On April 22, 2017, 4 hot wallets of Youbit were stolen, lost 3,816 BTC, with a total value of about $5,300,000, accounting for 36% of the exchange's funds. On December 19, 2017, Youbit announced that it was attacked again, lost approximately 17% of its assets, and at the same time announced the exchange closed and entered the bankruptcy process [14].

Exchange DDoS. Due to the high demand for network bandwidth in the trading platform, once a DDoS attack occurs, it is very serious for the platform and the entire industry. If the trading platform is attacked by DDoS, not only will itself suffer losses, but the transaction volume of the blockchain currency will also be greatly reduced, which will indirectly affect the rise and fall of the blockchain currency [15].

According to the report of global DDoS threat landscape Q3 2017 by Incapsula [16], although its industry scale is still relatively small, Bitcoin has become one of the top 10 industries which are most vulnerable to DDoS attacks. This reflects to a certain extent that the entire blockchain industry is facing serious DDoS security challenges. For example, from November 2017 to December 2017 Bitfinex announced that it had suffered the DDoS attack for three times, and all the services of the exchange had been shut down for a long time [17]. The attacker creates pressure on the server by creating a large number of empty accounts, causing related services and APIs to go offline for hours.

Employees Host Security. On June 20, 2011, the large Bitcoin exchange Mt.Gox was attacked. Its server was not compromised, but the attacker gained access to a computer used by an auditor of Mt.Gox, and got a read-only database file, resulting in about 60000 users' username, email address, and encrypted password [18] to be leaked. After obtaining this sensitive information, the attacker cracked the password of one of the large accounts, issued a large sales message through this account, and sold 400,000 BTC [19] under it, trying to transfer funds through the legal transaction process. Fortunately, because the exchange protection measures are effective, it limits the maximum value of \$1,000 BTC per account per day, so it does not cause much damage to this account. However, a large number of BTC sale requests caused the exchange BTC price to drop to 1 cent, resulting in an impact of approximately \$8,750,000 in assets.

Malicious Program Infection. Once a malicious program is implanted into the exchange system, it is likely to cause a large amount of sensitive information leakage, including key and wallet files. The key is everything, and the leakage of sensitive information often means losing control of all assets. The exchange Mt.Gox was attacked in 2014. The key file of Mt.Gox was stored locally in clear text, and the key file wallet.dat leaked due to Trojan infection, resulting in a large amount of asset loss and eventually, Mt.Gox went bankruptcy [20]. It is worth noting that in this attack, the attacker used two years to gradually transfer assets in order to avoid the community recovering the loss through hard forks. The emergence of this type of APT attack means that monitoring of the threat of attack in the blockchain industry cannot rely solely on short-term anomaly transaction monitoring.

Initial Coin Offering. Tampering Attack: When ICO raises funds, it usually hangs the receiving address on the project official website, and then the investor will transfer money to this address for the corresponding token. Hackers can tamper with the collection address through attacks such as domain hijacking, web vulnerabilities, or social engineering.

Phishing attack: The attacker uses social engineering and other means to impersonate the official, allowing the user to transfer money to the attacker's wallet address. For example, an attacker can use an approximate domain name and highly phishing website to defraud investors or use email to disseminate fake information, such as ICO project's payment address change notice, etc. or disseminate phishing information on social software and media to defraud investors.

Mining Machine System. The cyber security awareness of mining device manufacturers is uneven, and because of its closed source characteristics, the security of its code cannot be checked by the public. Once a cyber security issue occurs, the result is fatal. And whether the device manufacturer will intersperse the back door for remote control of the device, or steal the mining output, is still remain to be discussed.

0day: Most mining system is a general-purpose system. Once a mining system is found to have a 0 day vulnerability, the security barriers of the system will be broken in an instant. The attacker can use the vulnerability to obtain the modify permission and then tamper with reward receiving address and then hijack the user's reward.

Weak password attack: At present, the mining system in the market is based on the B/S architecture. Access to the mining system is usually through the web or other means. If the weak password is used, it will be vulnerable to intrusion.

Mining Pool. By June 2018, the top five Bitcoin mining pools in the world are BTC.com, AntPool, SlushPool, BTC.TOP and F2Pool. About 60% of the world's hash power is in the hands of Chinese miners [21].

Hash power forgery attack: The mining pool will test the actual hash power of the current miner through a certain proof of work test algorithm. The hacker can falsely report the hash power by finding the vulnerability of the algorithm, and then obtain the excessive reward that doesn't match the actual contribution.

Selfish mining attack: A malicious mining pool decides not to release the block it finds, and thus creates a fork. When the private fork is longer than the public chain, the malicious mining pool issues the private fork. Because the fork is the longest chain in the current network, it will be recognized as a legal chain by honest miners, so the original public chain and the honest data it contains will be discarded. The results of the study indicate that the malicious mining pools will yield more benefits normally by using selfish mining strategies. But such attacks usually require huge hash power as a support.

Centralization: The existence of the mining pool violates the principle of decentralization of the blockchain. Theoretically, if it can control at least 51% of the hash power of entire network, it will be able to monopolize the mining right, billing right and distribution right, which will affect the ecological security of the blockchain, so that the credit system of the cryptocurrency will cease to exist and the cryptocurrency system will be completely destroyed.

Possible Methods. It is impossible for any one party to respond to various attacks at the application layer. The application developers should ensure that the softwares don't contain discovered vulnerabilities and are thoroughly tested. As the central node, such as a trading platform, real-time monitoring of system health and some protected methods (e.g. data encryption storage, etc.) are required to ensure that the system is not subject to internal and external attacks. All employees should be systematically trained before they are employed to avoid becoming an attack portal. As a user, you should be able to keep your own account and key properly, distinguish between true and false information and be cautious in trading to avoid phishing attacks.

Smart Contract Layer. A smart contract is more than just a computer program that can be executed automatically. It is a system participant. It responds to the received message, it can receive and store value, and it can send out information and value [22]. For the security risks of smart contracts, the following attacks are summarized.

Reentrancy Attack. The essence of reentrancy attack is to hijack the contract control flow and destroy the atomicity of the transaction, which can be understood as a logical race condition problem. For example, The DAO was attacked, and the attacker used the vulnerability in the contract to launch a reentrancy attack and gained 60 million dollars. In order to recover this part of the funds, the Ethereum community decided to perform a hard fork, roll back all the transaction records since the start of the attack and fix the contract vulnerabilities in the new branch. The vulnerability is described below. Here is a simplified version of The DAO contract:

```
contract SimpleDAO {
  mapping (address => uint) public credit;
  function donate(address to){credit[to] += msg.value;}
  function queryCredit(address to) returns (uint){
    return credit[to];
  }
  function withdraw(uint amount) {
    if (credit[msg.sender]>= amount) {
      msg.sender.call.value(amount)();
      credit[msg.sender]-= amount;
    }
  }
}
```

Participants call the donate function to donate their own Ether to a contract address, the donation information is stored in the credit array, and the recipient contract calls The DAO's withdraw function to receive funds. Before actually sending the transaction, The DAO checks if there is enough donation in the credit array, and after the transaction is over, the transaction amount is reduced from credit.

The attacker first constructs a malicious contract Mallory, as follows:

```
contract Mallory {
  SimpleDAO public dao = SimpleDAO(0x354...);
  address owner;
  function Mallory(){owner = msg.sender; }
  function() { dao.withdraw(dao.queryCredit(this)); }
  function getJackpot(){ owner.send(this.balance); }
}
```

After Mallory deployed, the attacker calls The DAO's donate function to donate a bit of Ether to the Mallory contract. After triggering Mallory's fallback function (unnamed function), there are many trigger methods, such as transfer money to Mallory. The fallback function will call The DAO's withdraw function and extract all the funds that belong to it. It seems to be no problem so far. However, after msg.sender.call.value(amount)() in the withdraw is executed, Mallory's fallback function is automatically called after the transfer is completed due to the transfer operation feature, so the withdraw function is called again. Because credit is not updated at this time, so you can still withdraw money normally, then you fall into a recursive loop, and each time you can extract a part of Ether in the DAO to the Mallory contract.

This loop will continue until one of three conditions occurs, gas is exhausted, the call stack is full, and The DAO balance is insufficient. An exception is thrown when one of the above conditions occurs. Due to the characteristics of the Solidity exception handling, all previous transactions are valid. Theoretically, repeating this operation can extract all the Ether of The DAO's to Mallory.

Unauthorized Access Attack. Most of this attack due to failure to make explicit function visibility, or fails to do sufficient permission checks, which can cause an attacker to access or modify a function or variable that should not be accessed.

For example, a multi-signature contract vulnerability in the Parity wallet was exploited by an attacker to steal a total of 153,037 Ether in three times. Then Parity official blog and Twitter released security alert [23] and updated the new version of the library contract. The bug comes from the Multi-Sig library file enhanced-wallet.sol written by Parity's founder Gavin Wood. The attacker exploited the bug to reset the wallet owner, took over the wallet and stolen all the funds. This is essentially a breach of authority in the contract.

Solidity Development Security. Possible bugs when writing smart contracts include:

Race condition: The biggest risk of calling an external function is that the calling behavior may cause the control flow to be hijacked and accidentally modify the contract data. This type of bug has many specific forms, such as reentrant and cross-function race conditions.

Transaction-Ordering Dependence: A attacker can construct his own transaction based on the order information contained in the pending transactions, and try to get his transaction to be written into the block before others.

Integer overflow and underflow: When programming, you should think about whether integer overflows can occur, how the state of uint variables will be transferred, and who has the authority to modify those variables.

Denial of Service Attack Based on Exception Rollback: For example, a crowdfunding contract gives a refund to a participant. The contract may need to traverse an array to process a refund for a group of users. The simple idea is that every refund is successful, otherwise the program should be rolled back. The consequence of this practice is that one of the malicious users forced the refund to fail and all users were unable to receive the refund. It is recommended to use a pull payment mechanism, which separates the refund operation into an independent function, which is called by the refund recipient to pull the refund.

Possible Methods. Once a smart contract is deployed in a distributed, decentralized network, it is difficult to change. It prevents data manipulation and establishes a trust mechanism based on the encryption algorithm. On the other hand, when the blockchain is facing a security attack, it lacks an effective correction mechanism and is difficult to reverse. Therefore, before the development of smart contracts, it is necessary to guard against the vulnerabilities that have already occurred. It should conduct sufficient security tests before issued. Professionals perform code optimizations in a timely manner, conduct regular code audits, and monitor abnormal behavior of deployed contracts to reduce losses.

Incentive Layer. The purpose of the incentive layer is to provide certain incentives to encourage nodes to participate in the security verification of the blockchain. The security of the blockchain depends on the participation of many nodes. For example, the security of the Bitcoin blockchain is based on the great hash power that many nodes participate in the proof of work which makes it impossible for an attacker to provide a higher amount of computation. The verification process of a node usually consumes computing resources and electric power. In order to encourage node participation, the blockchain usually rewards participants in the form of virtual currency. Bitcoin, Litecoin, and Ether are all products of this mechanism.

Blockchain projects need to adapt to the market to automatically adjust the rewards, rather than simply reducing them. In the blockchain project reward mechanism, when the node's working cost is close to or greater than the income, they often choose not to work for this blockchain, which can easily lead to centralization problems.

Consensus Layer. The consensus mechanism gives the blockchain the soul to differentiate it from other P2P technologies. Commonly used consensus mechanisms are Proof of Work (PoW), Proof of Stake (PoS), and Delegated Proof of Stake (DPoS). The possible attacks include Bribe Attack, Long-Rang Attack, Accumulation Attack, Precomputing Attack and Sybil Attack. Table 1 shows the application scope of the attacks for the consensus mechanisms.

Table 1. Attack methods and application scope for consensus mechanism

Attack methods	PoW	PoS	DPoS
Bribe Attack	−	+	−
Long-Range Attack	−	+	+
Coin Age Accumulation Attack	−	+	+
Precomputing Attack	−	+	−
Sybil Attack	+	+	+

At present, the existing consensus mechanisms are not perfect, and it is necessary to explore a more secure and faster consensus mechanism while increasing the difficulty of existing attacks.

Network Layer. The information transmission of the blockchain mainly depends on the peer-to-peer network. The P2P network relies on nearby nodes for information transmission in which it must expose each other's IP. If there is an attacker in the network, it is very easy to bring security threats to other nodes. The node of the public blockchain network may be an ordinary home PC, a cloud server, etc., and its security must be uneven. There must be a node with poor security, and attacking it will directly threaten the other nodes. The main attacks are as follows.

Eclipse attack: The node is kept in an isolated network by hoarding and occupying the victim's slots. This type of attack is designed to block the latest blockchain information from entering the eclipse node, thereby isolating the nodes [24].

BGP hijacking: At present, the security researchers have proved the conceptual feasibility of the attack. From November 5, 2015, to November 15, 2016, through the analysis and statistics of the node network, most of the bitcoin nodes are currently hosted in a few specific Internet Service Providers (ISP), while 60% of Bitcoin connections are in these ISPs. Therefore, these ISPs can see 60% of Bitcoin traffic, and can also control the traffic of the current Bitcoin network. The researchers verified that at least two attacks are conceptual feasible through the hijacking scenario, and given validation code [25].

The security defense for the network layer can be mainly improved from two aspects: P2P network security and network authentication mechanism. In the transmission process of the network, a reliable encryption algorithm is used for transmission to prevent malicious attackers from stealing or hijacking the node network. Strengthen the validity, rationality and security of data transmission in network. Client nodes should do the necessary verification for important operations and information.

Data Layer

Block Data. Malicious information attack: Write malicious information, such as virus signatures, politically sensitive topics, etc. in the blockchain. With the data undelete feature of the blockchain, information is difficult to delete after it is written in the blockchain. If malicious information appears in the blockchain, it will be subject to many problems.

A team of researchers at the RWTH Aachen University and the Goethe University Frankfurt in Germany pointed out that among the 1,600 documents added to the Bitcoin blockchain, 59 files contained links to illegal children's pictures, politically sensitive content or privacy violations [26]. Currently, only a few Bitcoin blockchain transactions contain other data. In the Bitcoin blockchain, about 1.4% of the 251 million transactions contain other data, that is, only a few of these transactions contain illegal or undesirable content [26]. Still, even such small amounts of illegal or inappropriate content can put participants at risk.

Signature and Encryption Method. Cryptography is the key to ensure the security and tamper resistance of blockchain, and blockchain technology relies heavily on the research results of cryptography, which provides a key guarantee for the information integrity, authentication and non-repudiation of the blockchain.

As a mainstay of the blockchain, the encryption technology is particularly important. For example, the MD5 and SHA1 hash algorithms popular in previous years but have been proved to be insufficiently secure. At present, the SHA256 algorithm is widely used in bitcoin. So far, this algorithm is still safe, but with the development of new technology and research, it may not be safe in the future. Therefore, when designing blockchain applications, it is important to carefully choose the encryption method. Current mainstream signature methods include aggregate signature, group signature, ring signature, blind signature, proxy signature, interactive incontestable signature (IIS), blinded verifiable encrypted signature (BVES), and so on.

Attacks on cryptographic algorithms, especially the hash functions, include brute-force attack, collision attack, length expansion attack, back door attack and quantum attack.

3.3 Network Supervision of Blockchain

While blockchain brings technological innovation, it also brings huge challenges for network supervision. The traditional supervision mode is mostly centralized management. How to use the blockchain technology and the current legal system to supervise the application of the blockchain is one of the problems that the government and the industry pay attention to.

In order to overcome the problems of blockchain in network supervision, it is necessary to cross the underlying technology and think about how to combine the specific cases of technology application with supervision. At present, by classifying application cases, they can be divided into three categories, "Recycling Box", "Dark Box" and "Sandbox" [27]. The application cases in each category bring many challenges for the legal, supervision and decision-making departments. The three categories are fully analyzed below.

3.4 "Recycling Box"

"Recycling box" are those cases that attempt to solve industry pain points through blockchain solutions in a better, faster, and cheaper way. Their goals are not illegal, and the motivation is simple. In the process of the application launched, the network supervision authorities can implement supervision only by making minor modifications to the current supervision framework.

The most typical example is the interbank settlement system developed by Ripple. The payment solution uses a single distributed ledger to connect the world's major financial institutions and cross-bank transactions that occur between each other can be done in real time. Compared with the traditional method, it not only saves a lot of time, improves efficiency, but also saves a service fee [27].

3.5 "Dark Box"

"Dark box", its source is similar to "dark net". Cases belonging to this category, without exception, all contradict the current law. Such cases are numerous, for example, the online drug market, the arms market or other illegal goods market, human trafficking networks, terrorist financing and communication networks, money laundering and tax evasion can all be classified as such. These illegal services have existed in the dark network for a long time. Nowadays, because of the application of blockchain technology, some of them are like discovering the New World. It's easy to identify the "dark box", but it can be difficult to try to stop them [27].

The reason why the "dark box" is difficult to be stopped is that in recent years, the digital currency has become an important tool for money laundering, illegal transactions, and escaping foreign exchange control due to its anonymity and decentralization. Digital currency does not require a credit card and bank account information. Criminals can avoid the supervision agencies and cannot trace the source and destination of funds through traditional capital transaction records, which makes traditional supervision methods malfunction.

3.6 "Sandbox"

The "sandbox" is one of the most exciting and headaches for legislators in these three categories, and many of the most disruptive and public interest cases fall into this category. The term "sandbox" was taken from a recent initiative by the Financial Conduct Authority (FCA) called "Regulatory Sandbox". Application cases belonging to this category have very valuable business objectives, but the current situation is that due to the various characteristics of the distributed ledger technology, most of these cases cannot meet the existing supervision requirements. Their common feature is what the business pursued is legal, but it may cause various risks, so the government will not let it go and will have appropriate supervision.

The typical case is peer-to-peer(P2P) funding. It is necessary to mention the venture capital fund The DAO based on the blockchain. Although The DAO's ICO is no different from ordinary venture capital, their goals are all to invest in a startup. It seems to have nothing to do with illegality. However, the way The DAO works is not normal at all, which is one of the reasons why it will be incompatible with the existing legal system.

The DAO has no physical existence, no legal status in any jurisdiction, no leadership, management, or even employees. All operations are automatically done by the blockchain in a decentralized manner. It is not responsible to anyone except those anonymous donors. TechCrunch commented on such organizations as "completely transparent", "shareholders have full control", and "unparalleled flexibility and self-governance".

At present, the skills possessed by most of the regulators are highly specialized, and they are only suitable for a certain place. The applications of blockchain are mostly global, and the coverage area is very wide. This also explains why the

FCA's proposed regulatory sandbox program has suffered a cold spot as soon as it was launched, and many blockchain startups have expressed no interest in it.

4 The Current Status of Blockchain Security Protection

Blockchain technology is currently in the early stage of development. There are many security issues from the underlying technology to the upper application. The third chapter has analyzed the vulnerabilities of each layer of the blockchain and the possible attacks. At present, when studying blockchain security, most of the scholars mainly focus on integrity, privacy protection and scalability [4].

Defenses against these attacks have been given in some papers. In the blockchain integrity protection aspect, for example, for selfish mining attacks, Eya [28] and Heilman [29] both proposed defensive measures. The existence of Proof of Work mechanism and the large number of honest miners make the blockchain integrity protected.

Although the blockchain provides anonymization, it is not completely anonymous. The attacker can still perform certain mapping by analyzing network traffic and transaction information. In the literature [30–32], scholars analyzed and advanced a hybrid mechanism. It's main idea is that the user sends some bitcoin from an address and puts the bitcoin into another address in such a way that it is difficult to find the correspondence between the input and output addresses of the same user. At present, there are two main types of methods for blockchain privacy protection: One is to add an anonymous protection mechanism to an existing blockchain through a technology such as "secure transmission". Another possible approach is to create a new blockchain that is incompatible with the Bitcoin system, such as Zerocash, which provides anonymity by using new primitives in its block [33]. In fact, some more forward-looking technologies have been studied to obtain a better anonymity guarantee, such as Coin join solutions, software that provides anonymous functionality (e.g. Mimble wimble) and next-generation encryption technology represented by attribute-based encryption.

Cryptography is the cornerstone of blockchain technology. Once the hash function or encryption algorithm is no longer secure, the security of the blockchain will no longer exist. The hash function SHA256 and the encryption algorithm elliptic curve cryptography used for the blockchain are still safe, but with the development of new technologies (e.g. quantum computing), its security remains to be discussed. Therefore, we should pay attention to new research results in a timely manner and actively seek more secure algorithms.

Blockchain technology currently has many security problems, but any innovative technology needs a process of continuous problem solving from birth to maturity, so as the blockchain. What's more, features of the blockchain like eliminating the center, eliminating trust, and tamper-resistance, can solve problems exist in many industries.

5 Conclusion

As an emerging technology, the inherent data security and effective privacy protection make the blockchain industry be used more and more widely. However, it is worth noting that with the expansion of its application, more and more new types of security threats are emerging targeted on the blockchain. The way to strengthen the security protection of the blockchain needs further research indeed.

The second chapter of this paper introduces the application scenarios of blockchain technology in different fields and analyzes the corresponding projects. The third chapter focuses on the security analysis of the technology and application of each layer of the blockchain, and summarizes the vulnerabilities and possible attacks. The fourth chapter summarizes the current status of blockchain security protection, it shows that more research is needed on the security aspect.

According to a large number of papers have been researched, most users and researchers of the blockchain pay more attention to the application of blockchains and technology itself, but less attention and researches to security. We think blockchain anonymity research and upper-level security, especially smart contract layer and application layer security requires continuous attention and research. I hope that the work of this paper can alert the practitioner "network security of the blockchain is still waiting for deeper research".

References

1. Nakamoto, S.: Bitcoin: a peer-to-peer electronic cash system (2008)
2. Zhao, G.: Blockchain: the cornerstone of the value Internet. Publishing House of Electronics Industry, Beijing (2016)
3. Yang, B., Chen, C.: Blockchain Principle, Design and Application. China Machine Press, Beijing (2017)
4. Fang, W., Zhang, W., Pan, T., et al.: Cyber security in blockchain: threats and countermeasures. J. Cyber Secur. **3**(2), 87–104 (2018)
5. Distributed ledger technologies in securities post-trading. https://www.ecb.europa.eu/pub/pdf/scpops/ecbop172.en.pdf. Accessed 4 July 2018
6. IBM News. https://www.ibm.com/news/cn/zh/2016/10/19/D468881I72849Y25.html. Accessed 4 July 2018
7. Benet, J.: IPFS - Content Addressed, Versioned, P2P File System. https://github.com/ipfs/papers/raw/master/ipfs-cap2pfs/ipfs-p2p-file-system.pdf. Accessed 4 July 2018
8. RedChain White Paper. https://cdn.thiwoo.com/RedChain/reeed_white.pdf. Accessed 4 July 2018
9. U Network: A Decentralized Protocol for Publishing and Valuing Online Content. https://u.network/U_whitepaper_en.pdf. Accessed 4 July 2018
10. YOYOW White Paper. https://yoyow.org/files/white-paper3.pdf. Accessed 4 July 2018
11. BIHU White Paper. https://home.bihu.com/whitePaper.pdf. Accessed 4 July 2018
12. BCSEC Security Trend Analysis. https://bcsec.org/analyse. Accessed 4 July 2018
13. CHAITIN TECH, ConsenSys.: Blockchain Security Guide. https://chaitin.cn/cn/download/blockchain_security_guide_20180507.pdf. Accessed 4 July 2018

14. Youbit Files for Bankruptcy After Second Hack This Year. https://www.ccn.com/south-korean-exchange-youbit-declares-bankruptcy-after-second-hack-this-year. Accessed 4 July 2018
15. Blockchain Security v1. https://bcsec.org/report. Accessed 4 July 2018
16. GLOBAL DDOS THREAT LANDSCAPE Q3 2017. https://www.incapsula.com/ddos-report/ddos-report-q3-2017.html. Accessed 4 July 2018
17. Bitfinex Attacked Statement. https://twitter.com/bitfinex/status/940593291208331264. Accessed 4 July 2018
18. MtGox Account Database Leaked. https://news.ycombinator.com/item?id=2671612. Accessed 4 July 2018
19. LulzSec Rogue Suspected of Bitcoin Hack. https://www.theguardian.com/technology/2011/jun/22/lulzsec-rogue-suspected-of-bitcoin-hack. Accessed 4 July 2018
20. Bitcoin Trading Platform Mt.Gox Filed for Bankruptcy Protection. http://www.bbc.com/zhongwen/simp/business/2014/02/140228_bitcoin. Accessed 4 July 2018
21. Pool Distribution. https://btc.com/stats/pool?pool_mode=month. Accessed 4 July 2018
22. Smart Contract Wiki. https://github.com/EthFans/wiki/wiki/%E6%99%BA%E8%83%BD%E5%90%88%E7%BA%A6. Accessed 4 July 2018
23. Parity Security Alert. https://paritytech.io/security-alert. Accessed 4 July 2018
24. Heilman, E., Kendler, A., Zohar, A., et al.: Eclipse attacks on Bitcoin's peer-to-peer network. In: Usenix Conference on Security Symposium (2015)
25. BGP Hijack-btc. https://github.com/nsg-ethz/hijack-btc. Accessed 4 July 2018
26. Matzutt, R., Hiller, J., Henze, M., et al.: A quantitative analysis of the impact of arbitrary blockchain content on bitcoin. In: 22nd International Conference on Financial Cryptography and Data Security. Springer, Curaçao (2018)
27. Depth Long Text Interpretation of Blockchain and Supervision: "recycling boxes", "black boxes" and "sandboxes". https://www.pintu360.com/a49882.html?s=87&o=1. Accessed 4 July 2018
28. Eyal, I., Sirer, E.G.: Majority is not enough: bitcoin mining is vulnerable. Commun. ACM **61**(7), 95–102 (2018)
29. Heilman, E.: One weird trick to stop selfish miners: fresh bitcoins, a solution for the honest miner (poster abstract). In: Böhme, R., Brenner, M., Moore, T., Smith, M. (eds.) FC 2014. LNCS, vol. 8438, pp. 161–162. Springer, Heidelberg (2014). https://doi.org/10.1007/978-3-662-44774-1_12
30. Valenta, L., Rowan, B.: Blindcoin: blinded, accountable mixes for bitcoin. In: Brenner, M., Christin, N., Johnson, B., Rohloff, K. (eds.) FC 2015. LNCS, vol. 8976, pp. 112–126. Springer, Heidelberg (2015). https://doi.org/10.1007/978-3-662-48051-9_9
31. Bissias, G., Ozisik, A.P., Levine, B.N., et al.: Sybil-resistant mixing for bitcoin. In: Proceedings of the 13th Workshop on Privacy in the Electronic Society. ACM (2015)
32. Meiklejohn, S., Orlandi, C.: Privacy-enhancing overlays in bitcoin. In: Brenner, M., Christin, N., Johnson, B., Rohloff, K. (eds.) FC 2015. LNCS, vol. 8976, pp. 127–141. Springer, Heidelberg (2015). https://doi.org/10.1007/978-3-662-48051-9_10
33. Sasson, E.B., Chiesa, A., Garman, C., et al.: Zerocash: decentralized anonymous payments from bitcoin. In: Security and Privacy, pp. 459–474. IEEE (2014)

Automatic and Accurate Detection of Webshell Based on Convolutional Neural Network

Zhuo-Hang Lv[1], Han-Bing Yan[1(✉)], and Rui Mei[2]

[1] National Computer Network Emergency Response Technical Team/Coordination Center of China, Beijing, China
{lvzhuohang,yhb}@cert.org.cn

[2] Institute of Information Engineering, Chinese Academy of Sciences, Beijing, China
meirui@iie.ac.cn

Abstract. The rapid development of the Internet has changed the way people live and work. Web security, as the foundation of network security, has received much more attention. Based on the variability of Webshells and the vulnerability of detection methods, this paper proposed a model that used deep learning to detect and implements the automatic identification of Webshells. For the shortcomings of the traditional detection models using machine learning algorithms, this paper proposed to apply convolutional neural network to Webshell detection process. The deep learning model does not require complicated artificial feature engineering, and the modeled features trained through model learning can also allow the attacker to avoid targeted bypassing in Webshell detection. The experimental results showed that this method not only has better detection accuracy, but also can effectively avoid the attacker's targeted bypassing. At the same time, with the accumulation of training samples, the detection accuracies of the detection model in different application environments will gradually improvements, which has clear advantages over traditional machine learning algorithms.

Keywords: Webshell · Convolutional neural network · Text classification

1 Introduction

When an attacker conducts attacks such as penetration tests, data theft, dark chain implantation, and intranet lateral movement on the websites, the backdoors (that is, Webshells) of the website are often implanted on the website servers to maintain the management authority of the websites. Even if the website vulnerabilities are patched, as long as the backdoors of the hackers are exist, the hackers can still easily penetrate the website servers. There are many kinds of Webshells, small one that can exploit vulnerabilities, and big one that can obtain administrator privileges. Using a variety of attack tools and Webshell scripts, hackers can quickly and effectively implement bulk website intrusion. In addition, Webshell connection tools have different application

This work was supported by the NSFC Foundation, No. U1736218.

The original version of this chapter was revised: The acknowledgment of the NSFC Foundation was missing. The chapter has been updated to include these corrections. The correction to this chapter is available at https://doi.org/10.1007/978-981-13-6621-5_15

X. Yun et al. (Eds.): CNCERT 2018, CCIS 970, pp. 73–85, 2019.
https://doi.org/10.1007/978-981-13-6621-5_6

environments, such as "China Chopper", "axe" and other tools are website management tools, and they are often used for website attack.

At present, the methods of Webshell detection are mainly divided into four categories. One is based on the experience of webmasters for manual identification, the second one is static feature detection, the third one is dynamic feature detection, and the last one is statistical analysis.

1.1 Manual Identification

Webmasters need to have a comprehensive grasp of the website pages and files, and have a high recognition ability for some newly added exception files, such as some special naming files, 1.asp, hello.php, abc. Jsp, etc. In addition, due to some common Webshell, such as "one sentence", the file is very small, so attention should be paid to extremely small files. Finally, the content of the file is analyzed and determined. The normal webpage source files have a large number of labels and comments, and the layouts are neat and clear at a glance. The backdoor files, especially the small one, often have only some functions that perform specific functions, and the content is simple and the elements are very few.

1.2 Static Feature Detection

It is based on the features of the script files. These features generally include multi-dimensional information such as keywords, high-risk functions, file permissions, and owners. If the feature setting is reasonable, the success rate of this detection method will be high, but the disadvantage is that this method is only effective for the existing Webshells, and is basically undetectable for 0day Webshells. In such methods, machine learning algorithms are fully applied and are the mainstream of current Webshell detection. The application of machine learning algorithms needs to extract features from black and white samples (i.e. Webshell pages and normal web pages). The feature settings are based on the number of words, total length of text, key function calls, etc., and then apply different algorithms. Detection. For example, the literature [1] proposed a detection method using matrix decomposition, which has higher detection efficiency and correct rate, and can also detect new type of Webshells with a certain probability. However, the rationality and effectiveness of the classification method have not been confirmed when classifying page features. Literature [2] proposed a Webshell detection method based on decision tree, which can quickly and accurately detect the mutated Webshell, overcome the deficiencies of the traditional feature-based matching detection method, and combine the Boosting method to select the appropriate number of sub-models. The detection capability can be further improved. However, there are fewer training samples used in this document. In [3], a Webshell detection method based on Naive Bayesian theory is proposed for Webshell with obfuscated encryption coding technology. This model can accurately detect Webshells that have been confusingly encrypted and encoded, effectively improving traditional feature-based detection methods. The lack of detection methods is also the small number of training samples during the experiment, the training test samples need to be added, so that the classification model can more accurately identify the Webshell, and the classification model should be optimized and improved through experiments to improve the performance.

1.3 Dynamic Feature Detection

The dynamic detection method detects traffic requests, responses, system commands, and state changes generated in BS activities, discovers abnormal behaviors or states, and finally detects the existence of Webshell. For example, if there is a user accessing or calling a file that has never been used, the probability of a Webshell in the file is greatly increased. This method has certain detection capabilities for the new Webshells, but it is difficult to detect for some specific backdoors, and it is difficult to deploy. Intruders can also put Webshell into existing code, which makes the difficulty of dynamic detection more difficult. Literature [4] introduced a real-time dynamic detection method for PHP Webshell. For the key functions and variables involved in the execution of Webshell, mark tracking is performed by using a method similar to stain propagation to perform black and white discrimination.

1.4 Statistical Analysis

The statistics-based Webshell detection method is tailored to the user's access characteristics. The normal range of these features is statistically calculated and compared with the user-uploaded script files to finally determine the existence of Webshell. This method is still valid for encoded and encrypted Webshells, as these Webshells also exhibit some special statistical features. Generally, there are statistical analysis techniques such as coincidence index, information entropy, longest word length, and compression ratio. This method is generally used to identify obfuscated, encrypted code and performs well in identifying fuzzy codes or obscuring Trojans. However, there are also obvious shortcomings. Unblurred code is more transparent to statistical detection methods. If the code is integrated into other scripts, it is likely to be considered a normal file. Literature [5] proposed a Webshell detection technology based on semantic analysis. Compared with the rule-based detection method, the false positives are reduced, and the linear growth in time after the rule is increased is avoided. However, there is only one language in the literature is envolved. The scripting language was designed systematically, the system compatibility was not enough, and there were fewer training samples.

2 Convolutional Neural Network for Webshell Detection

2.1 Advantages of Convolutional Neural Networks

The advantages of CNN compared with other deep learning algorithms are as follows:

- Compared with RNN, its training time is shorter
- Compared with DNN, its parameters are fewer and the model is more concise.

The CNN model limits the number of parameters and mines the local structure. The training time is short and the effect is ideal. More importantly, compared with the traditional machine learning algorithm, the CNN model has the greatest advantage that its feature set is "learned" by itself. As long as the computing resources are sufficient, it is not necessary to use statistical analysis data to find features. The advantages of applying CNN to Webshell detection are:

- As long as the sample quality is high, there can be a lower false positive rate.
- There is no clear feature extraction link, and the attacker could not bypass easily.
- Compared to traditional machine learning algorithms, CNN has better ability to discover 0day Webs hell or unknown attack scripts.
- The model is easier to accumulate and iterate. For new samples, just add them to training set.

2.2 Application in Text Processing

At first, the emergence of convolutional neural networks solved the problem that deep learning could not be done in the image processing field because the amount of computation was too large. The convolutional neural network greatly reduces the amount of computation of the network through convolution, weight sharing, pooling, etc., and the result is very satisfactory. The computer's storage of images is usually in the form of a two-dimensional array, and the convolutional neural network processes the small images by using a two-dimensional convolution function, so that advanced features can be extracted. Similarly, feature extraction and analysis of text segments can be performed using a one-dimensional convolution function, as shown in Fig. 1.

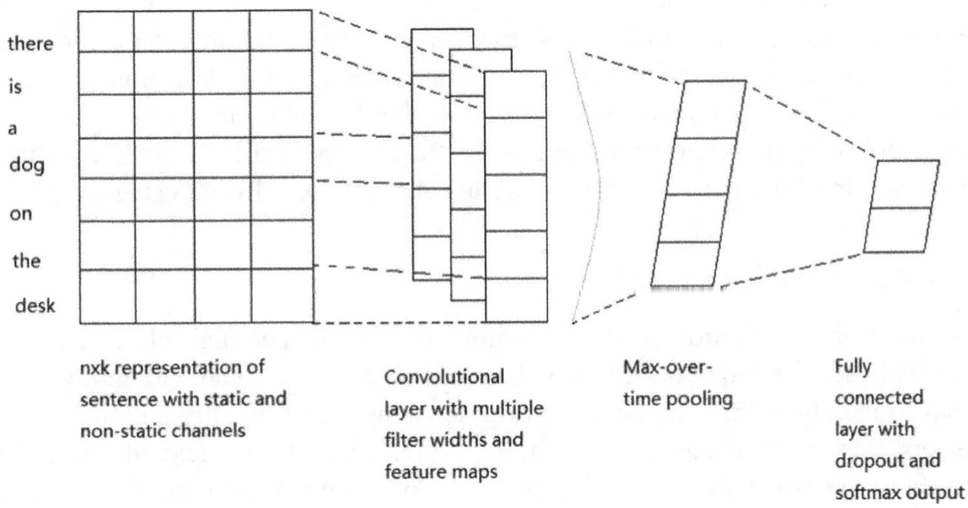

Fig. 1. Convolutional neural network for text processing

Assuming that $x_i \in R^k$ is a k-dimensional word vector corresponding to the i-th word in a sentence, a statement of length n can be expressed as:

$$x_{1:n} = x_1 \oplus x_2 \oplus \ldots \oplus x_n \tag{1}$$

Where $\oplus$ is the connector.

Thus, $x_{i:i+j}$ can be defined as a connection or combination of words or characters $x_i, x_{i+1}, \ldots, x_{i+j}$. Let $w \in R^{hk}$ be the filter in the convolution operation, also known as the convolution kernel, whose length is h, which can produce a feature after the convolution operation. For example, the feature c_i is generated by a word or character $x_{i:i+h-1}$ in a window.

$$c_i = f(w \cdot x_{i:i+h-1} + b) \tag{2}$$

Where $b \in R$ is the offset term and f is a nonlinear function, such as a hyperbolic tangent function.

The convolution kernel is slidably convolved with the sentence $\{x_{1:h}, x_{2:h+1}, \ldots, x_{n-h+1:n}\}$ to generate a feature layer.

$$c = [c_1, c_2, \ldots, c_{n-h+1}] \tag{3}$$

Where $c \in R^{n-h+1}$, Then use the max-over-time pooling operation, that is, for each value in this pooled operation window, only the maximum value is reserved:

$$\widehat{c} = \max\{c\} \tag{4}$$

By such a method, only the most important features in the feature layer can be retained, thereby obtaining a pooled layer, and such a pooling operation can correspond to a statement with a variable length.

For the above steps, a convolution kernel can generate a feature after a convolution operation, and multiple convolution kernels can generate multiple features. The window sizes of these different convolution kernels can be different.

The pooled layer is then connected to the fully connected layer with dropout and softmax, and the final output is the probability distribution of each category [6].

2.3 Sample Data Preprocessing

One of the main application areas of machine learning related algorithms is text processing and analysis. However, the raw data form used for text cannot be directly used as input to the algorithms, because the original sample data is only a combination of characters, and most of the input of the algorithm cannot be a text file of different length, but a fixed-length vector. Therefore, the relevant text files need to be preprocessed, some of the most basic methods for extracting data numerical features from text content are:

- Mark the text content and encode the result of the tag using an integer value. In the process of marking, special characters or punctuation in the text can be used as the dividing point to split the text data.
- Count the frequency of occurrence of characters or marks in a text file.
- Add weights, for the marks that often appear in the sample file, reduce their weight, and the marks appearing in fewer samples increase their weight.

2.4 Simplified Word Segmentation

For Webshell detection, this paper first classifies the sample, treats the characters in the sample except English letters and Arabic numerals as separators, and then uses the bag-of-words model to encode the divided words, numbers, etc., to generate a dictionary, and then For each sample page, take the fixed number of character codes (such as 200) with the highest frequency appearing as the representative vector for this page, as shown in Fig. 2.

```
e pageEncoding utf 8 page import java io page import java util page import java util regex page import java sq
static void readFromRemote final Socket soc final Socket remoteSoc final DataInputStream remoteIn final DataOu
eplaceAll gt str str replaceAll char 13 char 10 br str str replaceAll n br out write str toCharArray 0 str len
 public static String getStr String s return s null s public static String null2Nbsp String s if s null s nbsp
ction return this replace s s function fso obj this currentDir JSession getAttribute CURRENT DIR this filename
bold head td span font weight normal form margin 0 padding 0 h2 margin 0 padding 0 height 24px line height 24p
nect new InetSocketAddress ip Integer parseInt port iTimeout s setSoTimeout iTimeout if Util isEmpty banner r
ents db value form elements url value v split 1 form elements driver value v split 0 form elements selectDb va
 getColumnCount out println b style margin left 15px Query 0 Util htmlEncode sql b br br out println table bor
d td width 98 input class input name folder value path2View type text style width 100 margin 0 8px td td nowra
rFile EnterFile file close catch ZipException e JSession setAttribute MSG JSession getAttribute ENTER toString
it type submit value Submit input class bt type button value Back onclick history back p form td tr table catc
ur input class input name hour value cal get Calendar HOUR id hour type text size 2 minute input class input n
se public boolean doAfter return false public void invoke HttpServletRequest request HttpServletResponse respo
get request getParameter to if Util isEmpty target Util isEmpty src File file new File src if file renameTo ne
r return false private boolean config false private String extFilter blacklist private String fileExts null pr
 len input read b while len 1 output write b 0 len len input read b catch Exception ex finally try if output n
an doBefore return true public void invoke HttpServletRequest request HttpServletResponse response HttpSession
 table div td tr table form catch Exception e throw e private static class BackConnectInvoker extends DefaultI
hods n Method ms cls getDeclaredMethods for int i 0 i ms length i Method m ms i sb append t m toString n sb ap
y option option value reg query HKEY LOCAL MACHINE SYSTEM RAdmin v2 0 Server Parameters v Parameter radmin has
class ExportInvoker extends DefaultInvoker public boolean doBefore return false public boolean doAfter return
 HttpServletRequest request HttpServletResponse response HttpSession JSession throws Exception ByteArrayOutput
ew JspEnvInvoker ins put smp new SmpInvoker ins put mapPort new MapPortInvoker ins put top new TopInvoker ins
```

Fig. 2. Sample of word segmentation

2.5 Vectorization Model

One-Hot

The One-hot vector method first extracts the words in the sample set and extracts only the repeated words. This results in a vocabulary, assuming a size of V. The text is then represented by a vector of size V. If a word in the vocabulary appears in the text segment, the value in this dimension in the vector is 1, and no words appear in the text, the value of its corresponding bit is 0.

In the Webshell detection, this method is improved. Firstly, the dictionary is built. In order to avoid the sample matrix being too sparse, the dictionary size is controlled, and then the sample page is vectorized. Here the words that appear repeatedly in the text accumulate the corresponding bits on their vectors and words that do not appear in the simplified dictionary are ignored. This avoids excessive computational complexity and incorporates word frequency information.

Bag-of-Words

The so-called bag-of-words model is to treat the entire contents of a text file as a whole, and then add an index to all words, characters or positions in the whole. Thus, a text file can be represented by a word document matrix, where each column represents a word and each row represents a document. However, the disadvantage of this method of characterization is that:

- The matrix representing the document is too sparse in most cases and will consume a lot of storage resources.

- For the processing of a large number of different corpus samples, the representation of the document matrix will take up a lot of computing resources.
- The bag-of-words model ignores the relative positional information of words or characters in the text.

In view of the balance between the accuracy of the processing results and the computational complexity, this strategy can be optimized in special cases.

Word2vec

Word2vec is an NLP tool launched by Google in 2013. It is used to vectorize the words in the file, and the generated word vector can measure the relationship between the quantity and the distance, so word characterization and artificial word habits can be added to the process of vectorization.

In the past, neural networks were used to train word vector models. In order to calculate the classification probability of all words, such as the use of softmax in the output layer, you need to calculate the probability of softmax, and then find the maximum value. This process involves a very large amount of calculation.

For the Word2vec model, in order to avoid the heavy computation from the hidden layer to the output layer, the network structure has been modified and optimized. It uses the Huffman tree instead of the neuron structure in the output layer and the hidden layer [7]. In the Fuman tree, the number of leaf nodes is the size of the vocabulary composed of the input samples. At the same time, the leaf nodes have the same function as the neurons of the original output layer, and the internal nodes of the network act as the neurons of the original hidden layer. So, there is no need to calculate the softmax probability, which greatly reduces the amount of computation of the network.

Compared with the bag-of-words model, the Word2vec model incorporates the contextual relationship of lexical semantics, and the similarity between words can be obtained by calculating the Euclidean distance. This article uses the Word2vec library in Python. First, all the samples are trained to get the dictionary, and then each word in each sample is vectorized. In the process of vectorizing a single sample page, averaging and averaging all vectorized characters as a vector for this sample [8].

2.6 Convolutional Neural Network Structure

The convolutional neural network used in the experiments in this paper consists of the Embedding layer, the convolution layer, the pooling layer, the dropout layer, and the fully connected layer. The network is built on Tensorflow. TensorFlow is Google's second-generation artificial intelligence learning system based on DistBelief. It is most suitable for machine learning and deep neural network research, but the versatility of this system makes it widely used in other computing fields. The structure is shown in Table 1.

Table 1. Convolutional neural network structure

```
network = input_data(shape=[None,
MAX_DOCUMENT_LENGTH],name='input')
network = tflearn.embedding(network, input_dim=n_words+1, output_dim=128)
branch1 = conv_1d(network, 128, 14, padding='valid', activation='relu',
regularizer="L2")
branch2 = conv_1d(network, 128, 15, padding='valid', activation='relu',
regularizer="L2")
branch3 = conv_1d(network, 128, 16, padding='valid', activation='relu',
regularizer="L2")
network = merge([branch1, branch2, branch3], mode='concat', axis=1)
network = tf.expand_dims(network, 2)
network = global_max_pool(network)
network = dropout(network, 0.5)
network = fully_connected(network, 2, activation='softmax')
network = regression(network, optimizer='adam',
learning_rate=0.001,loss='categorical_crossentropy', name='target')
model = tflearn.DNN(network, tensorboard_verbose=0)
```

In the convolutional layer, setting padding does not add new elements based on the original data, that is, the boundary data is not processed, and the convolution is only performed in the original data.

The activation function uses ReLU:

$$f(x) = \max(0, x) \tag{5}$$

The advantage of using ReLU as an activation function is that its SGD will converge faster than tanh or sigmoid. ReLU can get the activation value based on only one threshold, no complicated operation, and it is linear. The disadvantage is that it is not suitable for inputs with large gradients during training, because as the parameters are updated, the ReLU neurons will no longer have an active function, which will cause their gradient to always be zero.

The regularization term uses the L2 norm, that is, each element in a vector is first summed to its square root, and then its square root is obtained. During the optimization process, the regularization term adds a penalty term to the activation value of the parameter in the layer, and the loss function together with this penalty term becomes the ultimate optimization goal of the network.

The pooling layer uses global_max_pool, that is, the feature point maximum pooling, and the maximum pooling can extract features better.

For the over-fitting problem in convolutional neural networks, the dropout layer is used to reduce its impact, which is equivalent to the effect of regularization. The essence of the dropout layer is to randomly delete some hidden neurons in the neural network. Thc input and output neurons are kept unchanged, and then the input data is forwardly propagated through the modified neural network, and then the error value is propagated back through the modified neural network. However, after randomly deleting some hidden layer neurons, the fully connected network has a certain sparseness at this time, and finally the synergistic effects of different features are effectively reduced.

Classifier using softmax regression:

$$f(z_j) = \frac{e^{z_j}}{\sum_{i-1}^{n} e^{z_i}} \tag{6}$$

The dimension of the output vector is the number of required categories, and the value of each bit is the probability value of each one.

For the encrypted Webshells, such as the Base64-encoded Webshells, based on the above-mentioned bag-of-words model, has not been specially processed. After the word segmentation, the Base64-encoded part will be treated as a whole. The method does not reduce the final effect, and the same can be done for the other encoding encryption methods.

3 Experiments

3.1 Sample Collection

The so-called web page source code files are script files that can be parsed by the server side and written by the script language asp, jsp, php and so on. Common Webshells are also written by these scripting languages and then uploaded to the servers. The content of the webpage source file is shown as Fig. 3.

```
function sendpacket() //2x speed
{
  global $proxy, $host, $port, $packet, $html, $proxy_regex;
  $socket = socket_create(AF_INET, SOCK_STREAM, SOL_TCP);
  if ($socket < 0) {
    echo "socket_create() failed: reason: " . socket_strerror($socket) . "<br>";
  }
  else {
    $c = preg_match($proxy_regex,$proxy);
    if (!$c) {echo 'Not a valid proxy...';
    die;
    }
  echo "OK.<br>";
  echo "Attempting to connect to ".$host." on port ".$port."...<br>";
  if ($proxy=='') {
    $result = socket_connect($socket, $host, $port);
  }
  else {
    $parts =explode(':',$proxy);
    echo 'Connecting to '.$parts[0].':'.$parts[1].' proxy...<br>';
    $result = socket_connect($socket, $parts[0],$parts[1]);
  }
  if ($result < 0) {
    echo "socket_connect() failed.\r\nReason: (".$result.") " . socket_strerror($result) . "<br><br>";
  }
  else {
    echo "OK.<br><br>";
    $html= '';
    socket_write($socket, $packet, strlen($packet));
    echo "Reading response:<br>";
    while ($out= socket_read($socket, 2048)) {$html.=$out;}
    echo nl2br(htmlentities($html));
    echo "Closing socket...";
    socket_close($socket);
  }
  }
}
```

Fig. 3. Sample of source code

The Webshell sample in this article is mainly from related projects on Github, as shown in Table 2.

Table 2. Webshell related projects

Project name	Description
tennc/Webshell	This is a Webshell open source project
ysrc/Webshell-sample	Webshell sample
xl7dev/Webshell	Webshell & Backdoor Collection
tdifg/Webshell	Webshell Collection
testsecer/Webshell	A project for Webshell Collection

In addition, there are also common Webshell samples on the Internet, direct extraction from attacked websites, and samples shared by professionals. A total of three data sets of PHP, JSP, and ASP are collected:

- PHP Webshells: 2103
- JSP Webshells: 712
- ASP Webshells: 1129.

The white samples are derived from open source CMS, open source software, etc. Since there is no evidence that these open source software contain backdoor code, they are considered to be white samples. The collected data sets of PHP, JSP and ASP are as follows:

- PHP white samples: 3305
- JSP white samples: 3927
- ASP white samples: 3036.

3.2 Comparison of Three Vectorization Models

In this paper, the above three models are compared experimentally. In the processing of Webshell detection and classification tasks, the same structure of convolutional neural network is used. The final effect is shown in Table 3.

Table 3. Comparison of three vectorization models

Models	Accuracy
Improved One-hot (1000 dimensions)	90.43%
Improved One-hot (5000 dimensions)	97.26%
Improved One-hot (10000 dimensions)	98.39%
Bag-of-words (200 dimensions)	99.21%
Bag-of-words (400 dimensions)	99.31%
Bag-of-words (600 dimensions)	99.16%
Word2vec (average)	65.66%
Word2vec (sum)	70.23%

It shows that the improved one-hot vectorization model works well when the dictionary size is above 5000. The bag-of-words model is also very good, but the Word2vec model has the worst effect. It shows that the word2vec model is not suitable for document-based classification tasks. At the same time, the improved one-hot model consumes a longer time and consumes more computing resources when the dimension is very high. In contrast, the bag-of-words model is a simple and effective way to deal with it.

For the source code sample, since there is a difference in the writing language, the experiment uses a separate training method. First, for the PHP samples, the sample is trained firstly, and then the ten-fold cross-validation is used, as shown in Fig. 4.

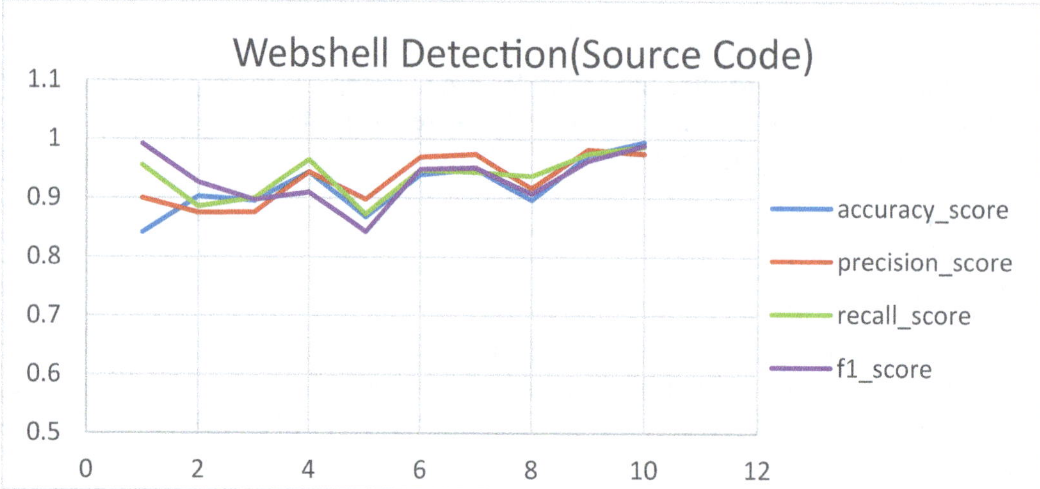

Fig. 4. Webshell source code detection curve

For the Webshell samples in various languages, the final indicators are shown in Table 4. The convolution function used in the experiment is 128 cores, one-dimensional, the processing length is 3, 4, 5 respectively, using relu as the excitation function, L2 norm processing over-fitting, and the dimension of the bag-of-words model is 400.

Table 4. Webshell sample testing indicators

Index	Accuracy	Precision	Recall	F1
PHP	99.5%	99.2%	99.7%	99.4%
ASP	98.3%	99.2%	99.5%	99.3%
JSP	97.5%	98.2%	99.4%	99.4%

It can be seen that the detection method based on convolutional neural network works pretty good in the application of Webshell detection. At the same time, due to different script languages, the generated lexicon is different. So Webshell source codes of different languages generate different detection models will have a better detection effect. The trained model is then compared with the existing detection methods.

The total number of Webshells used in this comparative experiment was 1,637, all written in PHP language. The detection accuracy of the convolutional neural network model compared with the decision tree, Webshell detector, D shield and 360 Trojan detection is shown in Table 5, in this case, the CNN network that has been used is the same as above:

Table 5. Comparison of test results

Methods	C4.5	D shield	360 detection	Webshell detector	CNN
Checkout	1347	1518	362	413	1553
Accuracy	82.28%	92.73%	22.11%	25.23%	94.87%

It shows that the trained CNN detection model has a higher detection accuracy.

3.3 The Impact of Filter Window

According to the research results of Zhang [9], for statements with a maximum word size of no more than 100, the size of the filter window in a convolutional neural network is generally between 1 and 10. But for statements with a maximum number of words over 100, the most appropriate window size (also known as a convolution kernel) will be larger. Moreover, for different data sets, there is a most suitable matching window size for each one. At the same time, the experiment confirms that more filtering windows with the same size that is near the most suitable size are added, the more final effect will be improved, but if the added filtering window sizes far apart from the most suitable size, the effect will be reduced. Based on this, for the 200-dimensional convolutional neural network model using the fixed sample vector of the bag-of-words model, the effects of different window sizes in the experiment are tried respectively. The results are shown in Table 6.

Table 6. Impact of filter window size on recall rate

Window size	5	9	12	15	30	60
Recall rate	82.4%	87.5%	85.8%	92.4%	83.2%	90.6%

The best window size for this experiment is 15.

Therefore, the window sizes of the convolution kernel in the experiment are 14, 15, 16. As shown in Table 7.

Table 7. Convolution kernel

```
branch1 = conv_1d(network, 128, 14, padding='valid', activation='relu', regularizer="L2")
branch2 = conv_1d(network, 128, 15, padding='valid', activation='relu', regularizer="L2")
branch3 = conv_1d(network, 128, 16, padding='valid', activation='relu', regularizer="L2")
```

4 Conclusion

This paper proposed the idea and process of using convolutional neural network model for Webshell detection. In this process, the most important thing is the quantity and quality of samples. A good training sample set can train very good models. Sample sets need to be expanded in the future. The training of the deep learning model does not require complex artificial feature engineering, which means that it is difficult for the attackers to bypass. Therefore, the deep learning model is stronger when facing some potential bypassing me thods. That is to say, the application of convolutional neural network to Webshell detection can prevent unknown attacks to a certain extent.

References

1. Dai, H., Li, J., Lu, X.-D., Sun, X.: Machine learning algorithm for intelligent detection of webshell. Chin. J. Netw. Inf. Secur. **3**(3), 71–77 (2017)
2. Hu, J., Xu, Z., Ma, D., Yang, J.: Research of webshell detection based on decision tree. J. Netw. New Media **6** (2012)
3. Hu, B.: Research on webshell detection method based on bayesian theory. Science Mosaic (2016)
4. Du, H., Fang, Y.: PHP webshell real-time dynamic detection. Netw. Secur. Technol. Appl. (2014)
5. Yi, N., Fang, Y., Huang, C., Liu, L.: Semantics-based webshell detection method research. J. Inf. Secur. Res. **3**(2), 145–150 (2017)
6. Kim, Y.: Convolutional neural networks for sentence classification. EprintArxiv (2014)
7. Goldberg, Y., Levy, O.: word2vec explained: deriving Mikolov et al.'s negative-sampling word-embedding method. EprintArxiv (2014)
8. Rong, X.: Word2vec parameter learning explained. Computer Science (2014)
9. Zhang, Y., Wallace, B.: A sensitivity analysis of (and practitioners' guide to) convolutional neural networks for sentence classification. Computer Science (2015)

End-Link Collaboration Control Mechanism in Intelligent Networks Based on Traffic Classification

Songer Sun(✉), Li Zhang, Xiaoping Han, and Chengjie Gu

Security Product Line, H3C Technologies Co., Ltd., Innovation Industrial Park Phase II, Gaoxin District, Hefei, Anhui, People's Republic of China
{sunsonger, billchang}@h3c.com

Abstract. In order to meet special requirements of service transportation and improve integral network performance, we propose self-adaptive control mechanism in intelligent networks based on traffic classification. The self-adaptive control mechanism which considers end-link cooperation in intelligent network implements service transportation with control method of the distributed-centralized combination. The mechanism optimize relevant network elements devices and reasonably allocates limited resources to improve end-to-end target depending on given strategies.

Keywords: End-Link · Collaboration control mechanism · Intelligent networks · Traffic classification

1 Introduction

Intelligent network is considered a new way of improving entire network performance and end-to-end system performance as well as simplifying network management [1]. It is the trend of next-generation communication. Intelligent networks are important for ensuring performance in complex and isomerism networks. Self-adaptive control technology can plan and allocate limited network bandwidth effectively so that network performance is improved [2]. The technology also manages and controls network traffic according to service features in order to improve the revenue of unit bandwidth. Therefore, intensive self-adaptive control is essential to solving network QoS problems in next-generation communication.

The foundation of traffic classification is the rapid perception of network environment. Situation awareness needs to observe current network environment information in appropriate time [3]. The information is used in later planning and decision making to determine whether the current network meets user requirements [4]. If not, a suitable reconfiguration method is used to meet user requirements.

The key concept is the network's ability to perceive changes in the intelligent network environment and adjust itself in real time. We propose the self-adaptive control mechanism in intelligent networks based on traffic classification. The remainder of this paper is organized as follows. In Sect. 2, we discuss the traffic classification

X. Yun et al. (Eds.): CNCERT 2018, CCIS 970, pp. 86–95, 2019.
https://doi.org/10.1007/978-981-13-6621-5_7

using traffic classification base machine learning method. Section 3 gives End-Link collaboration control mechanism in intelligent networks. Finally, we conclude our paper and discuss future work in Sect. 4.

2 Traffic Classification Using Traffic Classification Based on Sparse Proximal SVM

2.1 Intelligent Networks Need Traffic Classification

Intelligent networks need to be self-aware in order to provide resilient applications and services. Such networks should exhibit cognitive properties where actions are based on reasoning, autonomic operations, adaptive functionality and self-manageability [5]. Therefore, the best way to perceive, analyze, determine, and control transmission service initiatively is by using traffic classification (SA) technology. The network system initiatively perceives services on the network, including end user service status and NE (Network element) service status.

Initiative perception and classification based on the service stream is the foundation of service-centered resource configuration, route adjustment, and dynamic self-adaptive traffic control [6]. In service-aware technology, before the SA is introduced, traditional static port method, payload feature method, and stream statistical feature method are used. The methods are effective for perceiving regular services, but they cannot perceive many new services respectively [7].

Environment information perceived by the traffic classification includes network type, network topology, available resources, interface protocols, and network traffic, all of which affect end-to-end transmission performance [8]. Context perception is an important way of improving network intelligence. It determines changes in context information and adjusts itself accordingly. When the network environment changes dynamically, the network makes relevant self-adjustments. This self-adjustment uses a reflection mechanism and a policy mechanism. From the policy definition, the network can pre-define an adjustment method when the context changes.

2.2 Proximal Support Vector Machine

Support vector machine (SVM) based on the statistical learning theory by Vapnik is a new and powerful classification technique and has drawn much attention in recent years [9]. The optimal classifier can be obtained by solving a quadratic programming (QP) problem.

Support Vector Machine (SVM) is known as one of the best machine learning algorithms for classification purpose and has been successfully applied to many classification problems such as image recognition, text categorization, medical diagnosis, remote sensing, and motion classification [10]. SVM method is selected as our classification algorithm due to its ability for simultaneously minimizing the empirical classification error and maximizing the geometric margin classification space [11]. These properties reduce the structural risk of over-learning with limited samples. But standard SVM are still some limitations [12]. Proximal support vector machine

(PSVM) is proposed instead of SVM, which leads to an extremely fast and simple algorithm for generating a system of linear equations. The formulation of PSVM greatly simplifies the problem with considerably faster computational time than SVM.

Assume that a training set S is given as $S = \{(x_1, y_1), \cdots, (x_l, y_l)\}$, where $x_i \in R^n$, and $y_i \in \{-1, +1\}$. The goal of SVM is to find an optimal separating hyperplane

$$w'x - b = 0 \tag{1}$$

that classifies training samples correctly or basically correctly, where $w \in R^n$, and the scalar $b \in R^n$. Now to find the optimal separating hyperplane is to solve the following constrained optimization problem

$$\min \frac{1}{2} w'w + ce'\xi \tag{2}$$

$$s.t. \quad D(Aw - eb) + \xi \geq e \tag{3}$$

$$\xi \geq 0 \tag{4}$$

Where $\xi = (\xi_1, \xi_2, \cdots, \xi_l)'$, ξ_i is slack variable, $i = 1, 2, \cdots, l$, e denotes a column vector of ones of arbitrary dimension, $A = (x_1, x_2, \cdots, x_l)'$, D is a diagonal matrix whose entries are given by $D_{ii} = y_i$, and $C > 0$ is a fixed penalty parameter of labeled samples. It controls the tradeoff between complexity of the machine and generalization capacity.

PSVM modifies SVM formulation based on maximizing the separating margin $1/w'w + b^2$ in the space of R^{n+l} and changes the slack variables ξ from the L_1 norm to the L_2 one. Note that the nonnegative constraint on the slack variables ξ in (3) is no longer needed. Furthermore, a fundamental change is replacing the inequality constraint with an equality constraint. This leads to the optimization problem as follows

$$\min \frac{1}{2}(w'w + b^2) + c\frac{1}{2}\|\xi\|^2 \tag{5}$$

$$s.t. \quad D(Aw - eb) + \xi = e \tag{6}$$

This modification not only adds advantages such as strong convexity of the objective function, but changes the nature of optimization problem significantly. The planes $w'x - b = \pm 1$ are not bounding planes any more, but can be thought of as "proximal" planes, around which points of the corresponding class are clustered. The formulation of PSVM greatly simplifies the problem and generates a classifier by merely solving a single system of linear equations. However, sometimes the result of PSVM is not accurate when the training set is inadequate or there is a significant deviation between the training and working sets of the total distribution.

In this section, we principally test on different datasets consists of public Moore_Set, Handmade_Set, and Univetsity_Set. For each dataset, we give the 10-fold average testing correctness. In this experiment we compared the performance using SVM methods for classification.

Table 1. Comparing algorithm performance

Dataset	PSVM Accuracy(%) Time(Sec)	SVM Accuracy(%) Time(Sec)
Moore_Set	91.66 **3.6**	91.92 63.7
Handmade_Set	92.73 **0.7**	92.94 17.3
Univetsity_Set	90.58 **75.3**	90.69 1668.4

As shown in Table 1, bold type indicates the best result, the accuracy of the four algorithm were very similar but the execution time including ten-fold cross validation for PSVM was smaller by as much as one order of magnitude or more than the other methods tested.

2.3 Real-Time Traffic Classification Framework

Network traffic classification schemes operate on the notion of network flows. A flow is defined to be as a series of packet exchanges between two hosts, identifiable by the 5-tuple (source address, source port, destination address, destination port, transport protocol), with flow termination determined by an assumed timeout or by distinct flow termination semantics. For each flow, network monitors can record statistics such as duration, bytes transferred, mean packet inter arrival time, and mean packet size.

Classifiers based on machine learning use a training dataset that consists of N tuples (x_i, y_i) and learn a mapping $f(x) \rightarrow y$. In the traffic classification context, examples of attributes include flow statistics such as duration and total number of packets. The terms attributes and features are used interchangeably in the machine learning literature. In our supervised Network traffic classification system, Let $X = \{x_1, x_2, \cdots, x_n\}$

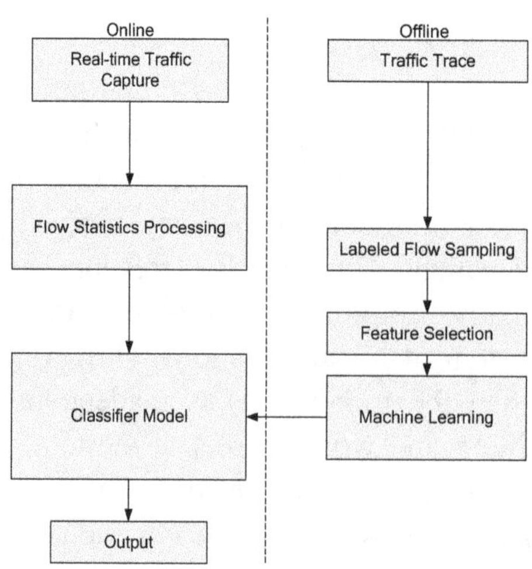

Fig. 1. Architecture of real-time network traffic classification based on proximal SVM

be a set of flows. A flow instance x_i is characterized by a vector of attribute values, $x_i = \{x_{ij} | 1 \leq j \leq m\}$, where m is the number of attributes, and x_{ij} is the value of the jth attribute of the ith flow, and x_i is referred to as a feature vector. Also, let $Y = \{y_1, y_2, \cdots, y_q\}$ be the set of traffic classes, where q is the number of classes of interest. The y_i can be classes such as "HTTP", "FTP", and "P2P". Therefore, our goal is to learn a mapping from an m-dimensional variable X to Y.

As illustrated in Fig. 1, the architecture of online network traffic classification based on proximal SVM includes two portions: off-line ML modeling and on-line ML classification. The system carries out feature selection to eliminate the redundant and irrelevant features to get optimal feature subset. In the stage of online ML classification, the flows which can be real-time collected are trained using the selected ML classifier. Flow statistics is computed in terms of each selected feature and stored them to the corresponding database in the flow preprocessing module. The output classifier model produced by off-line ML modeling is applied to classify the captured traffic. Eventually, the classification output would be applied to network activities such as network surveillance, QoS.

3 End-Link Collaboration Control Mechanism in Intelligent Networks

3.1 Intelligent Network Components

The Internet has become a large non-linear complex giant system in the past years. Early network management systems were limited to simple command line interfaces (CLI) provided to network administrators who were responsible for querying and manually configure every network component. The result is that the management of current and emerging network technologies is becoming the main bottleneck to any further advance [13].

If the network is not meeting the end-to-end requirements of users, the intelligent network adjusts the protocol stack parameters of the relevant NE to meet these requirements. The adjustment process is the reconfiguration of the network [14]. Intelligent network emphasizes the end-to-end target, and it should provide end-to-end re-configurability. Software radio technology is limited to reconfiguring the terminal, but intelligent network involves all layers of the NEs and protocol standards that a stream passes through. It is a scheme with foresight that ensures QoS targets are met. More factors are considered in end-to-end reconfiguration.

Realization of intelligent network is based on reconfiguration of the NE. The reconfiguration process can also be implemented through software, but the technical level of this reconfiguration is higher. Terminal reconfiguration, network reconfiguration, and service reconfiguration are contained, and this configuration is not limited to a single node. Multiple NEs on the end-to-end path are covered. This is called end-to-end reconfiguration (E2R). The complexity and importance of E2R is greater than terminal reconfiguration.

According to the existing literature, intelligent network should have at least the following five main functions. Self-aware should be able to know what is happening inside; then according to what it knows to determine appropriate actions to achieve goals and to learn. Self-configuration can adapt immediately—and with minimal human intervention to configure itself in the dynamically network environment [15].

3.2 Control Architecture in Intelligent Networks

As shown in Fig. 2, the network decision-making and control architecture has a three-level structure, composed of NE cognitive module, autonomous domain cognitive server, and central cognitive server. Each part provides cognitive capability (self-awareness, self-learning, and self-decision making). The NE cognitive module is the basic unit of the intelligent network awareness, analysis, and control system. It provides awareness and decision-making capability and dynamically adjusts NE parameters or configuration. The autonomous domain cognitive server deployed with cognitive module form a cognitive autonomous domain that is responsible for managing and controlling the NE device, service traffic, and network resources.

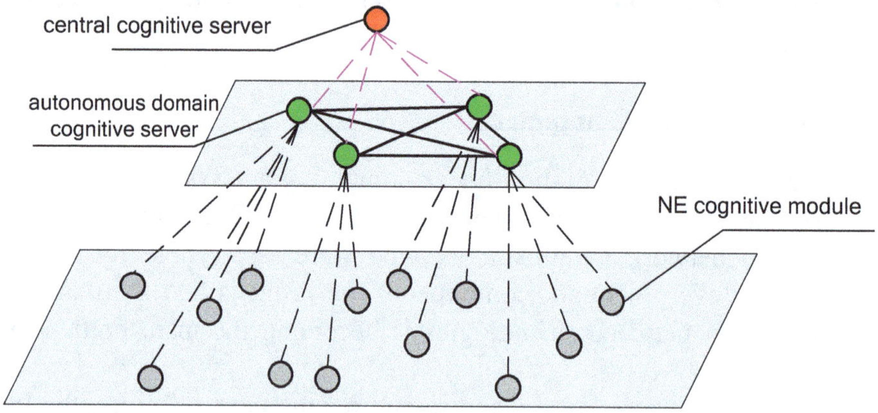

Fig. 2. The network decision-making and control architecture

At the same time, a central cognitive sever configured in the architecture is responsible for monitoring, awareness, and management of the running status of the entire network. The layered structure reduces the load on the central cognitive server. Even if the server fails temporarily, service QoS guarantee and management throughout the entire network is not affected.

Distributed networking and communication is enabled between autonomous cognitive servers so that information is exchanged in real time. The reason for using distributed management in the domain cognitive servers is to increase system reliability, flexibility, and expansibility. In the autonomous domain, adjacent nodes communicate so that distributed cooperative monitoring and self-adaptive processing is possible [16]. The architecture integrates the features of centralized architecture and distributed processing technology.

3.3 Self-adaptive Control Method Based on End-Link Collaboration

Network service types are varied, and network environments are complex and dynamic. Traditional end-to-end insurance technology lacks intelligent inference and self-learning capabilities. Therefore, it cannot adapt to provide ideal service under dynamically changing network conditions. Intelligent networks was different from the existing network of one of the most important characteristic is achieve end to end goals and its intelligence, autonomic, self-awareness and self-adaptive learning.

Intelligent network end-to-end targets is guaranteed by cognitive NEs. Cognitive NEs are cooperative or independent. The NEs perceive the network condition in real time, bring the trends together, and analyze the network condition. They configure themselves based on existing policies for achieving end-to-end targets.

The following describes the integration of service source-end control and link control in the intelligent network based on traffic classification, resource appointment concept, and control theory. A collaborative port and path policy-based self-adaptive control mechanism is proposed to solve the problem of end-to-end QoS guarantee for service traffic. The mechanism sends real-time network parameters to the autonomous domain server (or central cognitive server) through a feedback control. As a result, the self-adaptive control mode is integrated into the terminal NE and routers. The history of the network condition is compared with the current condition to form a control policy and to update the policy library through self-learning. At this point, the control policy is optimal. The mechanism can ensure the normal operation of a single NE and demonstrate the features of intelligent network. The mechanism uses relevant NE devices and reasonably allocates limited resources to improve end-to-end QoE and QoS. In this way, the performance of the entire network is optimized. Figure 3 shows the awareness-based service source end control layer and distributed awareness-based link control layer.

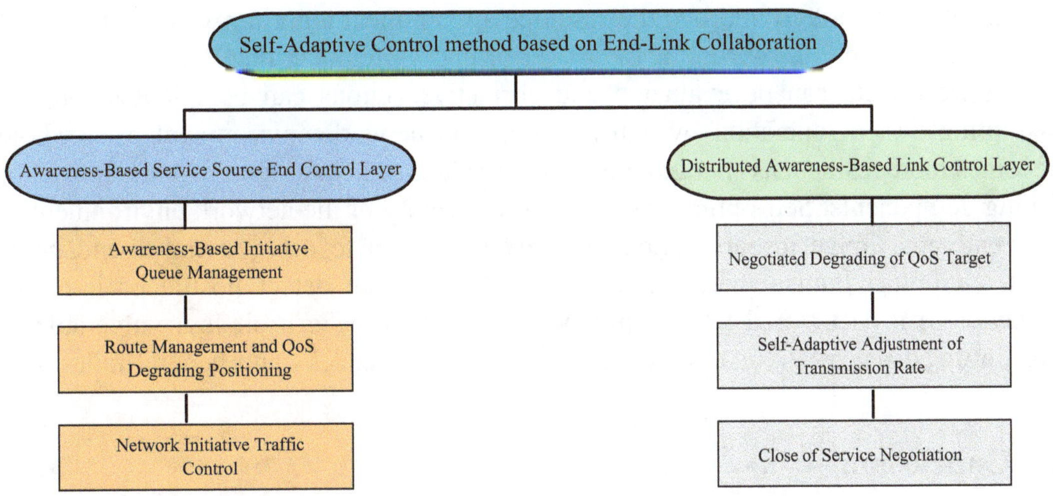

Fig. 3. Self-adaptive Control method based on End-Link collaboration

Awareness-based service control at the source end is implemented through self-adjustment of the source-end transmission rate, initiative closing of service, and initiative decrease of target. When the service source end launches a service in the traditional network, the current network condition is not considered. The intelligent network service end has certain cognitive functions; therefore, the cognitive information comes from the domain server or central control server. When certain conditions are met—for example, when bandwidth is sufficient—resources in the network can accept the access of other service traffic, and the service traffic can be transmitted to the peer end. When high-priority users need to transmit services, but the current network does not provide sufficient resources as required by the SLA, the central cognitive server (or domain cognitive server) negotiates with users at the service source end. If the user accepts a reduction of QoS, the source end transmits the service traffic according to the negotiated results. If QoS requirements cannot be reduced, the cognitive server recycles the network resources being used according to the resource distribution policy or even forcibly closes certain low-priority services.

Link control based on distributed awareness is implemented through initiative control of NE traffic, route management, QoS degradation positioning, and initiative queue management. By perceiving the network and making decisions based on this information, switches or routers with cognitive functions in the network can initiatively control traffic of different services and ensure the volume of trusted service traffic and key service traffic. They can also limit the volume of unsafe traffic or non-key traffic.

As service requirements and network resources are changing in real time, bottlenecks or QoS-degrading parts of the end-to-end network can be detected by cognitive route management and QoS degradation positioning. In addition, analysis and decision making can be performed, and service traffic can be re-routed. An intelligent and initiative queue management algorithm can also be used to determine congestion in the intelligent network. Awareness-based initiative queue management is oriented to the server's collaborative drive policy. This policy is integrated into the initiative queue management method to improve the resource appointment algorithm and router buffer management mode. Resources of the router or end system can then be reserved.

Network state can be evaluated and corrective actions can be initiated without disrupting system operation by self-healing. The network environment as a whole becomes more resilient as changes are made to reduce or help to eliminate the impact of failing components. Self-optimizing refers to the ability of the network environment to efficiently maximize resource allocation and utilization to achieve end-to-end goals with a minimal human intervention. Self-protecting can detect hostile or intrusive behavior as it occurs and take autonomous actions to make itself less vulnerable to unauthorized access and use, viruses, denial-of-service attacks and general failures.

4 Conclusion

Intelligent networks need to be self-aware in order to provide resilient applications and services. This paper proposes self-adaptive control mechanism in intelligent networks based on traffic classification. Drawing on control theory, network traffic can be controlled with a self-adaptive control mechanism that has end-link collaboration in intelligent networks. Such networks should exhibit cognitive properties where actions are based on reasoning, autonomic operations, adaptive functionality and self-manageability. Through self-learning mechanism and adaptive mechanisms of the network, it achieves the end-end goals. In this architecture, network flow can be identified and classified by intelligent situation-aware model. This mechanism can adjust resource allocation, adapt to a changeable network environment.

References

1. Kanaumi, Y., Saito, S., Kawai, E.: RISE: a wide-area hybrid OpenFlow network testbed. IEICE Trans. Commun. **96**(1), 108–118 (2013)
2. Bari, M., Chowdhury, S., Ahmed, R.: On orchestrating virtual network functions. In: International Conference on Network and Service Management, pp. 50–56 (2015)
3. Marias, J., Garay, J., Toledo, N.: Toward an SDN-enabled NFV architecture. IEEE Commun. Magzine **53**(4), 187–193 (2015)
4. Han, B., Gopalakrishnan, V.: Network function virtualization: challenges and opportunities for innovations. IEEE Commun. Mag. **53**(2), 90–97 (2015)
5. Moore, A.W., Papagiannaki, K.: Toward the accurate identification of network applications. In: Dovrolis, C. (ed.) PAM 2005. LNCS, vol. 3431, pp. 41–54. Springer, Heidelberg (2005). https://doi.org/10.1007/978-3-540-31966-5_4
6. Xia, M., Shirazipour, M., Zhang, Y.: Network function placement for NFV chaining in packet/optical data centers. J. Light. Technol. **33**(8), 1565–1570 (2015)
7. Sen, S., Spatscheck, O., Wang, D.: Accurate, scalable in-network identification of p2p traffic using application signatures. In: Proceedings of the 13th International Conference on World Wide Web, pp. 512–521 (2004)
8. Nguyen, T., Armitage, G.: A survey of techniques for internet traffic classification using machine learning. IEEE Commun. Surv. Tutor. **11**(3), 37–52 (2008)
9. Vapnik, V.: SVM method of estimating density, conditional probability, and conditional density. In: IEEE International Symposium on Circuits and Systems, pp. 749–752 (2002)
10. Yan, H., Xu, D.: An approach to estimating product design time based on fuzzy ν-support vector machine. IEEE Trans. Neural Netw. **18**(3), 721–732 (2007)
11. Hichem, S., Donald, G.: A hierarchy of support vector machines for pattern detection. J. Mach. Learn. Res. **7**(10), 2087–2123 (2006)
12. Tran, D.A., Nguyen, T.: Localization in wireless sensor networks based on support vector machines. IEEE Trans. Parallel Distrib. Syst. **19**(7), 981–994 (2008)
13. Benfano, S., Lucas, V., Ning, W.: Hybrid pattern matching for trusted intrusion detection. Secur. Commun. Netw. **4**(1), 33–43 (2011)
14. Chenfeng, Z., Christopher, L., Shanika, K.: A survey of coordinated attacks and collaborative intrusion detection. Comput. Secur. **29**(1), 124–140 (2010)
15. Sang, H., Won, S.: An anomaly intrusion detection method by clustering normal user behavior. Comput. Secur. **22**(7), 596–612 (2003)
16. Jing, J., Papavassiliou, S.: Enhancing network traffic prediction and anomaly detection via statistical network traffic separation and combination strategies. Comput. Commun. **29**(10), 1627–1638 (2006)

Malware Detection with Neural Network Using Combined Features

Huan Zhou(✉)

Onescorpion, 125 Malianwa North Road, Haidian District, 100000 Beijing, China
zhouhuan@onescorpion.com

Abstract. The growth in amount and species of malicious programs are now turning into a severe problem that strengthens the demand for development in detecting and classifying the potential threats automatically. Deep learning is an acceptable method to process this increment. In this paper, we propose an innovative method for detecting malware which uses the combined features (static + dynamic) to classify whether a portable executable (PE) file is malicious or not. A thorough experimental research on a real PE file collection was executed to make comparisons with the results that was performed in diverse situations and the performances of different machine learning models. The experiments prove the effectiveness of our model and show that our method is able to detect unknown malicious samples well.

Keywords: Malware detection · Neural networks · Feature engineering

1 Introduction

The amount of malware is growing annually and various types of attacks are more progressive and complex than before. One issue in computer security is thence to discover malware, so that it can be blocked before reaching its targets, or at least so that it can be wiped out in case it has been detected.

However, hackers keep on accelerating the automation of malware construction applying approaches such as polymorphism at a shocking rate. Obviously, automatic detection using highly precise intelligent models may be the only selection to fight against the issue in the future.

In recent years, a convergence of three evolutions have raised the probability for success in approaches using machine learning, keeping the commitment that these methods may reach pretty good detection performance at very low error rates without the trouble of human signature production required by non-automatic approaches.

The growth of commercial threat information feeds is the first of these tendencies which supplies great volumes of new malware, representing that for the first time, promptly, labeled malware samples are accessible to the security community. The second tendency is that computing power is much stronger and cheaper nowadays, implying that researchers are able to go over malware detection machine learning models more swiftly and train much more sophisticated and deeper models. Ultimately, machine learning as a subject has developed, suggesting that investigators have more

X. Yun et al. (Eds.): CNCERT 2018, CCIS 970, pp. 96–106, 2019.
https://doi.org/10.1007/978-981-13-6621-5_8

instruments to build models which can reach great performance not only in accuracy but also in scalability.

We propose an innovative method for detecting malware which uses combined features (static + dynamic) to classify whether a portable executable file is malicious or benign in this paper. Our method employs 2 kinds of neural networks to fit distinct property of respective work pipelines. The first type of neural network we use is recurrent neural network that is trained for extracting behavioral features of PE file, and the second type is convolutional neural network that is applied to classify samples. At the training stage of our method, we firstly extract static information of a PE file and use sandbox to record system API call sequences as dynamic behaviors. Then we extract static features based on predefined rules and dynamic features out of the trained RNN model. Next we combine them and use well design algorithm to create images. Lastly, we train and validate the concurrent classifier using images created in the previous steps labeled with 1(malicious) or 0(benign).

2 Related Work

In this section, we present published researches of deep neural network and malware detection.

2.1 Deep Neural Network

Neural networks (NN) have been studied for over thirty years which imitates the architecture referring to neuron collections in brain. NN consists of multiple layers. Deep neural networks (DNN) is a type of NN that comprises a lot of hidden layers.

Deep learning has become prevalent in many areas such as speech recognition [1] and computer vision [2] in recent times. Hinton et al. put forward an astonishing method called Dropout that can solve gradient vanishing problem well [3]. This approach decreases dependencies among neurons through omitting several results of neurons to prevent overfitting. The omitted neurons are selected stochastically. Therefore, all training is executed with distinct architectural network which decreases the dependency between neurons. Krizhevsky et al. use CNN which astonishingly reduced the false positive rate in the field of computer vision. Gers et al. put forward LSTM [4] which avoids the error disappearing issue.

2.2 Malware Detection

There are two types of malware detection approaches. The first type is detecting malicious files before they run to avoid endpoints being infected, and the second type is detecting endpoints which have been attacked to reduce the outspread of loss to the smallest possible degree.

Malware classification has been a popular research fields since 1990s. Mathur and Idika [5] proposed a good overview in this area. Kephart et al. [6] put forward an innovative method which utilizes neural networks for detecting malicious behaviors. Dahl et al. [7] made attempt to do malware classification utilizing neural networks and random projections on a large scale. Saxe et al. [8] try to do static analysis on samples by using feed-forward neural networks. Huang et al. [9] concentrated on assessing multi-task learning ideas and made use of deep feed-forward neural network. Pascanu et al. [10] built models based on system call sequences and utilized recurrent neural networks so as to build a "language model" for target files. They took measures to check performance on gated recurrent units (GRU) and long short-Term memory (LSTM) and reported good results.

3 Proposed Method

In this section, we propose an innovative method for detecting malware which uses combined features to classify whether a PE file is malicious or benign. We split the approaches into 4 stages. The first one extracts static feature information from PE file. The second stage records the system API sequences using sandbox and processes them by RNN. At the third stage, we combine the former static and dynamic features and convert them into fixed feature vectors which are going to be transformed into images. Finally, we train and classify the images using designed model based on CNN.

3.1 Overview

The overview of our proposal is shown in Fig. 1. For each file, many types of raw information are collected such as header, byte histogram, import list, etc., and a suit of application programming interface (API) call events.

Static information does not need thorough or sophisticated configuration for collection and multiplex static features have been raised for feature engineering of PE file: printable strings [11], opcodes, import tables, informational entropy [12] and byte n-grams [13]. We extract some basic features using approaches which have been used in previously published works.

File behaviors are consisted of a variety of activities such as registry operation, file management and so on which involve various operations. When we use API call sequences to represent dynamic information, a variety of API calls stand for an activity, and all of the recorded API calls will be regarded as dynamic features of target file. This hierarchical structure is the very picture of the composition of writings. A single writing is made up of multiple sentences which consist of various words. Therefore, we suppose that we are able to utilize language model like RNN to get the dynamic features of file.

The feature vectors extracted from static and dynamic information will be concatenated and converted into an image. And the generated image will contain combined information which will be use later. Our classifier is based on CNN since it has been proved to be very effective in image classification.

The training flow can be divided into four phases as shown in Fig. 1. First, collecting basic static and dynamic information of PE files. Second, the static features are extracted using predefined extractor and the RNN is trained using file API sequences to extract dynamic features. Third, features are combined and converted into feature images. At last, the neural network classifier will be trained and validated using labeled generated images.

After training the designed classifiers, we verify the effectiveness of our model. At the beginning, generating the images of PE files in validate dataset using the former steps. Finally, these files will be labeled whether 1 or 0 using model depended on the outputs and predefined threshold.

The specific details of every step are introduced in the following sections.

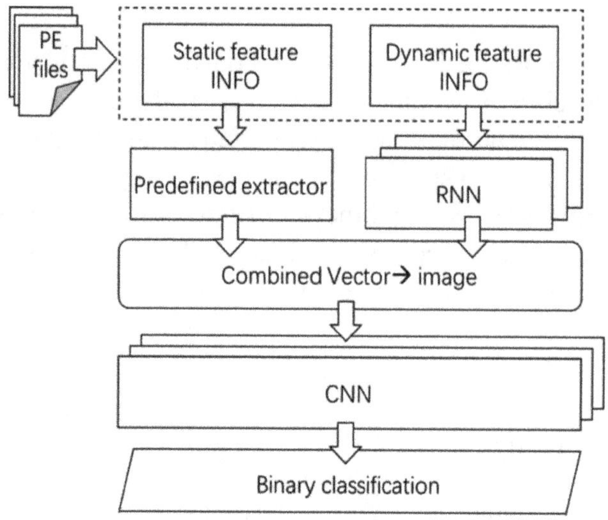

Fig. 1. Overview

3.2 Static Features

We predefined some basic features which will be extracted from PE file using methods employed in previously published works. The following Table 1 gives a summary of all target static features.

3.3 Dynamic Features

API Call Sequences. Before feeding the system API call sequences to designed models, we have to preprocess the input data. Dealing with redundant data and turning inputs into numerical vectors are two of the primary preparations. Firstly, we clean API sequences in which a single API is duplicate over 2 times. We merge these same API call sequences through applying maximum 2 successive duplicate system API call instances in the results. Moreover, we utilize 1-hot encoding method to create a specific binary vector for each system API call in our dataset. Along these lines, we get a set of numerical feature vectors rather than a suit of system API call names.

Table 1. Summary of target static features

Features	Description
Byte histogram	byte histogram (count + non-normalized) over the entire binary file
ByteEntropy histogram	2d byte/entropy histogram
Section information	section names, sizes and entropy: section_sizes_hashed, section_entropy_hashed, etc.
Imports information	imported libraries and functions from the import address table
Exports information	exported functions
General File information	general information about the file: size, vsize, has_debug, etc.
Header File information	machine, architecture, OS, linker and other information extracted from header: timestamp, machine, etc.
String extractor	extracts strings from raw byte stream: 'numstrings', 'avglength', etc.

Training LSTM. We employ LSTM which is a type of recurrent neural network to build our behavior model. Our model is consisted of an input layer X, multiple hidden layer (1 oridinary + 2 LSTM), and an output layer Y. The structure of our behavior model is illustrated in Fig. 2.

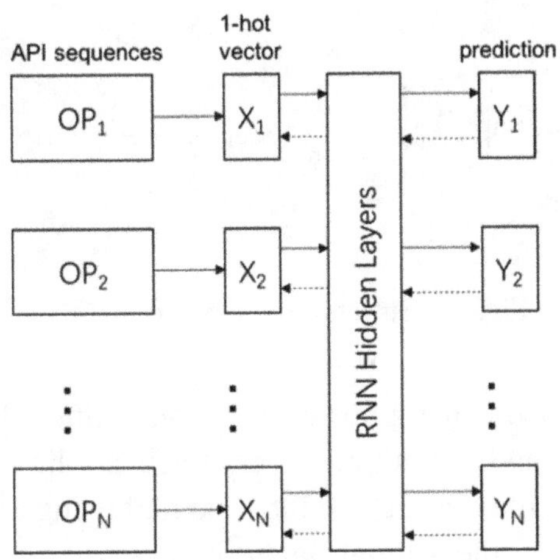

Fig. 2. RNN training process

Feature Extraction. We extract dynamic features of PE file by using trained model based on RNN. Our trained dynamic feature extractor is able to output the next predicted action from former sequences of inputs. Furthermore, fractional features are distilled in layers that near to the head of deep neural networks. And abstracted features are distilled in layers near to the bottom. Therefore, we are supposed to get behavioral features in deep layer of trained model.

3.4 Feature Selection and Imaging

Once getting static and dynamic features, we transform and concatenate them to build a combined vector. We design image classifier to receive fixed size of vectors. Thus, we have to transform the chains of vector to configured length since the sequences of system API are totally different between PE files.

$$\mathrm{V} = \begin{pmatrix} v_1 \\ v_2 \\ \cdots \\ v_n \end{pmatrix} = \begin{bmatrix} v_{11} & v_{12} & \cdots & v_{1m} \\ v_{21} & v_{22} & \cdots & v_{2m} \\ & & \cdots & \\ v_{n1} & v_{n2} & \cdots & v_{nm} \end{bmatrix} \tag{1}$$

We transform value of feature matrix to the range of [0,1] through using sigmoid function. Then we multiply each element in the matrix with 255 to constitute image of the source file. At last, the matrix V is calculated as feature image with size of $\mathrm{n} \times \mathrm{m}$.

3.5 Deep Neural Networks

Next, we train a deep feed forward concurrent neural network (CNN) for binary classification. The network architecture is shown in Fig. 3.

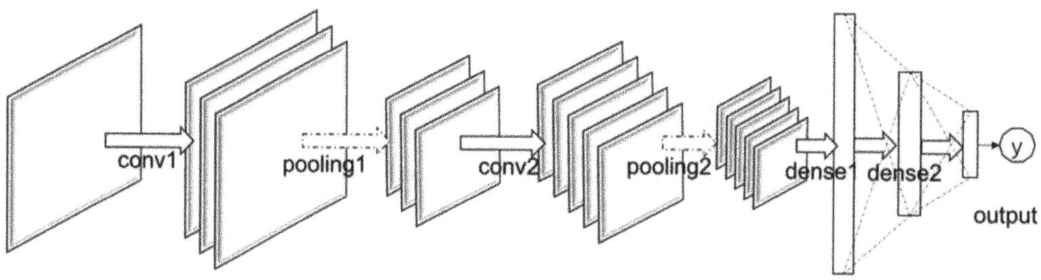

Fig. 3. Structure of CNN classifier

The CNN is consisted of an input layer, 2 convolution layers, 2 pooling layers, 2 fully connected layers, and an output layer. Each pooling layer obtains the result of the former layer and cut the output size into one half using average-pooling with step of two. The dimension of the output layer is 2 since we try to proceed binary classification.

By applying the classifier which has been trained, we compute the value of target file in the validation phase. When feed our trained classifier with a feature image of the validation file, it will output a 2 dimensional vector. And elements in the vector stand for benign and malicious extent. If the malicious value is bigger than the benign value, we can classify the source file as malicious. The probability value is computed through employing function below.

$$\mathrm{p} = \mathrm{sigmoid(y)} = 1/1 + \exp(-\mathrm{y}) \tag{2}$$

ReLU. The tanh and sigmoid activation function generally appear the gradient vanishing problem making models based on deep neural network difficult to train [14]. To overcome this trouble, we employ rectified linear unit (ReLU) and its activation function is as follows:

$$\mathrm{f(x) = max(0, x)} \tag{3}$$

Dropout. Dropout is a regularization method which is designed for the training phase of DNN. The key operation is that the algorithm makes a choice to update part of the hidden units randomly when updating hidden layer. The intuition for this method is that while ignoring units in hidden layers randomly, the network will be coerced to get multiple different patterns with the same dataset. In our designed classifier, we utilize Dropout to solve the gradient vanishing problem.

Loss function. Deep neural networks learn various patterns of inputs in different layers. The bottom layer uses function called softmax to calculate two dimensional vector which stands for benign and malware. To fine tune our model, we employ the loss function called cross entropy to assess the quality of our model's results. The function is illustrated as

$$L_n(\theta(v)) = -\sum\nolimits_{n \in N} gtd_n(v) log \theta_n(\mathrm{v}) \tag{4}$$

where v stands for the input vector, n means category, N is the set of predicted categories, gtd stands for ground truth distribution, and θ(x) indicates probability distribution of classifier.

4 Experiment

4.1 Dataset

We use a published framework [15] to collect samples. Our dataset is consisted of files collected from 3 major sources: Virus Share [16], Maltrieve [17] and private collections. These origins offer a wide and multiplex amount of files for validation. Our final dataset contains 90,000 samples with 72,317 labeled as malicious and 17683 labeled as benign. We train our model on 60,000 of the collected samples. The test data contain 30,000 samples.

There are a lot of tools which are able to track the execution of files and record system API call sequences [18, 19]. We use an open source sandbox called Cuckoo which is very useful and the environment it provides is controllable. For each sample, we receive a set of system API calls and use them to train a RNN model which is able to extract dynamic features.

4.2 Evaluation Method

In the following part, we introduce the method applied to evaluate our experiment results.

In the evaluation phase, we utilize a type of 3-fold cross-validation. So we choose 2/3 of files as training data in each experiment, while the rest of data is allocated into the test set. As a matter of fact, in order to get a trustworthy capability estimation, we averaged the results of 10 cross-validation experiments, carried out with a different stochastic dataset arrangement each time.

Table 2. Confusion matrix

		Predicted value		
		$y = t$	$y \neq t$	
Original value	$x \in t$	True Positive (TP)	False Negative (FN)	P = TP + FN
	$x \notin t$	False Positive (FP)	True Negative (TN)	N = FP + TN

For multi-classification issue, Positive indicates a sample x can be classified as target class t because of surpassing a predefined threshold. On the contrary, it is Negative. Since we try to divide the sample into two categories, the issue turns into binary classification. y is the output of x. Under this circumstance, the confusion matrix is illustrated in Table 2 and we demonstrate the functions which we will use as follows.

$$TPR = TP/P \tag{5}$$

$$FPR = FP/N \tag{6}$$

$$AR = (TP + TN)/(P + N) \tag{7}$$

where TPR stands for true positive rate, FPR stands for false positive rate and AR means accuracy rate.

We assess the quality of our classifier using Area Under the Curve (AUC) that can be calculated from ROC curve which is a figure showing the relationship between FPR and TPR within threshold. In our method, samples are classified as benign or malicious based on output probability p calculated by (2). The value p and threshold both lie in the range of [0,1]. For each situation, we draw ROC curve through treating TPR as y axis and FPR as x axis. Furthermore, we evaluate classifier efficiency by comparing the AUC in each situation.

4.3 Result

In our first experiment, we want to know the performance of only using static features and the performance of only using dynamic features since we combined the static and dynamic features. Figure 4 show the ROC curve which illustrates that using combined features outperforms the other two methods.

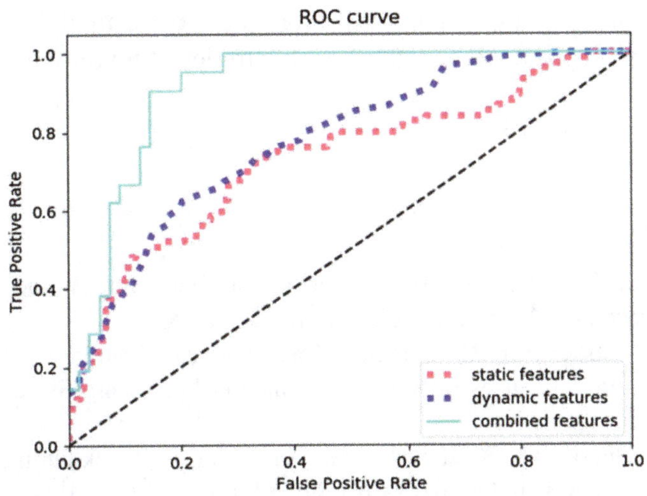

Fig. 4. ROC curves of different feature engineering methods

Then we want to evaluate the effectiveness of our methodology compared with the other machine learning methods. Thus, we compare the classification result of our designed neural network architecture with traditional machine learning methods such as Decision Tree, Random Forest, etc., as well as stat-of-the-art deep learning methods such as CNN, RNN because these models have been widely employed in researches which have been published. We show the results in Table 3 which proves the effectiveness of employing our designed method.

Table 3. Accuracy of different models

Methods	Models	ACC
Traditional machine learning methods	Decision Tree [20]	90.7%
	Random Forest [21]	95.4%
	Hidden Markov Models [22]	87.3%
	Support Vector Machine [23]	91.4%
	KNN [24]	94.7%
NN methods	CNN [25]	94.7%
	RNN [26]	95.6%
Our method	RNN + CNN	97.3%

5 Conclusion

We propose an innovative method for detecting malware which uses the combined features (static + dynamic) to classify whether a portable executable (PE) file is malicious or benign in this paper. Our method discovers malicious software through classifying the generated images using designed model. We make comparisons with the results that was performed in diverse situations and the performances of different machine learning models. The results show that our innovative method acquires the best results in all three situations and outperforms the other models which prove great effectiveness of the proposal. Our method is able to detect unknown malicious samples well.

References

1. Hinton, G., et al.: Deep neural networks for acoustic modeling in speech recognition. In: IEEE Signal Processing Magazine, vol. 29, pp. 82–97 (2012)
2. Krizhevsky, A., Sutskever, I., Hinton, G.E.: Imagenet classification with deep convolutional neural networks. In: Advances in Neural Information Processing Systems, pp. 1097–1105 (2012)
3. Srivastava, N., Hinton, G., Krizhevsky, A., Sutskever, I., Salakhutdinov, R.: Dropout: a simple way to prevent neural networks from overfitting. J. Mach. Learn. Res. **15**(1), 1929–1958 (2014)
4. Gers, F.A., Schmidhuber, J., Cummins, F.: Learning to forget: continual prediction with LSTM. Neural Comput. **12**(10), 2451–2471 (2000)
5. Idika, N., Mathur, A.P.: A survey of malware detection techniques. Technical report, Purdue University, February 2007. http://www.eecs.umich.edu/techreports/cse/2007/CSE-TR-530-07.pdf
6. Kephart, J.O.: A biologically inspired immune system for computers. In: Proceedings of the Fourth International Workshop on the Synthesis and Simulation of Living Systems, pp. 130–139. MIT Press (1994)
7. Dahl, G.E., Stokes, J.W., Deng, L., Yu, D.: Large-scale malware classification using random projections and neural networks. In: IEEE International Conference on Acoustics, Speech and Signal Processing (ICASSP) (2013)
8. Saxe, J., Berlin, K.: Deep Neural Network Based Malware Detection Using Two Dimensional Binary Program Features. arXiv preprint arXiv:1508.03096 (2015)
9. Huang, W., Stokes, J.W.: MtNet: a multi-task neural network for dynamic malware classification. In: Conference on Detection of Intrusions and Malware & Vulnerability Assessment (DIMVA) (2016)
10. Pascanu, R., Stokes, J.W., Sanossian, H., Marinescu, M., Thomas, A.: Malware classification with recurrent networks. In: IEEE International Conference on Acoustics, Speech and Signal Processing (ICASSP) (2015)
11. Schultz, M., Eskin, E., Zadok, E., Stolfo, S.: Data mining methods for detection of new malicious executables. In: Proceedings of the 2001 IEEE Symposium on Security and Privacy, 2001. S P 2001, pp. 38–49 (2001)
12. Weber, M., Schmid, M., Schatz, M., Geyer, D.: A toolkit for detecting and analyzing malicious software. In: Proceedings of the 18th Annual Computer Security Applications Conference, pp. 423- 431. IEEE (2002)
13. Abou-Assaleh, T., Cercone, N., Kesˇelj, V., Sweidan, R.: N-gram-based detection of new malicious code. In: Proceedings of the 28th Annual International Computer Software and Applications Conference. COMPSAC 2004, vol. 2, pp. 41–42. IEEE (2004)
14. Hochreiter, S., Bengio, Y., Frasconi, P., Schmidhuber, J.: Gradientflowinrecurrent nets: the difficulty of learning long-term dependencies. In: Kolen, J.F., Kremer, S.C. (eds.) A Field Guide to Dynamical Recurrent Neural Networks. IEEE Press. Wiley- IEEE Press (2001)
15. Webster, G., Hanif, Z., Ludwig, A., Lengyel, T., Zarras, A., Eckert, C.: SKALD: a scalable architecture for feature extraction, multi-user analysis, and real-time information sharing. In: International Conference on Information Security (2016)

16. Roberts, J.-M.: Virus Share, July 2018. https://virusshare.com/
17. Maxwell, K.: Maltrieve, April 2015. https://github.com/krmaxwell/maltrieve
18. Guarnieri, C., Tanasi, A., Bremer, J., Schloesser, M.: The Cuckoo Sandbox (2012)
19. Lengyel, T.K., Maresca, S., Payne, B.D., Webster, G.D., Vogl, S., Kiayias, A.: Scalability, fidelity and stealth in the drakvuf dynamic malware analysis system. In: Annual Computer Security Applications Conference (ACSAC) (2014)
20. HUANG Quanwei: Malicious Executables detection based on N-Gram System call Sequences. Harbin Institute of Technology (2009)
21. Zhang, J., Li, Y.: Malware detection system implementation of Android application based on machine learning. Appl. Res. Comput. **6**, 1–6 (2017)
22. Annachhatre, C., Austin, T.H., Stamp, M.: Hidden Markov models for malware classification. J. Comput. Virol. Hack. Tech. **11**(2), 59–73 (2014)
23. Arp, D., Spreitzenbarth, M., Hubner, M., Gascon, H., Rieck, K.: Drebin: effective and explainable detection of android malware in your pocket. In: Proceedings of NDSS (2014)
24. Dahl, G.E., Stokes, J.W., Deng, L., et al.: Large-scale malware classification using random projections and neural networks. In: 2013 IEEE International Conference on Acoustics, Speech and Signal Processing (ICASSP). IEEE 2013
25. Kolosnjaji, B., et al.: Empowering convolutional networks for malware classification and analysis. In: 2017 International Joint Conference on Neural Networks (IJCNN). IEEE (2017)
26. Athiwaratkun, B., Stokes, J.W.: Malware classification with LSTM and GRU language models and a character-level CNN. In: 2017 IEEE International Conference on Acoustics, Speech and Signal Processing (ICASSP), pages 2482–2486. IEEE (2017)

Cyber Threat Detection and Defense

Malicious Websites Identification Based on Active-Passive Method

Xue-qiang Zou[1,2,3](✉), Peng Zhang[2], Cai-yun Huang[2,3], and Xiu-guo Bao[1,2,3]

[1] National Computer Network Emergency Response Technical Team/Coordination of China, Beijing 100029, China
[2] Institute of Information Engineering, Chinese Academy of Sciences, Beijing 100093, China
{zouxueqiang, zhangpeng, huangcaiyun, baoxiuguo}@iie.ac.cn
[3] School of Cyber Security, University of Chinese Academy of Sciences, Beijing 100049, China

Abstract. Nowadays, massive numbers of malicious websites are endeavored to change their hosts/IP addresses to avoid tracking. This paper fills a gap in the study of tracking this kind of websites and offers approaches to detection and identification by combining both active and passive methods. The active method, as bootstrap, is based on crawling traffic from Internet, we can extract title, keywords and picture as features and store them as feature sets. What we do in passive filtering is to match online traffic using the feature sets. Other than finding out those malicious websites, we can extract extra features such as cookie and users information, which is unavailable by using active method, from online traffic and add them to the feature sets created by proceeding active method. According to the experiment, we can have 95.43% true positive rate and 3.90% false positive rate under real data flow in this way.

Keywords: Website identification · Feature extraction · Active detect · Passive monitoring

1 Introduction

With the rapid development of the Internet, websites have become the most important way for people to obtain information. At the same time, many malicious websites spread information such as fraud, violence, pornography, etc. through the Internet, posing a serious threat to cyberspace. Therefore, analyzing and extracting the effective features of websites can identify malicious websites more accurately, reduce the spread of malicious information, and improve the security of network.

At present, some malicious websites are struggling to survive by changing the domain name and IP address. On the one hand, the traffic information of all the domain names under the website cannot be captured by directly matching the known host and IP address. On the other hand, for a website that uses a LAN or a cloud server, its IP address is probably not fixed. For the website service provider, the value of the host

X. Yun et al. (Eds.): CNCERT 2018, CCIS 970, pp. 109–121, 2019.
https://doi.org/10.1007/978-981-13-6621-5_9

field of the HTTP message can be changed by itself, which also makes it possible to forge host information. For the above reasons, the way to directly match the host and IP does not guarantee that the traffic matching the hit is the traffic to the target website.

In view of the above problems, this paper proposes a new method for recording and identifying specific website features. The main research results include:

(1) Based on the identification of website access traffic by matching host and IP attributes, other feature information, including keywords, title, logo picture and cookie, are introduced. Firstly, the cookie is used for website identification. Then, the simhash is used to calculate the value and the similarity comparison is performed by using the simhash algorithm. Finally, the comparison hashing algorithm is used to perform the falsification operation on the comparison result through the logo image of the website. This can eliminate the impact of fake host and IP address uncertainty on website identification, and improve the accuracy of website identification.

(2) According to the characteristics of the website in the traffic, a system of extracting and identifying the active module and passive module linkage is established. After the active discovery of some features, the features are complemented by passive detection, and the host information of the same website whose domain name or IP constantly changing is found. The information is recorded and input into the active acquisition module for further analysis.

The second section of this paper mainly introduces the related work of website detection and identification. The third section describes the extraction system based on active-passive combination, and introduces the way to determine the similarity of the website. The fourth section uses the experiment to quantitatively evaluate the results obtained by the model; Finally, we summarize the paper and point out the next step.

2 Related Work

The current research on automatically identify websites is mainly based on three types of methods: blacklist, active detection and passive monitoring. The blacklist-based technology is mainly implemented by maintaining a blacklist with IP address and domain name. It can be judged the malicious website by checking whether the domain name/IP address appears on the blacklist. Active detection mainly uses crawler to obtain static data, such as keyword in webpage html, and then analyze it through machine learning. Passive detection allows direct analysis of online traffic.

Specifically, some browsers use a built-in blacklist to provide users with lightweight, real-time malicious web page identification services to meet the needs of rapid response. However, most of the blacklists are obtained through manual reporting and client analysis, and the workload is large. Ma et al. [1–3] use machine learning algorithms to identify malicious URLs based on DNS information, WHOIS information, and grammatical features of URLs. Canal et al. [4] added JavaScript and HTML features to improve the accuracy of malicious web page identification by detecting web content. However, such active methods often fail to detect malicious websites in time. In addition, with the popularity of network services, attackers will continue to adopt some new technical means (for example, automatic domain name generation [5], web page hiding technology [6], etc.) to enhance the concealment of malicious web pages and improve attack efficiency. This further increases the difficulty of malicious website identification.

Therefore, this paper proposes a combination of active and passive methods for malicious website identification. This method can solve the untimely problem of traffic discovery and processing in the active mode, and provides effective features for passive traffic filtering. At the same time, combined with the file content of html and the field content of HTTP head, it can extract more useful information to improve the accuracy of website identification.

3 Proposed Method

There are a large number of malicious websites hiding their existence by constantly changing their domain names and IP addresses. This type of website cannot be detected by filtering traffic directly by specifying the IP or domain name. Here, this paper proposes a method of detecting with the combination of active and passive. By establishing the feature information set of the website, the traffic of particular dynamic website is detected to achieve the purpose of identifying the website. The way of collecting website feature information is mainly divided into two types: active acquisition and passive acquisition. The basic framework of the model is given in Fig. 1. The following sections will illustrate the main parts of the framework.

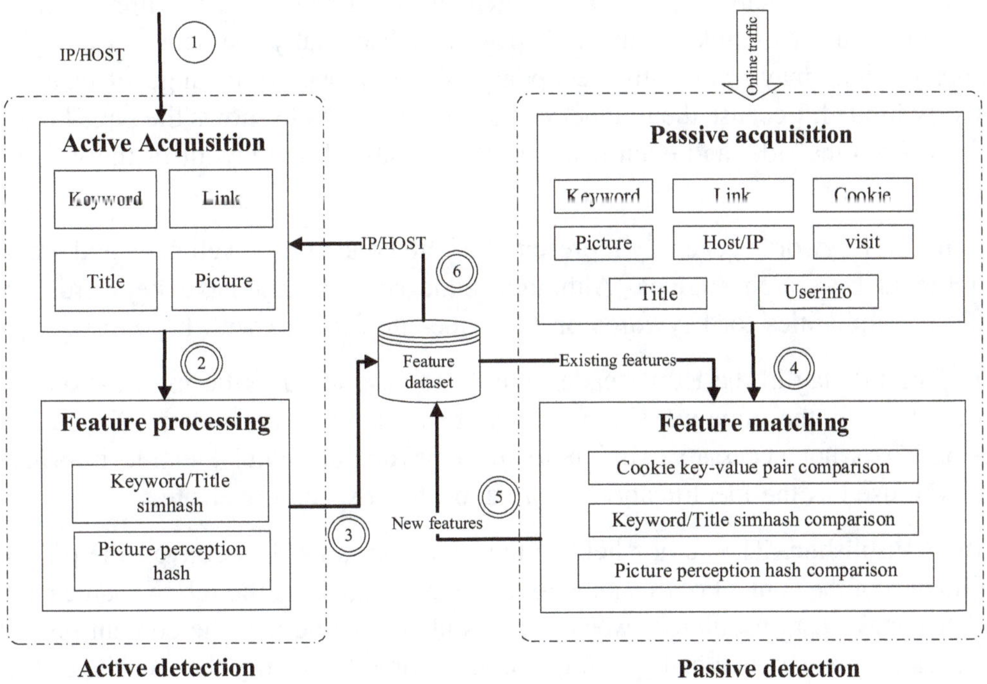

Fig. 1. Website feature feedback identification model

3.1 Active Detection

HTTP response message content plays an important role in network traffic analysis. On the one hand, it truthfully reflects information such as web page content during transmission; on the other hand, HTTP messages have a strict encapsulation format to facilitate data extraction.

Traffic active acquisition is the guide part of the whole model. It mainly sends out GET requests to specific websites by the operator, and extracts the useful information to identify specific websites based on the return HTTP response message content. These feature information mainly include the following two kinds:

(1) HTTP message header field information, such as server, last-modified, x-powered-by and other field information;
(2) HTML file content information, such as title information in HTML, meta information, general software system information, link information, and so on.

These feature information is then saved to a local database to form feature information set for the particular website. At the same time, the crawling data may have some noise, such as the display result is garbled due to different coding methods of the website, and the href tag in the webpage points to the intra-site URL. The active traffic acquisition will pre-process the data before it is saved, such as performing corresponding decoding operations on the webpage content and complementing the link content in the webpage will help to reduce the noise in the dataset.

Specifically, this article selects the following factors that may have an impact on identification accuracy:

Links. For the malicious websites detected, even in the case of different domain names, the number of links in the web page is substantially the same. Although the number of links may vary with the update of the website, the range of changes is relatively limited. Because the number of links on the website shows the page layout of the page from the side, and even if a website is updated, the layout of the website is similar.

Keywords. Keywords generally represent the core content of a web page and are used for retrieval by search engines. Although some sites do not have keywords, there should be similarities for keywords on the same site for sites with keywords.

Title. The title tag in the Html header is used to describe the title information of the website. Usually the same website will have the same title information. Since the title information is not necessary, similar to the keyword attribute, the title information should be used as the identification information for a specific website.

Content Publisher. The author field in the Meta tag is used to convey the publisher information of the content of this page to the search engine. Although the same content publisher may post on different websites, it is also possible that the content publisher has the same name, which makes it impossible to directly identify the website or falsify the website through this option, but this is a property of the website itself. At the same time, the inclusion of content publisher information in the site's feature information set can also provide conditions for similar site queries in the future.

Logo. Most websites have their own logo patterns. Since these logo images may have different height and width, the picture information can be extracted and the two-image similarity calculation is performed using a perceptual hash algorithm.

Host/IP. Recording known URLs for specific websites visited does not reflect the characteristics of such URLs, but helps to more accurately filter specific URL traffic during passive traffic acquisition.

3.2 Passive Detection

Passive traffic detection mainly obtains online traffic information by accessing ISP traffic. Compared with active traffic detection, the feature information obtained through passive mode includes the following points:

(1) The IP address and port, the agent of the sending and receiving parties, and so on, are available in the active acquisition by the operator itself, or are preset by the operator, which is not characteristic.
(2) The information sent to the server when requested by the client, such as cookie information. Since the operator can set the value of the information he wants to send, this information cannot be recorded as part of the signature database in active traffic acquisition. At the same time, this information is also reinforcing for the judgment of the website.
(3) Statistics. The active requester for the service is only the operator's individual, but once the overall traffic is available, the overall request information can be statistically analyzed by sampling. For example, the amount of visits, users accessing the website, and the ratio of traffic to the site.

When the operator obtains a partial information set of a specific website from the active traffic detection, the feature information is pushed to the passive traffic detection. Passive traffic detection compares these feature information with the online traffic it has acquired. If the features can be matched, it is regarded as obtaining the traffic accessing the specific website, and the above three kinds of information can be sequentially recorded and added to the feature information set of the specific website.

Specifically, passive traffic acquisition module mainly records and adds the following feature information:

User. User information including the source IP address of the TCP layer, source port information, and user login time information. Although the user information cannot mark the website, the user-related information can be used to monitor and analyze the IP access traffic in the future to obtain similar sites.

Traffic. These two values are recorded as statistical information in the feature information set. As attribute information that cannot directly filter the traffic filtering, recording it has a certain effect on the network mapping work.

Cookies. Cookies are mainly used by the server to record the basic information of the visitor and some statistics of the access. Chen et al. [7] provide a way to judge the same website through cookies. When there are two or three cookie key pairs in the passively acquired traffic, it can be judged that the traffic belongs to the same website.

Additional Features. Initially, the feature information of active traffic acquisition, such as keywords, title information, etc., may not be complete. The use of passive traffic can obtain more information about the specific feature of a specific website and complement it, so that a higher rate of flow matching can be obtained in the next screening.

Host/IP. The known host and IP information is limited. Using passive traffic for matching may result in more host and IP address information for the homologous website, which can continue feature extraction in the next active acquisition.

3.3 Homologous Website Identification

Homogenous website refers to a website that provides the same content although the domain name or IP address changes. Such websites have similar feature information. For the identification of such websites, it is necessary to use the specific attributes in the feature set to detect and filter online traffic after the feature information set of the website is generated. At this time, features that can be used to judge the similarity of the website include: keyword, title, logo hash value, and cookie.

Based on the above information, the identification process of the homologous website proposed in this paper is shown in Fig. 2.

First, the cookie is selected as a strong feature to identify the website. When there are three or more cookie key-value pairs in the test website traffic, it is determined to be a homogenous website. However, experiments have shown that the cookie value of the same website may be completely different. Therefore, when using cookies can't judge the flow of the passive traffic to the target site, the similarity of the string generated by the keyword and the title, as well as the similarity between the logo pictures of the website can be used. Finally, the hash value of the logo image is used to falsify the homologous websites determined by keywords and titles. The homologous websites with logo pictures are similar in image features. When the keyword and the title information are similar, if the passive traffic does not find a picture similar to the feature set, it can be considered that the detected website is not the homologous site of the target website.

In the following, the identification criteria are described in terms of features, wherein the feature information set includes feature information represented by A, and the corresponding feature information extracted from the traffic is represented by B:

Step1: For cookies, select T_{cookie} as a critical value. When the same number of cookie keys reaches the critical value, it is judged to be the same website [7], which is recorded as $c_{sim}(A, \mathrm{B})$. The method of determining the similarity between two websites by using the cookie key-value for the same number is as shown in the formula (1):

$$c_{sim}(\mathrm{A}, \mathrm{B}) = \begin{cases} 1, & |\mathrm{A} \cap \mathrm{B}| \geq T_{cookie} \\ 0, & |\mathrm{A} \cap \mathrm{B}| < T_{cookie} \end{cases} \tag{1}$$

Where $|\mathrm{A} \cap \mathrm{B}|$ indicates the number of identical key-value pairs of the cookie in the signature database and the cookie detected in the traffic.

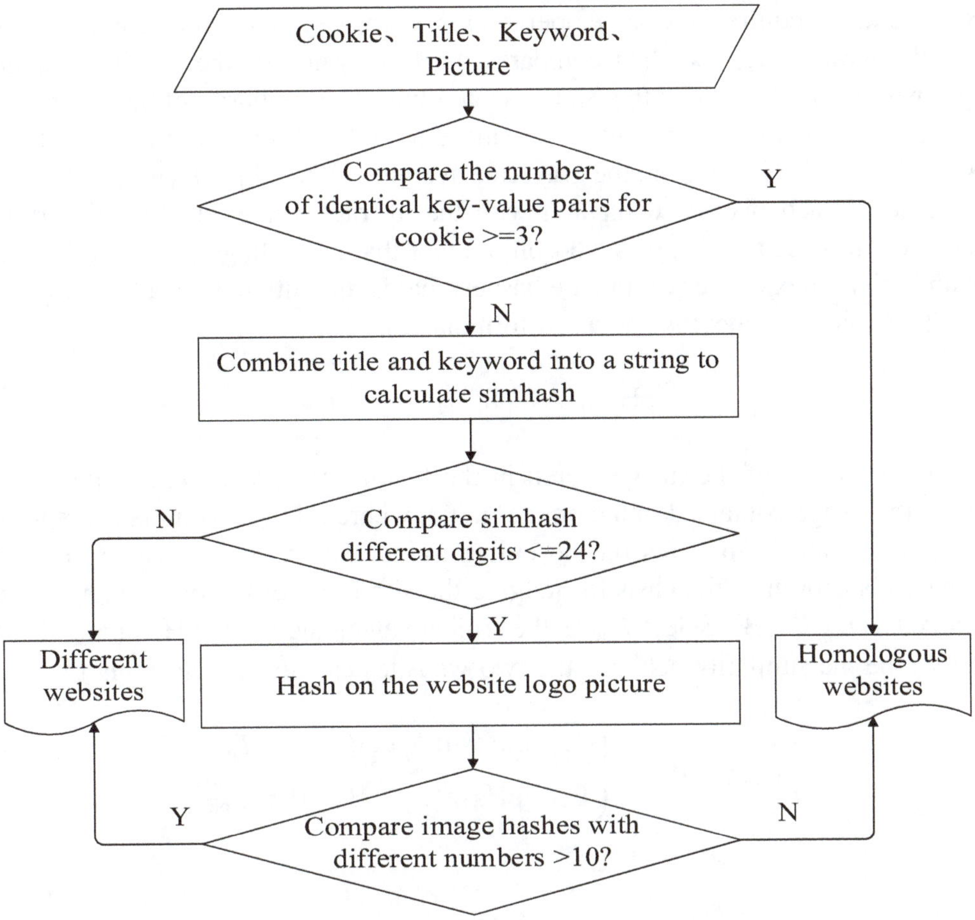

Fig. 2. The process of homologous website identification algorithm

Step2: For keyword and title information, we used LSH (locally sensitive hash) [8] to combine the keyword and title information of the website into a input string. Then extract the keywords that identify the website from this string. These keywords are given a specific weight, and each keyword is hashed to obtain a 64-bit binary string. Multiply the hash value of each keyword by its weight, and add the results of each keyword in bits. Finally, if a value obtained by bit is greater than 0, the bit is marked as 1; otherwise it is marked as 0. For keyword and title information, we used a locally sensitive hash algorithm [8] to combine the keyword and title information of the website into a string input. Then extract the keywords that identify the website from this string. These keywords are given a specific weight, and each extracted keyword is hashed to obtain a 64-bit binary string. Multiply the hash value of each keyword by its weight, and add the results of each keyword in bits. Finally, if a value obtained by a bit is greater than 0, the bit is marked as 1, otherwise it is marked as 0. Then, a 64-bit binary fingerprint based on the website keyword and title is finally generated. When the fingerprint extracted in the passive traffic differs from the fingerprint in the signature database by less than a certain distance, it is determined to be a homogenous website.

Step3: For the logo picture, this paper uses the perceptual hash algorithm [9] to obtain the hash value of the logo image in the active traffic acquisition. When the passive traffic is acquired, the same operation is performed on the image in the traffic to obtain the hash value, and then compares the hash value of the passively acquired images with the hash value in the feature set to obtain the similarity of the image. In the perceptual hash algorithm, the image is reduced to an 8 * 8 size, so it is converted into a 64-level grayscale image, and the grayscale average of the 64 pixels is calculated. The gray value of each pixel is compared with the average value and then 0 and 1 are respectively recorded. This gives a 64-bit number that is the fingerprint of this picture. The similarity index of the two picture hashes, that is, the different data bits of the hash value (Hamming distance) is shown in formula (2):

$$\mathrm{pHash}\left(\mathrm{A}_{pic}, \mathrm{B}_{pici}\right) \quad i\epsilon[1, n] \tag{2}$$

The hash value of the image stored in the feature set is compared with the hash value of the image contained in the online traffic, where n in the formula (2) represents the number of all the pictures on the online traffic. The minimum value of the two differences is chosen as the basis for judging the similarity of the two websites, which is denoted as $\mathrm{p}_{sim}(\mathrm{A}, \mathrm{B})$. Select T_{pic} as the critical value, and use the Hamming distance to determine the similarity between the two websites as shown in formula (3):

$$\mathrm{p}_{sim}(\mathrm{A}, \mathrm{B}) = \begin{cases} 1, & \left|\mathrm{pHash}\left(\mathrm{A}_{pic}, \mathrm{B}_{pici}\right)\right| \leq T_{\mathrm{pic}} \\ 0, & \left|\mathrm{pHash}\left(\mathrm{A}_{pic}, \mathrm{B}_{pici}\right)\right| > T_{\mathrm{pic}} \end{cases} \tag{3}$$

4 Experimental Evaluation

4.1 Data Collection

In order to evaluate the effectiveness of the active-passive combination detection method, this paper conducts deployment experiments according to the model diagram shown in Fig. 1, and performs data collection in a real Internet environment. In terms of active detection, this article has conducted several random interviews on websites such as the Caoliu Forum. Use the script program written in python 2.7.11 to get the corresponding keyword value on the website and save it to the database after processing. For passive detection, this paper obtains passive data acquisition and analysis by accessing certain ISP traffic.

The data actively obtained in this paper mainly comes from three adult websites whose names/IP addresses will change, such as the Cailiu Forum, Maya Forum, and sis001, and the data is mainly crawled for the website homepage. Compared with the method of detecting the website by using only the keyword/title information, the method of this paper can well realize the identification of the website without the keyword/title; and the way of using only the domain name/IP address Compared with the method of detecting the website, the method of this paper can well realize the identification of the website with the domain name/IP change.

4.2 Parameter Setting

The models used in this paper include the active detection phase and the passive filtering rediscovery phase. The most important measurement metrics are the accuracy of the final passive filtering website and the false positive rate of the website, as described in 4.3. At the same time, as rediscovery progresses, the data in the feature set will become more and more, and the results obtained will be more accurate.

In the experiment, the value of the same cookie key-value to the number of the number, the value of the hash value of the hash value of the logo picture and the value of the simhash value of the keyword and the title information synthesis string will have an effect on the accuracy of the final judgment of the specific website.

Since the cookie information is used as a strong feature to judge the website, so when the number of the same key-value pairs is greater than or equal to 3, the site of the passive traffic is judged to be the homologous website of the target website [7]. At the same time, when the similarity between two pictures is calculated by the perceptual hash algorithm [9], when the hash value of the two pictures is less than 5, it is judged that the two pictures are basically the same picture; When the Hamming distance of the hash value is greater than 10, it is judged that the two pictures are basically different. Here, because the picture information is used for falsification, in order to ensure a certain recall rate, the picture hash Hamming distance 10 is selected as the demarcation value.

4.3 Evaluation Method

True Positive Rate (TPR), False Positive Rate (FPR), Accuracy and Recall are the common evaluation indicators for classification effects, considering the characteristics of malicious website identification in real traffic environment. We choose TPR and FPR that is ROC curve, as the evaluation criteria.

For a category of Class, the category that belongs to the category is usually called positive, and the one that does not belong to the category is usually called negative, as shown in Table 1.

Table 1. Double classifier model

	True	False
Positive	TP	FN
Negative	FP	TN

For a certain class, those belonging to this category are usually called positive cases, which are not usually called negative cases, as shown in Table 1.

Where TP indicates the number of identified in the positive case, and FN indicates the number identified in the negative case, and FP indicates the number that is not identified in the positive case, and TN indicates the number that is not identified in the negative case. The definition of TPR and FPR is shown in formula (4) and formula (5):

$$\text{TPR} = \frac{TP}{TP + FN} \tag{4}$$

$$\text{FPR} = \frac{FP}{FP + TN} \tag{5}$$

At the same time, the area AUC (Area Under Curve) under the ROC curve is used to judge the effect of the classifier. The larger the AUC, the better the classifier.

4.4 Experimental Result

Among them, the blue line indicates the ROC curve obtained by using the homologous website identification algorithm proposed in this paper, and the orange line indicates the ROC curve obtained by direct matching with the host. It can be intuitively seen that the AUC obtained by the simhash algorithm is much larger than the AUC obtained by using the host, which proves that the proposed algorithm has a better effect.

For the selection of the hash value of the final keyword and the title synthesis string, we tested the different URLs of the Cailiu Forum, Maya Forum and sis001 websites, and obtained the values under different simhash (A, B). The TPR and FPR identified by the website are shown in Fig. 3.

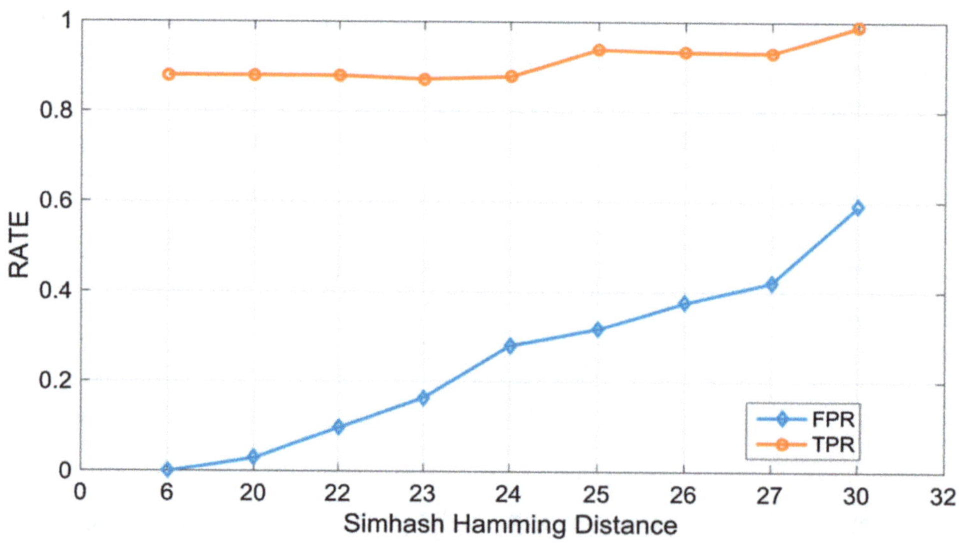

Fig. 3. TPR and FPR graphs obtained using simhash (Color figure online)

Among the Fig. 3, the blue line indicates the FPR obtained by simhash, and the orange line indicates the TPR obtained by the same way. It can be seen that the greater the value of the simhash value, the higher the TPR for the identification. But at the same time, the FPR also has a big rise in the trend. When the cutoff value of the simhash value is 30, the TPR can reach 99%, and the FPR will reach 59.09%. However the Logo will be used for falsification later, when the simhash cutoff value is 24, the TPR obtained is 93.93% and the FPR is 31.81%, the growth rate of FPR is less than the growth rate of TPR.

After adding the cookie and the logo information to judge, the method is compared with the method of identifying the website through host, and the obtained result is shown in Fig. 4.

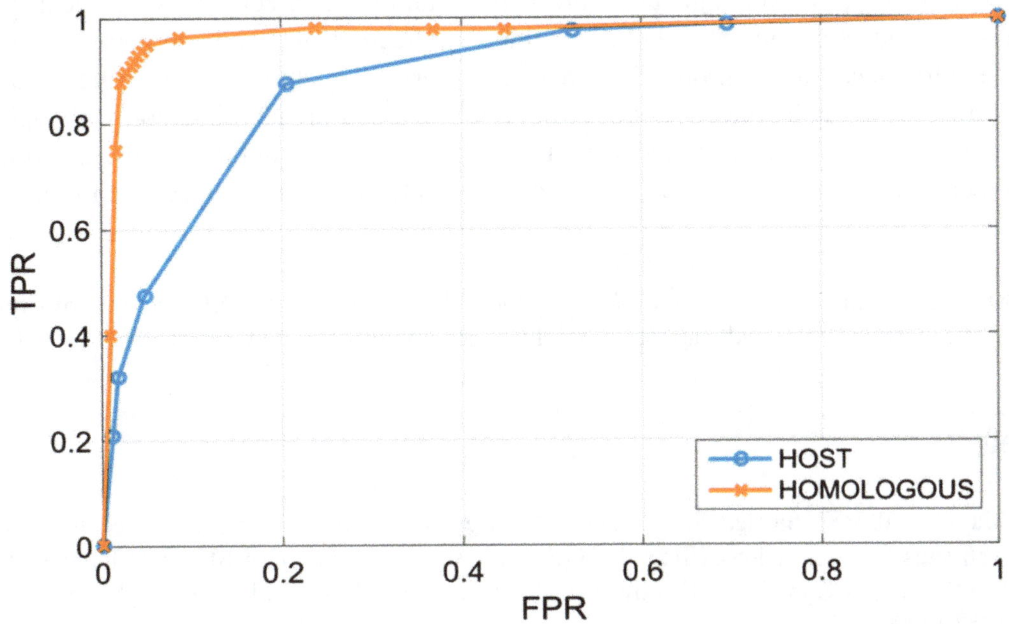

Fig. 4. Identification comparison of homologous website algorithm with host (Color figure online)

In Fig. 4, the blue line indicates the ROC curve obtained by using the homologous website identification algorithm proposed in this paper, and the orange line indicates the ROC curve obtained by direct matching with the host. It can be seen intuitively that the AUC obtained by the simhash algorithm is much larger than the AUC obtained by using the host, which proves that the proposed algorithm has a better effect.

5 Conclusion

In view of the identification of specific websites, this paper uses the combination of active and passive to discover and record the key attributes of specific websites based on the content of http header and html files, and proves that this method is validity and accuracy to identify the website especially when the domain name/IP changes.

We have found that user detection and content publisher information for accessing specific websites can be reversed detected. For visitors, it is possible to capture the source IP/port as the traffic of the visitor and perform keyword matching on the access traffic, because the visitor often knows not only a specific website but also such a website. Have some understanding. For content publishers, when they post a malicious website, we have reason to believe that he has a tendency to post other malicious websites. Therefore, in the next step of the work, the two will be monitored to try to get the same type of malicious website.

Not only the user information, but also the statistical information obtained by analyzing the feature data set of a specific website has a great effect. For example, statistics on websites with domain name/IP changes are more likely to use information such as what kind of framework/server to build, and the threshold for the number of links to such sites. Although this information cannot be directly used to identify a website, it has a certain contribution to the identification of a website because it has these attributes. Later, through the machine learning method, the website feature information set can be directly reduced in dimension, and the identification with higher accuracy can be obtained. At the same time, statistics on the number of users and the number of visits to such sites can be used to estimate how much impact such sites can have.

Acknowledgment. The research work is supported by National Key R&D Program of China (No. 2017YFB0801701) and National Natural Science Foundation under Grant (No. 61300206).

References

1. Ma, J., Saul, L.K., Savage, S., Voelker, G.M.: Beyond blacklists: learning to detect malicious web sites from suspicious URLs. In: Proceedings of the 15th ACM SIGKDD International Conference on Knowledge Discovery and Data Mining, New York, NY, USA, pp. 1245–1253 (2009)
2. Ma, J., Saul, L.K., Savage, S., Voelker, G.M.: Identifying suspicious URLs: an application of large-scale online learning. In: Proceedings of the 26th Annual International Conference on Machine Learning (ICML), Montreal, Quebec, Canada, pp. 681–688 (2009)
3. Ma, J., Saul, L.K., Savage, S., Voelker, G.M.: Learning to detect malicious URLs. ACM Trans. Intell. Syst. Technol. (TIST) **2**(3), 1–24 (2011)
4. Canali, D., et al.: Prophiler: a fast filter for the large-scale detection of malicious web pages. In: Proceedings of the 20th International Conference on World Wide Web (WWW), Hyderabad, India, pp. 197–206 (2011)
5. Yadav, S., Reddy, A.K.K., Reddy, A.L., et al.: Detecting algorithmically generated malicious domain names. In: Proceedings of the 10th ACM SIGCOMM Conference on Internet Measurement (IMC), New York, NY, USA, pp. 48–61 (2010)
6. Kolbitsch, C., Livshits, B., Zorn, B., et al.: Rozzle: de-cloaking internet malware. In: Proceedings of the IEEE Symposium on Security and Privacy (SP), San Francisco, CA, USA, pp. 443–457 (2012)
7. Chen, Z., Zhang, P., Zheng, C., Liu, Q.: CookieMine: towards real-time reconstruction of web-downloading chains from network traces. In: 2016 IEEE International Conference on Communications (ICC), pp. 1–6. IEEE (2016)
8. Manku, G.S., Jain, A., Das Sarma, A.: Detecting near-duplicates for web crawling. In: International World Wide Web Conference (2007)
9. Schneider, M., Chang, S.-F.: A robust content based digital signature for image authentication. In: Proceedings of IEEE International Conference on Image Processing, Lausanne, Switzerland, vol. 3, no. 3, pp. 227–230 (1996)

A Model of APT Attack Defense Based on Cyber Threat Detection

Yue Li[1], Teng Zhang[2(✉)], Xue Li[1], and Ting Li[2]

[1] Dongxun Tech (Beijing) Co., Ltd., Beijing 100097, China
[2] National Computer Network Emergency Response Technical Team/Coordination Center of China, Beijing 100029, China
zt@cert.org.cn

Abstract. The targets of Advanced Persistent Threat (APT) are mainly concentrate on national key information infrastructure, key research institutes, and large commercial companies, for the purpose of stealing sensitive information, trade secrets or destroying important infrastructure. Traditional protection system is difficult to detect the APT attack, due to the method of the APT attack is unknown and uncertain. And the persisted evolution ability destroyed the traditional protection methods based on feature detection. Therefore, this paper based on the theory of red-blue confrontation, to construct the game model of attack and defense. And then combined the APT offense and defense experience, presents a model based on cyber threat detection to deal with APT attacks.

Keywords: Cyber security · Advanced Persistent Threat · Unknown attack · Red-blue confrontation · Threat detection

1 Introduction

Advanced Persistent Threat (APT) is a kind of complex and multi-dimension advanced cyber penetration attack aimed at specific organizations [1]. First of all, the attackers usually conducted long-term information gathering and monitoring to the target or its associated organizations from different sources. And then aimed at the existing defense methods to deal with some targeted confrontation and penetration researches. Through the persistent multi-dimension hidden penetration attack (including Cyber, Realistic, Fraudulent), ultimately achieved the purpose of long-term control, information steal, or target destroy.

From the typical APT attack events, APT attacks have the following features:

Long incubation (or implement) period. As the Fig. 1, these cyber attack incubation periods were about 5 years such as Stuxnet [2], Duqu [3], OceanLotus [4], Mermaid action [5]. And some advanced information stealing APT attack have even longer incubation period, such as Flame.

The attackers had already acquainted the defense systems of the targets. The attackers tried their best to find out the target's protection methods as much as possible, and conducted targeting evaluations such as Anti-Antivirus and penetration abilities before they released the malicious programs, in order to bypass the Antivirus software detection installed on host and evade the detection by mainstream cyber security devices.

X. Yun et al. (Eds.): CNCERT 2018, CCIS 970, pp. 122–135, 2019.
https://doi.org/10.1007/978-981-13-6621-5_10

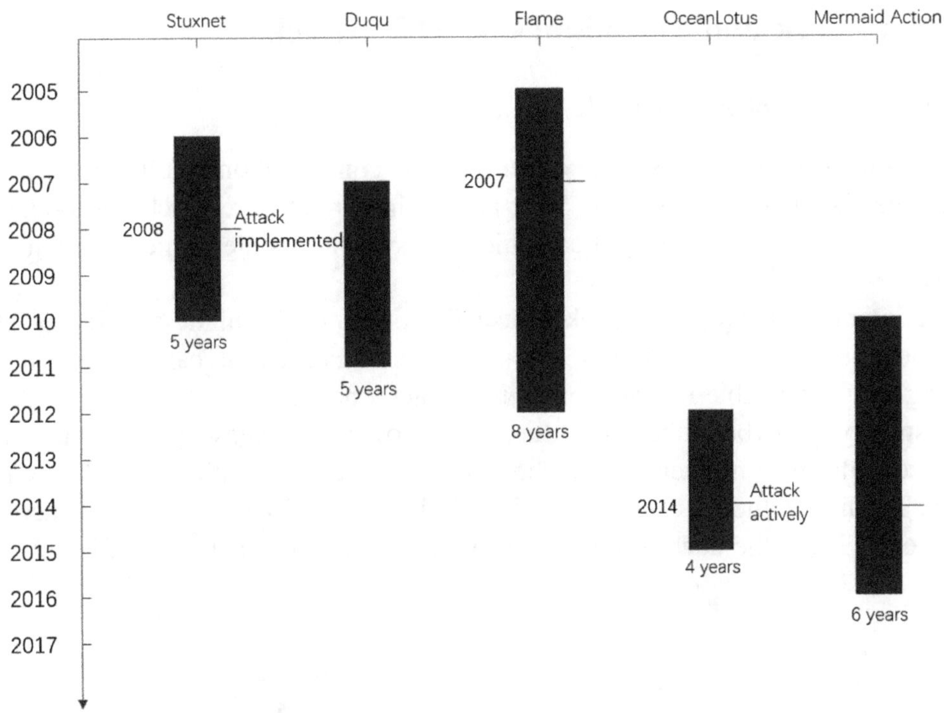

Fig. 1. Typical APT attack events

Various attack techniques and different combinations. From the case studies, the most commonly used APT attack techniques are the Spear Phishing attack and the Watering Hole attack. These two attack techniques could be used with a variety of different social-engineering attack scenarios, created multiple patterns of attack. For example, created a spear Phishing e-mail to trick the developers by simulating the leader's tone. Besides, there still have some other attack techniques which barley reported. Such as exploited the website vulnerabilities to invade into the Demilitarized Zone (DMZ), and then infiltrated into the Intranet.

The occurred cases shows that the traditional defense system has a lot of limitations to deal with the APT attacks. In order to elaborate the defense of APT attack, this paper were focused on the theory of red-blue confrontation to gradually depth the description through the way from APT attacks to APT defenses. Contributes of this paper are as follows:

1. Proposed a model to interpret the thought of APT attacks based on its characteristics.
2. Classified and summarized the common network attack steps and techniques based on cyber kill chain classifications.
3. Proposed a defensive model based on APT threat detected theory, which faced on current limitation of the defense system.
4. Proposed a new framework of APT attack detecting, which is collaborated with "cloud, transport layer, terminals, and manual response".

2 Framework and Techniques of APT Attack

2.1 Framework of APT Attack

The prerequisite to win the battle of cyber red-blue confrontation is fully understanding the enemies' strategies and tactics. So it is very important to research the thoughts of APT attack and establish theoretical guidance systems in the game of offense and defense.

The intention of an APT attack is usually to obtain the highest authority of the target network in order to access the information. Further, it can be described as grasping all the valuable information in the target's network.

Abstractly, the cyber-attack procedure is the process to increase the authority and the volume of information. Each step of the attack acquires new authority and new information. The new authority determines what kind of new information could be acquired. On the other hand, the new information promoted to get new authority (Fig. 2).

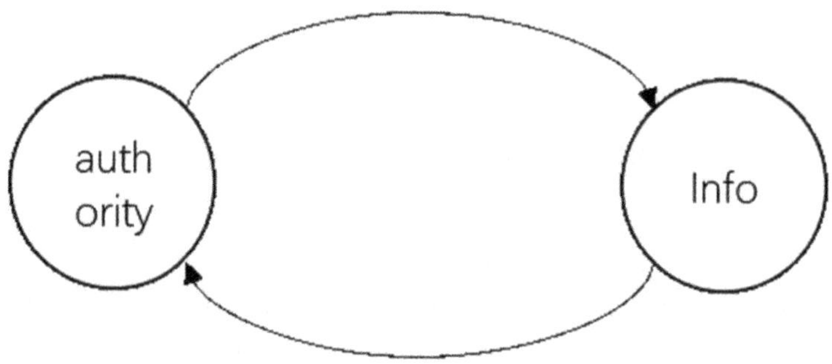

Fig. 2. The view of APT attack

Information is the necessary part during an entire attack. A successful attack is to maximize the effort of information collection, analysis and utilization.

In this paper, we present different views of APT attacks on time dimension and spatial dimension.

On time dimension, attackers generally use the following four methods, and an abstract view of APT attack is shown as Fig. 3.

1. Discovering. To discover new information and clues of sources
2. Detection. To detect the accessed information in order to acquire more sources of information based on acquired authority.
3. Analysis. To analyze effective intelligence based on combining various information and clues.
4. Exploiting. To exploited the acquired information and resources to get more advanced authorities.

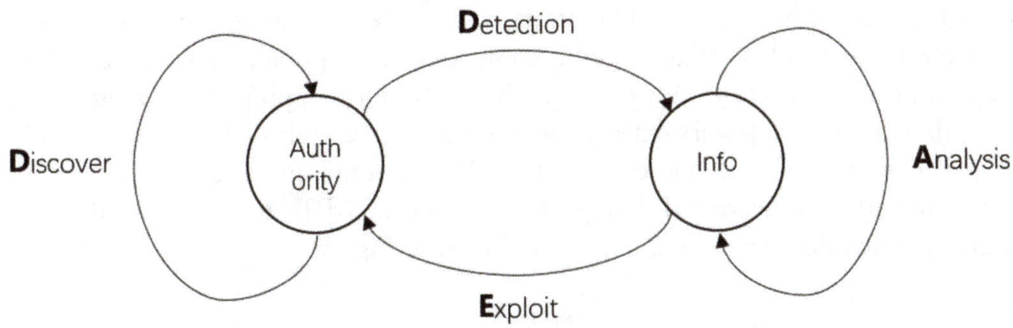

Fig. 3. The view of APT attack on time dimension

On spatial dimension, the APT attack presented the vertical and horizontal features, as shown in Fig. 4.

1. Vertical break refers to acquire more advanced and depth authorities through penetration and breakthrough attack by exploiting the known information. That is the deepening of the authorities.
2. Horizontal break refers to acquire more the same level authorities of different users through penetration and breakthrough attack by exploiting the known information. That is the deepening of the extended authorities.

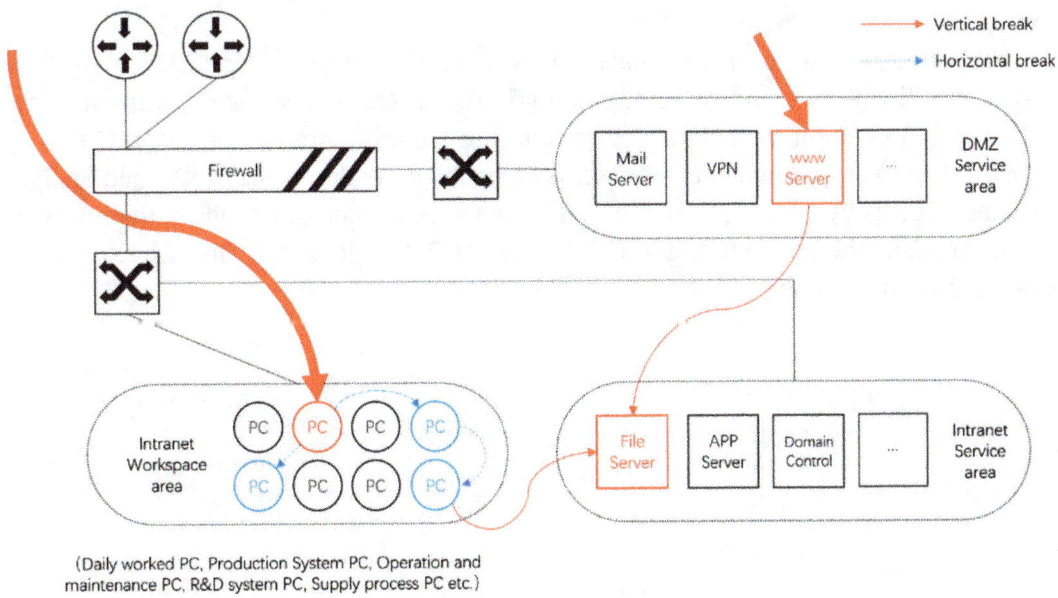

Fig. 4. The view of APT attack on spatial dimension (Color figure online)

Common attacks typically involved both vertical and horizontal break. After each successful breakthrough, the attacker will acquire new authorities. And at the same time the additional information obtained by the new authorities will become an important prerequisite for the next breakthrough.

In Fig. 4 is shown a topological intranet graph of the enterprise. Assuming that the attack target is a file server, and the red solid line is shown as a vertical break. For example, a vertical break for a PC often by using Spear Phishing emails or Watering Hole websites to attack and exploit, commonly known as "point attack". After obtained the control right of a certain PC, by using this PC as the stepping stone to attack other PCs within the Intranet workspace area to obtain more rights of the same level. In Fig. 4, it is indicated by a blue dotted line, which is a horizontal breakthrough.

In summary, the abstracted thought and method of APT attack in time dimension and space dimension can be expressed as shown in Fig. 5.

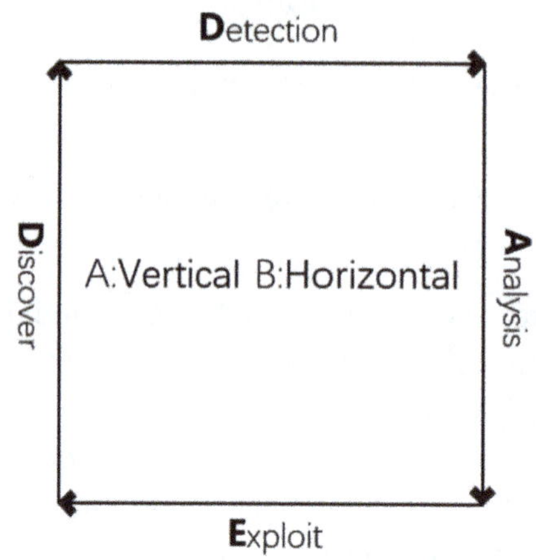

Fig. 5. The thought and method of APT attack

ATP attack could be further analyzed by using the Intrusion Kill Chains [6]. The Intrusion Kill Chains could be divided into 7 layers: Reconnaissance, Weaponization, Delivery, Exploitation, Installation, Command & Control, Actions on Objectives.

Each layer is represented as a phase. It helps the defender to recognize and analyze the attack events by abstracted and classified the attack process. Based on the Intrusion Kill Chains and the above thought and method of APT attack, the attack event can be presented in the manner of Fig. 6.

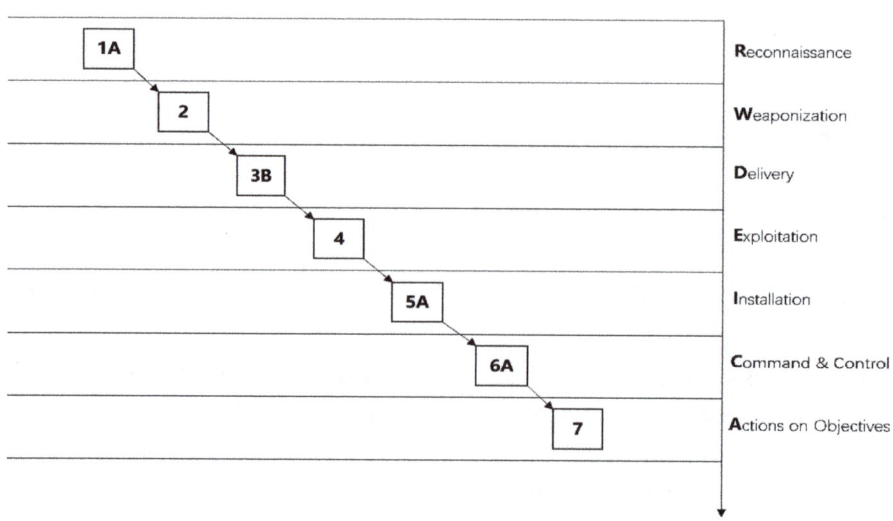

Fig. 6. The Schematic of APT attack event

In Fig. 6, the squares represent a method of attack, the A or B is used to indicate the breakthrough modes, and the serial number is used to indicate the attack implementation steps. The schematic diagram can be used to visualize the whole process from reconnaissance, weaponization, delivery, exploitation, installation, command & control, actions on objectives.

Actually, the APT attack events are often presented as shown in Fig. 7. Before the final attack launched on the target (indicated in red in the figure), large number of pre-attacks (shown in black in the figure) had been implemented for a long time.

Fig. 7. The Schematic of actually APT attack event (Color figure online)

2.2 Techniques of APT Attack

Although different steps and techniques used in each attack phases may have lots of crossovers, it could be described by the Intrusion Kill Chains model shown as Table 1. When the suspicious actions such vulnerability scanning, port scanning, password cracking were detected in the networks, it could be inferred to the attack is in the reconnaissance stage. After some controlled actions were detected, such as webshell, advanced Trojan, Command & Control actions etc., it could be inferred to the attacker was about to control or had already controlled the target. Therefore, combing the attack procedures and techniques helps the defenders to accurately estimate the current situation and make reasonable inferences after the threat was discovered.

The development of cyberattack technology is essentially based on the current defense technology. At the same time the development of defense technology is essentially base on the currently discovered attack techniques. Therefore, adhering to the thought of red-blue confrontation, classified the attack techniques, and discovered more new methods and new modes of attack are the effective ways to improve the technical capabilities of the defenders.

Table 1. Common used network attack steps and techniques

Intrusion kill chains	Serial	The attack procedures and techniques
Reconnaissance	1	External information acquisition
	2	Vulnerability scanning
	3	Password cracking
	4	Port scanning
Weaponization	5	Carrier selection (file carrier, flow package)
	6	Choices about vulnerabilities and ways to exploit
	7	Choices about penetration tools
	8	Choices about the control weapons
	9	Anti-antivirus techniques (packing, feature confusion etc.)
Delivery	10	Spear Phishing attack
	11	Watering Hole attack
	12	Supply chain attack
	13	Proximity attack
	14	Ferry attack (USB ferry attack etc.)
Exploitation	15	Overflow vulnerabilities exploit
	16	Web vulnerabilities exploit
	17	Logical vulnerabilities combined exploit
	18	Verity of elevated privileges techniques
Installation	19	Botnets, Trojans, worms
	20	Backdoors of operation systems or devices
	21	RootKit embed
	22	WebShell
	23	Advanced Trojans
Command & Control	24	Command and Control
	25	Covert channels
	26	Abnormal communication modes
Actions on objectives	27	Destroyed the data or devices
	28	Data leakage
	29	Data defacement
	30	Long-term monitoring

3 A Model of APT Attack Defense

The starting point for both sides of the offense and defense is the same. Attackers understood the target network and the defense system to find breakthroughs by using various information gathering tools. Defenders also needed to deploy enough probe suites in the network system to detect malicious behavior, recognize attackers, and block attacks. However, in the network security constructions the managers of the security department had a common understanding of security protection as shown in Fig. 8. Deployed moderate security products and implemented the emergency response by professional security practitioners after a security incident event occurred.

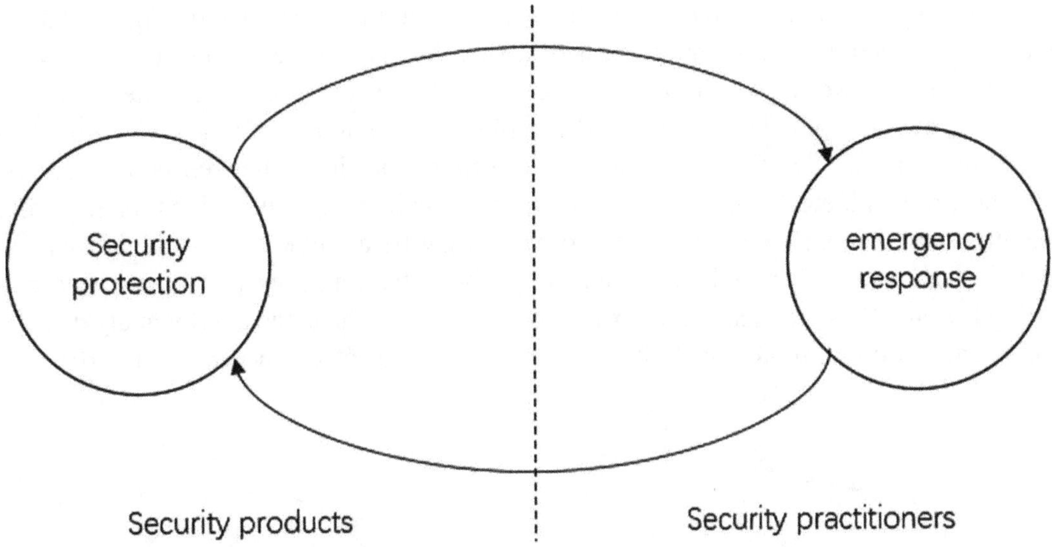

Fig. 8. Traditional thought of defense

In the procurement of products, they also did not analyze their own business scenarios in detail, blindly pursued coverage, and purchased a large number of technical homogenized protective products. The security modules crossed each other. By this way built a seemingly stable defense system. But during the event of a major cybersecurity incident, all deployed security products lost their utility at the same time. And the employed security administrators were also at a loss. At this time, it may be necessary to find a more professional external security team for emergency response, resulting in waste of resources.

Through the analysis, the root cause for this passive situation was that during the construction of cybersecurity systems, the idea of offense and defense game model and red and blue confrontation was not been introduced, and didn't pay enough attention at the detection of potential risks and unknown threats. Eventually, the information on both sides of the offensive and defensive was seriously unequal. The security operation and maintenance employees didn't know what the attackers were doing, what they wanted to do next and what they had done before. Therefore, it must transform the thought of defense and it is the key to build the protection system concentrated on threat detect which based on the theory of the red-blue confrontation.

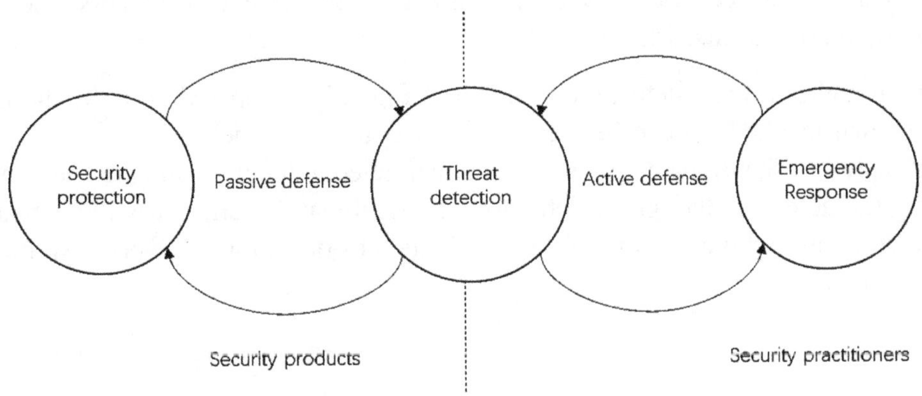

Fig. 9. Defensive thought based on red-blue confrontation

The defensive thought based on the threat detection is shown in Fig. 9. Threat detection refers to the discovery process of attack threats and the compromised hosts in the attacked network. Attack threats are descriptions of attack attributes such as attackers, attack tools, delivery methods, exploits, and control methods. The compromised host are the description of the target attributes such as attacked hosts, servers, switches, firewall, etc. Threat detection is the process by which the defenders acquiring the attackers. The starting point of the process may be an attack threat event that has already occurred, or it may be a compromised host that has been discovered. By analyzing the attack threats, more compromised hosts may be detected and by analyzing the compromised hosts, more attack threats may also be detected. Shown as Fig. 10.

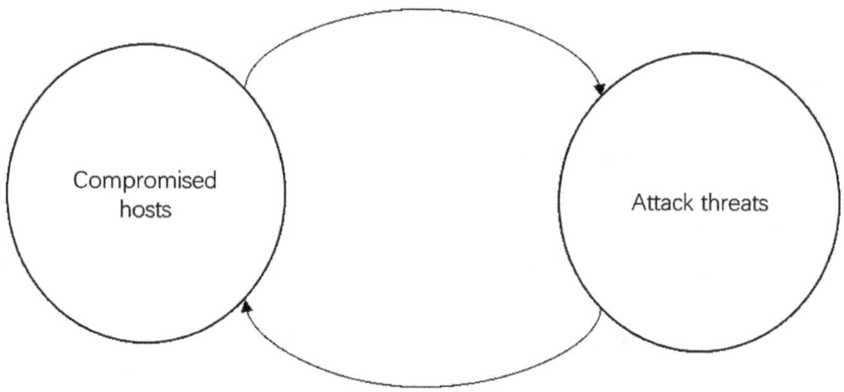

Fig. 10. Threat detection model

Corresponding to the thought of attack, threat detection could be used the following four methods:

1. Analysis: Analyze the system, log, abnormal operation and other information of the compromised host to get more intrusion cues.
2. Inference: Infer attack threats by associating all clues, including attack tools, malicious samples, C&C flow, etc.
3. Discovery: Discover the purpose of the attack by reversely mining value information of the threats such as attack tools and samples.
4. Detection: By leveraging the newly discovered attack threats to create new detection features or scenarios. By using them to scan the entire network and detect unknown compromised hosts.

The thought of threat detection is shown in Fig. 11. Compared with the thought of attack shown in Fig. 3, it can be seen that it is a mutual game.

Defensive work will be no longer just concentrated at the beginning of the attack by adopting the defensive thought which based on the threat detection. It will be changing and adapting around the process of the attack such as detection, delivery, exploitation, installation, control, etc.

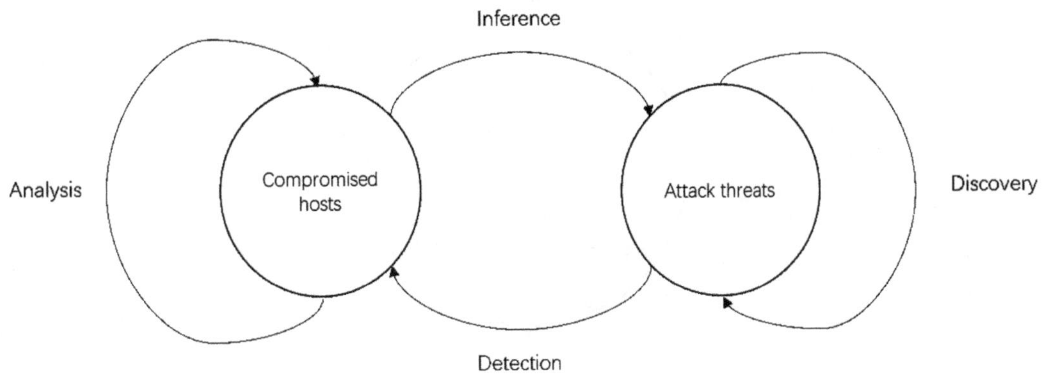

Fig. 11. The thought of threat detection

4 APT Attack Defense Based on Threat Detection

4.1 APT Attack Defense Model Based on Threat Detection

Most of the traditional protection products adopt feature-based detection technology. For example, the antivirus engines mainly detect the file characteristics of malicious samples, and network devices such as IDS and IPS are mainly detected the features of network flow. The advantages of feature detection are identifying the known malicious files or attack techniques quickly, and telling the threats accurately. But the limitations are also obvious, which is, if the features of threats are not contained in the database, the protection will lose its effectiveness.

Therefore, if we meet unknown threats, we will build our protection based on a high view of red-blue confrontation instead of using a single feature-based detection. As shown in Fig. 12, adopting the integrated security technology framework collaborated with "cloud, transport layer, terminals, and manual response", collecting program behavior and network traffic behavior in the system at the terminal and network nodes by the probes, focus on threat intelligence and big data platform, combined with threat perception and anomaly detection model, to analyze the unknown threats semi-automatically.

1. Cloud: Threat intelligence big data platform

Threat Intelligence Big Data Platform is a platform for monitoring and related intelligence data analysis and processing the advanced threats. It can be deployed in the intranet machine rooms. Adopt artificial intelligence technology, combined with Indicator of Compromise information [7] (IOC) to automatically collect and clean threat data, intelligently integrate clue data, automatically mine high-value threat intelligence, and long-term track and analyze the potential threat sources. Targeting on the advanced attacks in cyberspace, it can conduct specific services such as event restoration, attacker intent analysis, attack investment evaluation, attack source tracing, and identification, and at the same time build efficient threat detection and event handling capabilities.

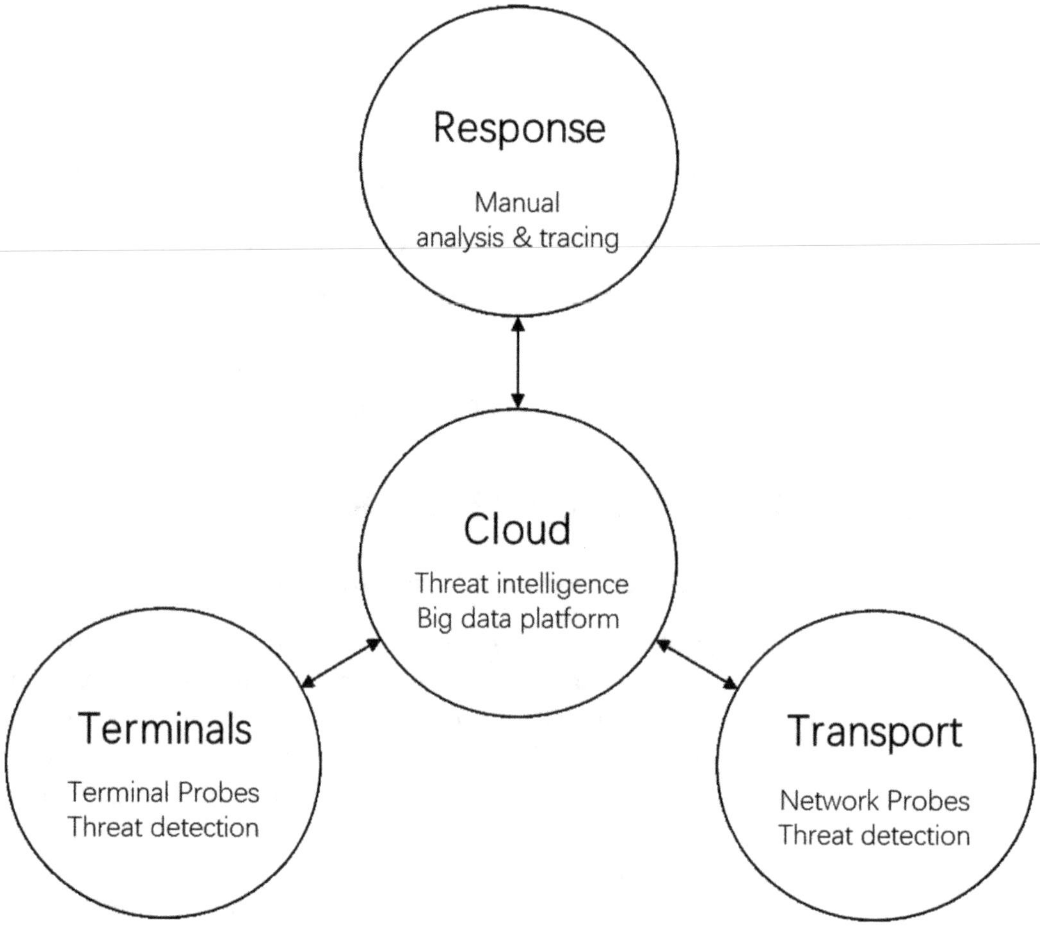

Fig. 12. Techniques framework for unknown threat detection

2. Transport layer: Network probes and threat monitoring

The network probes bypass deployed on the network gateway to collect transmission flow, identifying and filtering the protocols of the data link layer, the network layer, the transport layer, the session layer, the presentation layer, and the application layer, restoring the file and traffic characteristics in the flow, and performing preliminary analysis and evidence collection. The benefit of adopting a bypass deployment was that it did not impact the flow and process of original system. Depending on the performance of the probe devices, additional detection modules such as anti-virus engine, file sandbox, traffic sandbox, hidden channel detection, User and Entity Behavior Analytic (UEBA) can be integrated to share the computing pressure of the cloud Threat Intelligence Big Data Platform.

3. Terminals: Terminal probes threat detection

The terminal probe works in the driver layer of the terminal system, and performs real-time, comprehensive and deep collection and forensic on suspicious data involved in malicious program execution such as terminal processes, files, services, memory, registry, hooks, and network flow. The terminal probe will spend a little amount of terminal system overhead, which has a certain impact on CPU performance.

4. Response: Manual analysis and tracing

It is necessary to conduct manual analysis and tracing for the high-risk threats or high-risk events based on threat intelligence big data platform, network probes and terminal probes.

The analysis process of malicious samples is also the process of recognizing the attackers [8, 9], from which the purpose and target of the attack can be inferred. Features extracted from the sample can be further correlated with merged homologous events, proactively detect potential compromised hosts, trace the source of attack, and even implement counter-attack strategies.

The security Operation Center (SOC) and Security Information and Event Management (SIEM) were two kind of mainstream platform which can represent the collaboration theory of "Cloud, Transport layer, Terminals and Manual Response". SIEM focused on statistical analysis of security logs, system assets, user behavior, and assisted analysts in threat monitoring and location. The SOC focused on the management of the security incident analysis process upon the SIEM, and it was adapt to the companies with independent security and maintenance department. But independent of what kind of the platforms used by the upper layer, the essential core capabilities were depend on the capabilities of the network probes and terminal probes, the analysis ability of the algorithms, and the experience of the security analysts.

4.2 Best Practices in WannaCry Ransomware Response

This kind of APT attack defense model had played an important role in the detection and response on the WannaCry ransomware attack. WannaCry ransomware spread and invaded the hoses by using the EternalBlue program which exploded the vulnerability of MS17-010. EternalBlue is an advanced exploit tool leaking from NAS (National Security Agency) [10]. Feature-based detection such as HASH detection and CVE detection were not able to detect this ransomware.

By adopting the thread detection model, the APT attack defense system of Dongxun Tech successfully detected the WannaCry ransomware. First of all, the network probes deployed in the transport layer discovered the attack package exploited the ms17-010 vulnerability and then locked the destination hosts. The terminal probes deployed at the destination hosts detect a suspected sample named 'wcry.exe'. The wrcy.exe evaded feature-based detection such as HASH detection and CVE detection. Terminal probes upload this sample to the cloud platform. Cloud platform analyzed the sample's behavior. The sample wrcy.exe could create three system processes: attrib. exe, taskdl.exe, cmd.exe, at the same time this sample invoked sensitive API, and existed obviously behavior of ransomware characteristics such as encryption behavior and writing behavior. Based on the above information, the defense system identified this sample as a high-risk threat. The defense system automatically cut off the attack traffic and alarmed to the cyber security administrator. The administrator responded to this alarm and further analyzed the assets under this threat. By adopting this thread detection model and the corresponding defense system, the WannaCry ransomware attack had been prevented timely.

5 Conclusion

APT attack offense and defense is a long-term continuous confrontation process. Focus on the problem of detecting unknown threats hidden in APT attacks, this paper presented a novel model of APT attack defense based on threat detection. Based on the model, this paper presented a technique framework with the collaboration theory of "Cloud, Transport layer, Terminals and Manual Response" to detect the threat of APT attack. Compared with traditional security methods, out method is more effective on detecting unknown attack threats. This paper is based on years of practical experience of Dongxun Tech. and try to deconstruct the APT attack framework and techniques from a more unique perspective by establishing an attack model. And then described the defense model according the features of APT attack. The authors of this paper hoped through this elaboration to inspire the readers of cybersecurity practitioners.

References

1. Daly, M.K.: Advanced persistent threat. Usenix **4**(4), 2013–2016 (2009)
2. Thabet, A.: Stuxnet malware analysis paper. Code Project (2011)
3. Bencsath, B.: The cousins of stuxnet, duqu, flame, and gauss. Future Internet **4**(4), 971–1003 (2012)
4. SkyEye: OceanLotus APT Report. https://ti.360.net/static/upload/report/file/OceanLotusReport.pdf. Accessed 29 May 2015
5. SkyEye. APT-C-07 Report. https://ti.360.net/uploads/2018/01/26/ea9d6d29c2218746acaf87a68a2bbc1e.pdf. Accessed 30 May 2016
6. Hutchins, E.M.: Intelligence-driven computer network defense informed by analysis of adversary campaigns and intrusion kill chains. Leading Issues in Information Warfare & Security Research, vol. 1(1), p. 80 (2011)
7. Indicator of compromise [EB/OL]. https://en.wikipedia.org/wiki/Indicator_of_compromise. Accessed 19 Jan 2018
8. Shufu, L.: Analysis of Typical APT Attack Cases. Netinfo Securtiy, pp. 85–88 (2016)
9. DongXun 2046Lab: APT Report: Harvest Event (DX-APT1) [EB/OL]. http://www.freebuf.com/articles/paper/111557.html. Accessed 22 Aug 2016
10. Nakashima, E., Timberg, C.: NSA officials worried about the day its potent hacking tool would get loose. Then it did, Washington Post. Accessed 19 Dec 2017. ISSN 0190-8286

A Generic Architecture to Detect Vulnerability Leaks at Crowdsourced Tests

Zhonghao Sun, Zhejun Fang, Yueying He, and Jianqiang Li(✉)

National Computer Network Emergency Response Technical Team/Coordination Center of China, Beijing, China
{sunzhonghao, fzj, hyy, ljq}@cert.org.cn

Abstract. Nowadays, there is a fundamental imbalance between attackers and defenders. Crowdsourced tests level the playing field. However, the concern about vulnerability leaks severely limits the widespread of crowdsourced tests. Existing crowdsourced test platforms have adopt various technical or management approaches to protect applications or systems under test, but none of them is able to remove the concerns about vulnerability leaks. This paper provides a generic architecture to discover the white hat who finds a vulnerability but conceals it. The architecture is not only valid for public vulnerabilities, but also valid for unknown vulnerabilities. Finally, the proposed architecture is tested by real vulnerabilities. The results show that, with proper rules, most of the concealing behaviors can be detected.

Keywords: Crowdsourced test · Intrusion detection · White hat · Vulnerability leak

1 Introduction

Nowadays, there is a fundamental imbalance between attackers and defenders, because the system designers and developers cannot work as security experts at the same time. Thus, to ensure the security of the system, professional test is necessary. However, traditional security test is expensive and with limited coverage. Fortunately, the emergence of crowdsourced test levels the playing field [10]. Crowdsourced test is a kind of new service pattern, where companies can publish their test projects on the crowdsourced platform and hackers can attend the projects they interested. Hackers are paid by the company if and only if they submit vulnerabilities. With this kind of pattern, both companies and hackers obtain a benefit. At present, various crowdsourced test platforms have arisen. In China, the mainstream platforms include Wooyun [16], VULBOX [15], Testin [14], 360 [1], Sobug [13], CNVD [5] and ICS-CERT [8] etc. In foreign countries, HackerOne [7] and BugCrowd [4] are widely accepted crowdsourced platforms.

Although crowdsourced tests have so many advantages, the concern about vulnerability leaks seriously limits the widespread of crowdsourced tests [17]. For some systems or applications, the security is mainly based on their privacy. So, exposing these systems or applications under the crowdsourced tests scenario will raise the concerns of the companies. For some hackers, concealing the vulnerabilities they find may bring more benefits instead of submitting them to the companies. Therefore, how to avoid vulnerability leaks is the primary issue that all crowdsourced platforms have to deal with.

X. Yun et al. (Eds.): CNCERT 2018, CCIS 970, pp. 136–144, 2019.
https://doi.org/10.1007/978-981-13-6621-5_11

Existing crowdsourced test platforms have adopt various technical and management approaches to avoid vulnerability leaks. The commonly used approaches can be summarized as three aspects: legal approaches, management approaches and technical approaches [11]. The legal approaches mainly include signing confidentiality agreements, conducting legal training, declaring authorized test boundaries, and real name certification etc. The management approaches include forming credible hacker teams, setting test projects with different secret levels, allowing companies choose hackers they trust etc. [18]. The technical approaches mainly include test traffic monitoring, VPN based accessing control for application/system under test (A/SUTs), accessing control for A/SUTs based on bastion host, test behavior auditing and screen recording etc. It is no doubt that the above-mentioned approaches considerably reduce the concerns about vulnerability leaks, but none of them is able to thoroughly remove the concerns.

Different from the indirect approaches above, this paper design a generic architecture to detect from the test traffic whether the white hats have found a vulnerability. The architecture do not need to install monitors on the various heterogeneous A/SUTs, thus having good operability. In the architecture, the rule-matching method based on Snort [3] is adopted to detect public vulnerabilities, and abnormal behavior monitoring method based on deep learning is adopted to detect unknown vulnerabilities. Finaly, the proposed architecture is applied to the ICS-CERT crowdsourced test platform [8]. The results show that, with proper rules, most of the concealing behaviors can be detected.

2 The System Architecture

The system architecture is shown in Fig. 1. The architecture includes three parts: the white hats, the A/SUT and the crowdsourced test platform. They are connected through Internet. The dotted lines in the figure denote the data flow.

2.1 The Crowdsourced Test Platform Architecture

The crowdsourced test platform acts as a bridge between A/SUTs and white hats. White hats apply for test projects on the platform and companies publish test projects on the platform. In order to achieve the monitor ability, the platform have to contain the web portal module, the VPN module and the monitor module at least.

(1) The web portal module provides access to the platform, where white hats can apply for test projects and companies can publish test projects.
(2) The VPN module provides white hats the only access to the A/SUT. In other words, without the VPN, white hats will not able to access the A/SUT.
(3) The monitor module gets the test traffic of VPN servers from the switch's monitor port. The traffic-based monitor software is deployed on the monitor servers. The architecture of the software will be given in the next section.

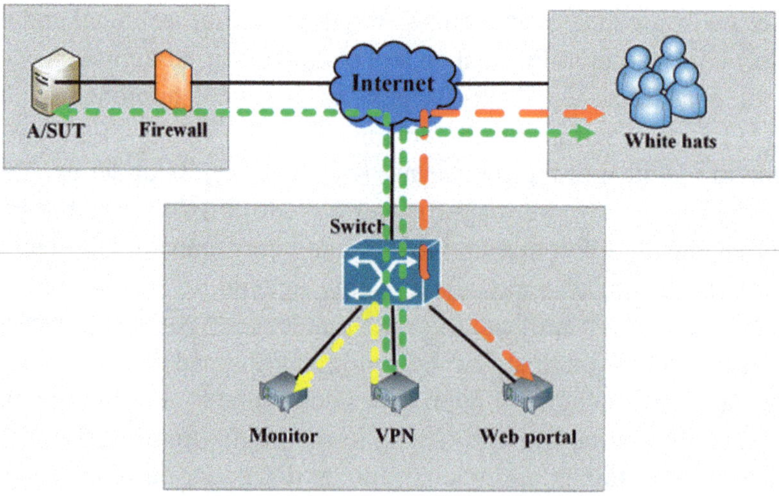

Fig. 1. The hardware architecture and data flow (Colopr figure online)

2.2 The A/SUT Configuration

To make sure that all the test traffic is under surveillance, we require the VPN to be the unique access to the A/SUT. So, a firewall is placed before the A/SUT and only the IP address of VPN is allowed to access the A/SUT. As shown in Fig. 1, the A/SUT part should contain two modules at least: the A/SUT itself and the firewall. The A/SUT is connected to Internet through the firewall.

Obviously, the crowdsourced test platform can be connected with more than one A/SUT. But every A/SUT should keep this kind of configuration.

2.3 The Data Flow

The dotted lines in the Fig. 1 denote the data flows. The red line denotes the white hats' access path to the web portal. It is obviously that the web portal can be accessed directly without the VPN. The green line denotes the white hats' access path to the A/SUT. If white hats want to test a A/SUT, they have to get through the VPN servers, because the firewall before the A/SUT only allows the access from the VPN servers. The yellow line denotes the data flow between the VPN servers and the monitor servers. All the test traffic flow through the VPN servers is completely copied to the monitor servers.

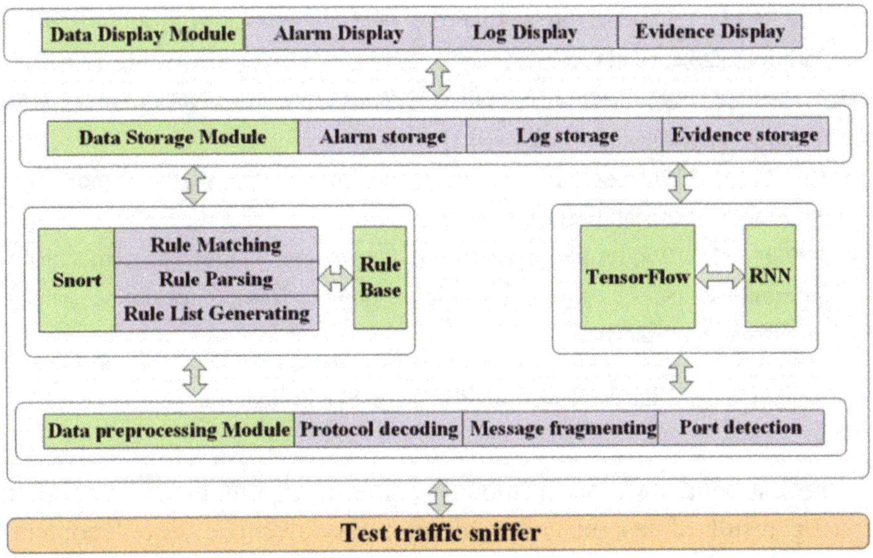

Fig. 2. The software architecture

3 The Software Architecture

The vulnerability detection software is deployed on the monitor servers shown in Fig. 1. In the software, the rule-matching method based on Snort [3] is adopted to detect public vulnerabilities, and Recurrent Neural Network (RNN) model based on TensorFlow [2] is adopted to detect unknown vulnerabilities. The detailed software architecture is shown in Fig. 2.

The software mainly includes three layers: the test traffic collection layer (the bottom layer), the vulnerability monitor layer (the middle layer) and the result display layer (the top layer).

(1) In the bottom layer, the main module is the traffic sniffer which collects the test traffic from the mirror port of switch.
(2) In the middle layer, the data preprocessing module is mainly responsible for the protocol decoding, message fragmenting and port scanning etc. After the pre-processing, the raw test traffic is converted to the format that the monitor algorithms can recognize.

Above the data preprocessing module is the test behavior monitor module. This module contains two algorithms: the rule-matching method based on Snort to detect public vulnerabilities, and RNN model based on TensorFlow to detect unknown vulnerabilities. The key technology of the rule-matching method is the rule base. In this paper, we obtain the rule base from EVERSEC [9]. The rule base is a kind long-term accumulated knowledge, which is important in engineering but plain in theory. So we do not illustrate the rule base in this paper. What we want to tell readers is that the rule matching based method is really effective in the detecting of concealing behaviors. The RNN model is trained with normal traffic of the A/SUT, and learned the normal behavior of the A/SUT. Then we use the test traffic as the input of the trained RNN model. If there is abnormal behaviors that the model cannot identify and no rule is matched, then we think a unknown vulnerability is detected.

```
POC1:http://47.94.131.119/index.php?option=com_fields&view=fields&layout=modal&list[fullor
dering]=updatexml(0x23,concat(1,user()),1)
POC2:http://47.94.131.119/index.php?option=com_fields&view=fields&layout=modal&list[fullor
dering]=updatexml(0x23,concat(1,database()),1)
POC3:http://47.94.131.119/index.php?option=com_fields&view=fields&layout=modal&list[fullor
dering]=updatexml(0x23,concat(1,select datse();),1)
POC4:http://47.94.131.119/index.php?option=com_fields&view=fields&layout=modal&list[fullor
dering]=updatexml(0x23,(select group_concat(table_name) from information_schema.tables
where table_schema=database()),1)
```

Fig. 3. The four POCs for SQL injection

Above the test behavior monitor module is the storage module. This module stores the processing result of test behavior monitor module. The stored content include alarms, logs and evidence.

(3) In the result display layer, the display module read the result data from the storage module and shows to administrators.

4 The Evaluation

The proposed architecture has been realized in the ICS-CERT crowdsourced test platform. To evaluate the effectiveness of the architecture, we test it with SQL injection vulnerability, XSS vulnerability, file upload vulnerability, file inclusion vulnerabilities and command execution vulnerability. For the space limitation, we just illustrate the detailed test of SQL injection and XSS.

4.1 SQL Injection Vulnerability

We use CVE-2017-8917 [6] and Joomla 3.7 as the test case. We configure a A/SUT with the vulnerabilities and the access address of the A/SUT is http://47.94.131.119/index.php. Four POCs shown in Fig. 3 are used to evaluate the effectiveness. Except the POC3, the other three POCs are valid.

The results show that all the four POCs are successfully detected. The detection result for POC1 is shown in Fig. 4. Especially, for POC3 shown in Fig. 5, we identify that it is a invalid SQL injection. For the space limitation, we do not show the detection results of the other POCs in the paper.

4.2 XSS Vulnerability

We configure a A/SUT with XSS vulnerabilities and the accessing address is: http://104.225.151.194/cshajx/xss/easyxss/.

The two payloads we used are shown in Fig. 6. The Payload1 will trigger an alarm window, as shown in Fig. 7. The detection result of Payload1 is shown in Fig. 8. For the space limitation, we do not show the running screenshot of Payload2.

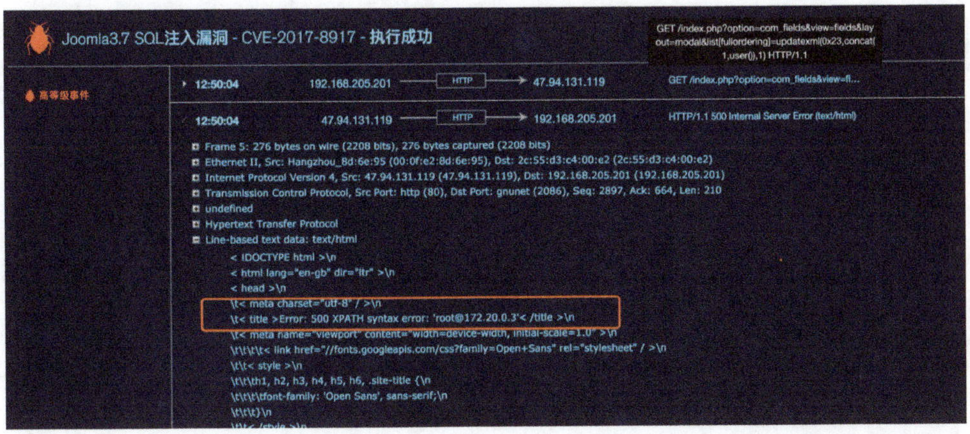

Fig. 4. The detection result for POC1

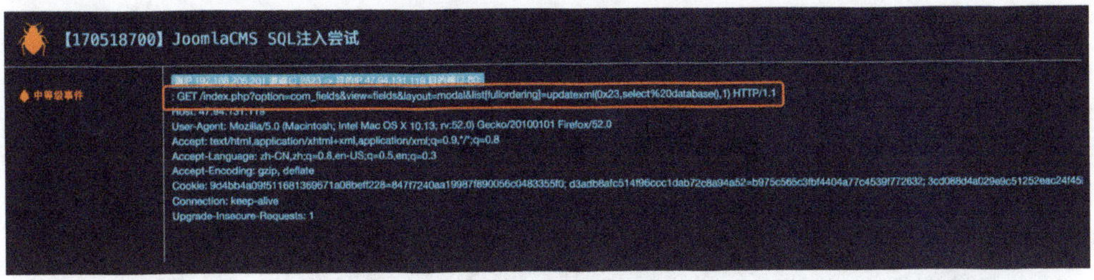

Fig. 5. The detection result for POC3

Payload1:http://104.225.151.194/cshajx/xss/easyxss/?input=<script>alert(/xss/)</script>

Payload2: http://104.225.151.194/cshajx/xss/easyxss/?input=<script>alert(xss)</script>

Fig. 6. The two XSS payloads used in the evaluation

The results show that reflective XSS vulnerabilities such as Payload1 can be successfully detected. For invalid XSS vulnerabilities such as Payload2, we can identify that it is a failed XSS attack.

4.3 Command Execution Vulnerabilities

For the command execution vulnerabilities, we use the ShellShock vulnerability [12] to test the detection ability. The result shows that we can identity that whether the vulnerability is successfully exploited.

4.4 Some Unknown Vulnerabilities

For the space limitation, we do not show the running screenshots for the tests of unknown vulnerabilities, but give the test results here directly. For an unknown vulnerability, we cannot find a rule that matches the vulnerability. So we can only detect it by the RNN model.

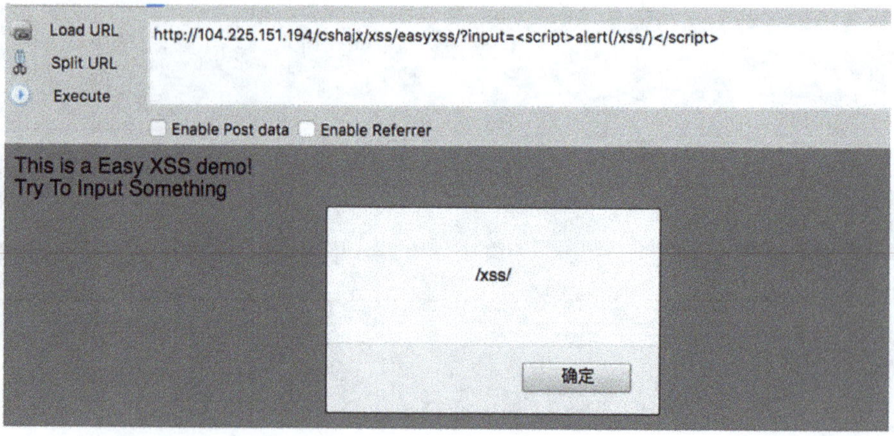

Fig. 7. The running screenshot of Payload1

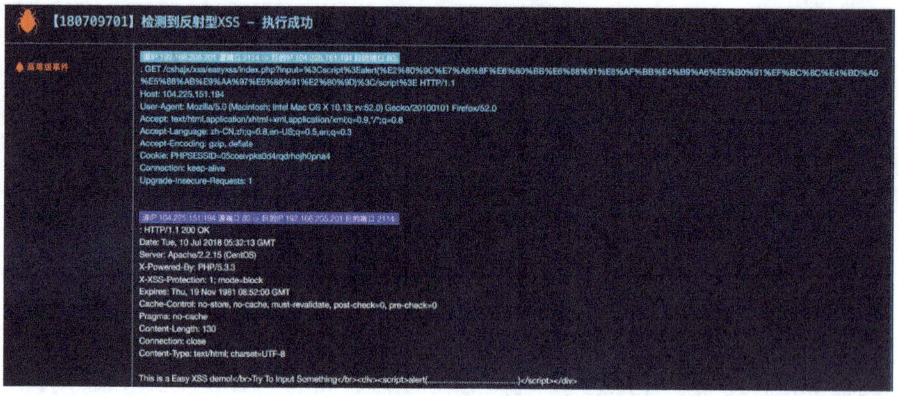

Fig. 8. The detection result for Payload1

For some unknown vulnerabilities that can cause file upload behaviors, though it is difficult to distinguish whether the file is harmful, but if the white hats try to connect or execute the file, we can successfully detect the connection and execution behaviors.

For some unknown vulnerabilities that can cause the file inclusion attacks, though we cannot identify the category of the vulnerability, but we can give alarms successfully once the vulnerability is exploited.

5 Conclusion

This paper proposes a generic architecture for crowdsourced test platforms to detect whether the white hats have found a vulnerability. In the architecture, the rule-matching method based on Snort is adopted to detect public vulnerabilities, and RNN model based on TensorFlow is adopted to detect unknown vulnerabilities. The proposed architecture is applied to the ICS-CERT crowdsourced test platform. We test it with SQL injection vulnerability, file upload vulnerability, file inclusion vulnerabilities, command execution vulnerability and XSS vulnerability. The results shows that, for most of vulnerabilities, the architecture can detect them successfully. With the technology, we can remove companies' concerns about vulnerability leaks, thus accelerating the application of crowdsourced test.

References

1. 360 Crowdsourced Test, August 2018. http://zhongce.360.cn
2. Abadi, M., et al.: TensorFlow: a system for large-scale machine learning (2016)
3. Beale, J., Foster, J.C., Posluns, J., Caswell, B.: Snort 2.0: Intrusion Detection. Syngress Publishing, Amsterdam (2003)
4. Bugcrowd Crowdsourced Test, July 2018. https://www.bugcrowd.com/
5. CNVD Crowdsourced Test, July 2018. http://zc.cnvd.org.cn/
6. CVE-2017-8917, June 2017. http://cve.mitre.org/cgi-bin/cvename.cgi?name=CVE-2017-8917
7. Hackerone Crowdsourced Test, June 2018. https://www.hackerone.com/
8. ICS-CERT Crowdsourced Test, July 2018. https://test.ics-cert.org.cn/
9. IDC/ISP Information Security Management System, August 2018. http://eversec.com.cn/idc-security/
10. Leicht, N., Blohm, I., Leimeister, J.M.: Leveraging the power of the crowd for software testing. IEEE Softw. **34**(2), 62–69 (2017)
11. Mao, K., Capra, L., Harman, M., Jia, Y.: A survey of the use of crowdsourcing in software engineering. J. Syst. Softw. **126**, 57–84 (2016)
12. Shetty, R., Choo, K.-K.R., Kaufman, R.: Shellshock vulnerability exploitation and mitigation: a demonstration. In: Abawajy, J., Choo, K.-K.R., Islam, R. (eds.) ATCI 2017. AISC, vol. 580, pp. 338–350. Springer, Cham (2018). https://doi.org/10.1007/978-3-319-67071-3_40
13. Sobug Crowdsourced Test, July 2018. http://www.sobug.com
14. Testin Crowdsourced Test, August 2018. http://www.testin.cn
15. Vulbox Crowdsourced Test, August 2018. https://www.vulbox.com
16. Wooyun Crowdsourced Test, May 2016. http://www.wooyun.org
17. Zogaj, S., Bretschneider, U., Leimeister, J.M.: Managing crowdsourced software testing: a case study based insight on the challenges of a crowdsourcing intermediary. J. Bus. Econ. **84** (3), 375–405 (2014)
18. Zogaj, S., Leicht, N., Blohm, I., Bretschneider, U., Leimeister, J.M.: Towards successful crowdsourcing projects: evaluating the implementation of governance mechanisms. In: Governance of Cowdsourcing Systems. Social Science Electronic Publishing, New York (2015)

Security Against Network Attacks on Web Application System

Yashu Liu[1,2](✉), Zhihai Wang[1], and Shu Tian[2]

[1] School of Computer and Information Technology, Beijing Jiaotong University, Beijing 100044, China
ly_s8020@163.com

[2] School of Electrical and Information Engineering, Beijing University of Civil Engineering and Architecture, Beijing 100044, China

Abstract. With the development of Internet, web applications are more and more. Network attacks have become increasingly serious problem. How to make network security administrators quickly discover vulnerabilities and protect networks against attacks has become an important part of network security protection. In this paper, it introduces the principle of web vulnerabilities and implements a forum system built in some web vulnerabilities. Then it simulates the process of web attacks according to various types of vulnerabilities and gives the defensive means separately. This system can be used to conduct security training, test security tools, and practice common penetration testing techniques for network administrators and web developers.

Keywords: Network attack · Defensive measure · SQL injection · XSS

1 Introduction

It was reported that "Coinhive" mining software intruded into Youtube video platform in 2018 [1]. The malicious software tried to hijack the users' CPU and excavated the encrypted currency, which is called "cryptojacking". It is a famous network attack. The 2018 global risk report released by the Davos world economic forum, showed that global leaders were worried that the threat of large-scale network attacks ware more than terrorism in January 23, 2018 [2]. The large-scale network attacks have been the third of the most likely major risks.

It is very important to be prepared for future attacks. In order to improve the network security administrators' defense skills, we implement a forum built in some common web vulnerabilities. On the forum, network attacks are simulated, and given defense means. Thus, it can provide a real attack and defense environment for users. It is very useful to users teach or learn web application security.

The rest of this paper is organized as follows. In Sect. 2, we discuss the related work in network attack. In Sect. 3 we describe common web vulnerabilities principle. Implementation of forum system is detailed in Sect. 4. Simulation of attack and defense process is shown in Sect. 5. We give the conclusion in Sect. 6.

X. Yun et al. (Eds.): CNCERT 2018, CCIS 970, pp. 145–152, 2019.
https://doi.org/10.1007/978-981-13-6621-5_12

2 Related Work

In foreign countries, the mainstream of vulnerability simulation environment is released by open source agencies. For example, Webgoat, dvwa, Metasploitable and so on. The most important one is Webgoat [3], which is a teaching environment released by OWASP based on OWASP TOP 10. Webgoat has common web vulnerabilities, such as SQL injection and cross site scripting. Damn Vulnerable Web App (DVWA) is a PHP/MySQL web application that is damn vulnerable [4]. Its main goals are to be an aid for security professionals to test their skills and tools in a legal environment, help web developers better understand the processes of securing web applications and aid teachers/students to teach/learn web application security in a class room environment. Metasploitable is an Linux virtual machine [5]. This VM can be used to conduct security training, test security tools, and practice common penetration testing techniques.

The main contributions of this paper are as follows:

- We develop a forum which has common functions, for example, registering, logging in, starting new topics, replying topics and so on.
- The forum has some vulnerabilities which are appear or disappear by hand. Users can understand the harm of vulnerabilities.
- It can simulate the process of network attack. Users can launch the attack according to the types of vulnerabilities by themselves. During the process, they can understand network attack and web vulnerabilities more deeply.
- It can provide defensive measures according to network attack. Users can learn how to defense various network attack and avoid web vulnerabilities.

3 Common Web Vulnerabilities Principle

In our forum application, it introduces some common web vulnerabilities, for example, brute force vulnerability, SQL injection vulnerability, XSS vulnerability, file upload vulnerability [6–8].

Brue force uses exhaustive methods to decipher passwords, verification codes, etc. It can calculate the password one by one until it finds the real one. Generally, it doesn't know the scope and specification of the password.

SQL injection means that it can insert some SQL codes into query strings of domain name or page request [9]. Thus, the server is deceived to execute malicious SQL codes. In another words, SQL injection makes the database server doesn't execute the correct SQL codes, but to execute the malicious codes if it has some vulnerabilities.

XSS is known as a cross station script attack, which is a type of vulnerability on web application [10–12]. It makes attackers inject JavaScript codes into some web pages which have some vulnerabilities. Then the users open the URL whose pages have malicious codes on the web browser, and the malicious script is executed.

Most websites and applications have file upload function. File upload function doesn't restrict the uploaded file suffix and file type on some websites strictly, which can be attacked by uploading various malicious files into Server, for example, PHP files. When PHP files are interpreted, Trojan horse, virus, malicious script, or WebShell will be executed on the server.

File upload vulnerability is a huge harmful one, WebShell has expanded the impact of harm. Most file upload vulnerabilities can be attacked, attackers will leave WebShell in order to access to the system later.

4 Implementation of Forum System

In order to provide a secure and legitimate website for web attack tests, we implement a forum system. Except general forum functions, it is also built in various vulnerabilities.

4.1 The Functions of Forum System

The forum has some common functions and been built in some web vulnerabilities. The forum system is designed by thinkPHP and MVC. It has three main function, "community management", "users management" and "post management". Each function is subdivided into sub functions. The function module diagram of the forum system is shown in Fig. 1.

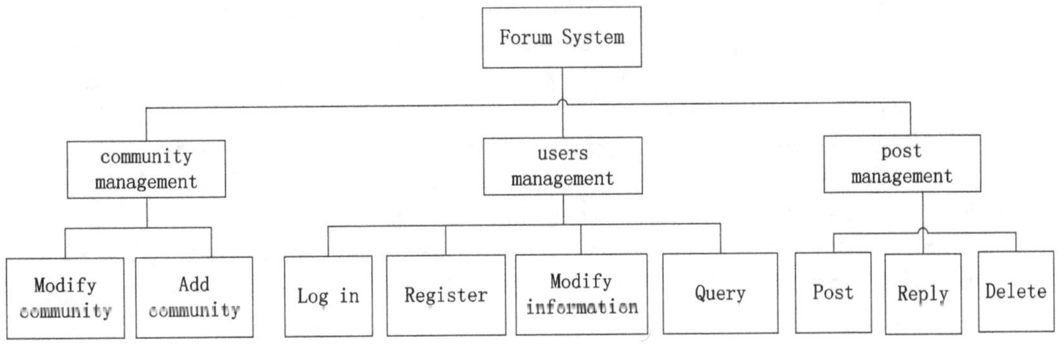

Fig. 1. The function module diagram of the forum system.

In addition to, we have created a database with four tables. They are "bbs_category", "bbs_user", "bbs_closeip" and "bbs_details". The information of topic category, users, IP and topics is stored in them separately. For example, the details of "bbs_details" are shown in Table 1.

4.2 Reserved Web Vulnerabilities

In the forum, it is reserved some web vulnerabilities, in order to simulate the attack. XSS vulnerability is built in registration module. In the module, it should check the users' data posted by form, but it ignores the process. The key codes are shown in Table 2.

Table 1. The table of bbs_details.

Field	Datatype
Id	Int(11)
Userid	Int(11)
Parentid	Int(11)
Title	Varchar(255)
Content	Text
Addtime	Datetime
Addip	Int(10)
Hitcount	Int(11)
Replycount	Int(11)
Isdelete	Int(11)

Table 2. The process of building in XSS vulnerability.

```
if(!isset($_SERVER['HTTP_REFERER'])){
    $this->notice('<font color="red">Please login in
</font>','index.php?m=index&a=reg');
        }
        //get the user's data
        $uname=trim($_POST['username']); //get user's name
        $pass=trim($_POST['password']); //get the password
        $repass = trim($_POST['repassword']);//get the password again
        if($pass!=$repass){
        $this->notice('<font color="red">Please input again, because
the values of the pass and repass are not equal
</font>','index.php?m=index&a=reg');
    }//here doesn't check and filter user's input, built in XSS
    vulnerability
        ......
        $data = [
            'username' =>$uname,
            'password' =>md5(md5($pass.$this->salt).$this->salt),
            'regtime' =>date('Y-m-d H:i:s',time()),
            'regip' =>$ip,
            'lasttime' =>date('Y-m-d H:i:s',time()),
            'money' =>200,
        ];
        if($userObj->add($data)){ //write the data into database
            $this->notice('<font color="gray">Successfully!
</font>','index.php?m=index&a=index');
        }
    $this->notice('<font color="red">Failure!
</font>','index.php?m=index&a=reg');
```

In login module, the forum doesn't check and filter user's data. It is built in SQL injection vulnerability. At the same time, the system doesn't limit the times of login requests by users, leaving a potential threat of brute force.

For file upload vulnerability, the forum is built in the module of modifying user's avatar. In the module, user can upload an avatar file, but it doesn't be limited the size and type. Thus, user upload the files which may be malicious ones. The codes are shown in Table 3.

Table 3. The process of building in file upload vulnerability.

```
......
$file_true_name=$_FILES['myfile']['name'];
$move_to_file=$user_path."/touxiang.jpeg";
  if(move_uploaded_file($uploaded_file,iconv("utf-8","gb2312",
$move_to_file))) {
       echo $_FILES['myfile']['name']."Upload successfully!";
       $this->notice('<font  color="green">  Upload  successfully!
</font>','/index.php');
    } else {
            $this->notice('<font   color="red">  Upload   Failed!
</font>','/index.php');
        }
......
```

In addition to, some vulnerabilities are built in the module of forum community modification, user permission modification and posting new topic, replying topic, deleting topic and so on.

5 Attack and Defense

On the forum, we can simulate web attack and defense which help web developers better understand the processes and means of securing web applications.

5.1 Simulate Attacks

In login module, the forum system doesn't check the data of form and filter the key SQL codes. It is built in vulnerabilities. To know if there is a SQL vulnerability, we write three SQL codes, as follows:

(1) **select * from bbs_user where username='username' and password='password'**
(2) **select * from bbs_user where username='username' and password='password' and '1'='1'**
(3) **select * from bbs_user where username='username' and password='password' and '1'='2'**

If (1) and (3) are executed abnormally, and (2) is executed normally, the system has SQL vulnerability. Thus, we can try to log in as an administrator using the following SQL code:

select * from bbs_user where username='admin' and password='XXX' or '1'

The SQL string implements to log in the forum as an administrator without password verification. Then, the information of the forum will be revealed.

In forum system, it doesn't filter "JavaScript" codes in controller layer and put the data from web form into database directly. Thus, we simulate XSS attack. On register page, we input the following string as username:

"<script>alert(\'h Attack, Just a kidding!\');</script>"

Once it is registered successfully, the malicious JavaScript code will be executed. Of course, it will cause more harm. When the followed codes are written into database, the users' information will be transferred to hacker website who open the pages built in malicious codes. The codes are as follows:

"<script>window.location.href=\'http://www.hacked.com/index.php/?c=\' + document.cookie + \'&url=\' + window.location.href </script></p>"

To simulate file upload attack, we use hacker software to test the vulnerability. In the module of avatar modification, we upload malicious php file from the website. Then the malicious file can modify the data or execute shell script to make more serious attack.

5.2 Defense Means

To secure web applications, there will be relative defense means against network attack. In this paper, it will give some means.

In order to prevent brute force attacks, we can take restrictions on the times of requests from users. It can also increase the difficulty and cost of brute force by encrypting passwords again. The example of encrypting is shown in Table 4.

Table 4. The example of encrypting.

```
// when registering
......
$data = [
        'username' =>$uname,
        'password'
=>md5(md5($pass.$this->salt).$this->salt),//encrypting
......
// when logging in
if($user[0]['password']  !=md5(md5($password.$this->salt).$this->salt))
```

It is strictly forbidden to connect directly to the database in the controller layer. The database can be accessed through the model layer, which greatly reduces the risk of SQL injection attack. Filtering user input data on form is also a common means to prevent it.

Checking user input data is the most effective and practical means to defense XSS attack. The example is shown in Table 5. In addition to, the field is limited by length and type in database which can defense many malicious attacks.

Table 5. The example of XSS attack

```
......
$obj = new Details();
        $deltails = $obj->getDetailsById($id);

$deltails[0]["content"]=strtr($deltails[0]["content"],"script","js"
);
        $this->assign('details',$deltails[0]);
```

Defensing file upload attack can be implemented by prohibiting all suspicious files uploaded to the server strictly. In forum system, it adds some codes to check the size and type of files. The details are shown in Table 6.

Table 6. Filtering JavaScript code.

```
......
if($file_size>2*1024*1024) { echo "The size of file is not over 2M. ";
        exit();   }
   $file type=$ FILES['myfile']['type'];
    echo $file_type;
    if($file_type!="image/jpeg" && $file_type!='image/pjpeg') {
        echo "only jpg！";
        exit();
    }
```

6 Conclusion

In this paper, it implements a forum built in some web vulnerabilities which can aid users to learn web application security. It can be provided to network administrators to learn how to defense web attacks. At the same time, it can give some advice to web application developers who can avoid web vulnerabilities. It presents defensive measure of brute force vulnerability, SQL injection vulnerability, XSS vulnerability and file upload vulnerability, but that's not enough. We will pay more attention to other network vulnerabilities later.

Acknowledgments. This work was supported in part by the National Key Research and Development Program of China under Grant 2018YFB0803604, 2015BAK21B01, in part by the National Science Foundation of China under Grant 61672086, 61672086.

References

1. Cryptojacking news. http://www.sohu.com/a/219580006_609556. Accessed 29 Jan 2018
2. 2018 global risk report. http://www.sohu.com/a/218458499_781333. Accessed 23 Jan 2018
3. Webgoat. https://sourceforge.net/projects/metasploitable. Accessed 22 Jan 2018
4. Damn Vulnerable Web App (DVWA). http://www.dvwa.co.uk. Accessed 25 Jan 2018
5. Metasploitable. https://www.owasp.org/index.php/Category:OWASP_WebGoat_Project. Accessed 1 Aug 2018
6. Kang, C., Zhu, Z.: Network attack and defense experimental platform based on cloud computing technology. J. Xi'an Univ. Posts Telecommun. **3**, 87–88 (2013)
7. Zhang, L., Zhou, H.: Design of network security attack and defense experimental platform based on cloud computing technology. In: Software Guide, vol. 9, pp. 188–191 (2015)
8. Huang, X.: Development and implementation of network attack and defense experimental platform. Exp. Technol. Manag. **5**, 73–76 (2017)
9. Liu, Y.: Brief discussion of the deployment and design of field exercises on Internet security. Cyberspace Secur. **8**, 88–90 (2017)
10. Huang, J., Zhang, H., Pei, J.: Design of virtual simulation experimental teaching system for network security. Res. Explor. Lab. **10**, 170–174 (2016)
11. Ma, L.: Design and implementation of network security attack and defense training platform. Wirel. Internet Technol. **22**, 75–77 (2017)
12. Ye, J., Zhang, P., Gao, Y.: Design and construction of a network attack and defense combat training platform based on Openstack. Exp. Technol. Manag. **3**, 86–89 (2016)

Association Visualization Analysis for the Application Service Layer and Network Control Layer

Mianmian Shi[1(✉)] and Huaping Cao[2]

[1] Institute of Network Technology, Beijing University of Posts and Telecommunications, Beijing 100876, China
shimian@bupt.edu.cn

[2] National Computer Network Emergency Response Technical Team, Coordination Center of China, Beijing 100029, China
caohuaping@cert.org.cn

Abstract. Most researches about complex networks are single-layer networks-based representation. However, in most cases, systems in the real world are not isolated but connective. In this paper, different from the traditional Open System Interconnection (OSI) model, our research pays attention to application service layer and network control layer for the view of application. Two layers connect with each other by using IP mapping relationship. Firstly, to avoid unnecessary loss of computational efficiency, we modify Louvain algorithm to divide the nodes in network control layer into several parts. Secondly, we add additional community attractive force and introduce Barnes-Hut force-calculation model to Fruchterman-Reingold algorithm in order to make nodes in network control layer aligned more structured and well-distributed efficiently. Finally, we merge the application service layer and the network control layer into a two-layer visualization model. Based on our two-layer model, the whole network trend, topology and incidence relation can be conveniently grasped.

Keywords: Two-layer layout · Network visualization · FR algorithm

1 Introduction

Visual analytics is based on the combination of automatic analysis technology and interactive visualization technology for efficacious exploring and decision making for users [1]. Converting complex datasets into graphics or images makes it easier for users to understand large-scale data and discover hidden information.

In many researches, network was just considered as a complex graph or a kind of data structure with nodes and edges. These studies are generally divided into two categories. One is visualization research for a single layer. The other is visualization of multi layers for complex network.

There are some works on displaying network status in single layer. For network control layer, VizFlowConnect [2] and PortVis [3] use Parallel—Coordinate and Scatter Plot to visualize Netflow data. IPMatrix [4] and Netvis [5] use Node-Link and

X. Yun et al. (Eds.): CNCERT 2018, CCIS 970, pp. 153–164, 2019.
https://doi.org/10.1007/978-981-13-6621-5_13

TreeMap to visualize IDS alarm data. Romero-Gomez [6] designs THACO (THreat Analysis COnsole) for DNS-based network threat analysis. In addition, researchers also use topology diagram of network routing information to analyze network events. BGP data is regularly used in some systems, such as BGPlay [7], BGP Eye [8], BGPfuse [9] and so on. From the view of application, Alsaleh [10] presents an extension to PHPIDS, which correlates PHPIDS logs with the corresponding web server logs to plot the security-related events. ThousandEyes [11] monitors internal and external network performance to improve application delivery and reduce service interruptions. Similarly, RIPE Atlas [12] is a global network of probes that measure Internet connectivity and reachability, providing an unprecedented understanding of the Internet in real time.

Some researchers also propose multi-layer visual model to show the complex network. Zhang [13] considers that all the subsystems in the real world are not isolates but connective. Iyad Katib [14] separates the logical layer form physical layer, and propose a three-layer named IP-OTN-DWDM to improve the convenience of resource management and fault detection in communication. In 2017, Wei [15] develops a research from the view of application and proposes two-layer network with carrier layer and business layer. In order to display the different levels of network topology and the relationships between the multi layers, researchers usually set each network's nodes and edges in a 2D plane, and put these 2D planes in 3D space. This method is called as two-and-a-half-dimensional (2.5D) visualization [16].

However, in most cases, it is hard for single-layer visualization to show the relationship between different layers in network. Simultaneously, traditional multi-layer social or biological network visualization always focuses on displaying the same type of data hierarchically based on community detection. Each communities are placed on different 2d planes and straight lines connect those planes. These visualization models always ignore the connection relation among different types of layers in real network.

To solve problem mentioned above, we use the 2.5D visualization method to design our two-layer visual model. Concretely, different with the traditional Open System Interconnection (OSI) model, we just consider the application service layer and network control layer from the view of application. These two layers connect with each other by using IP mapping relationship. To avoid unnecessary loss of computational efficiency, we modify Louvain algorithm via pruning the leaf nodes to divide the network control layer into several parts. In order to make the view structured and well-distributed, we add additional community attractive forces to Fruchterman-Reingold algorithm. Then, to minimize the number of the crossing lines between these two layers, the method is given that the nodes' locations of the application service layer can be obtained by using the locations of nodes in the network control layer. Finally, we merge the application service layer and the network control layer into a two-layer visualization model. Based on our two-layer model, the whole network trend, topology and incidence relation can be easily observed.

2 Preliminary Knowledge

In network control layer, we can abstract the Internet topology at the inter-domain level into an Autonomous System (AS) connection graph. Through this graph, network is just considered as a complex graph with AS nodes and BGP routing sessions' links. Similar to social networks, there are communities in the real network. The AS nodes in the community interact closely and the relationships between communities are relatively sparse. In order to present a good community structure layout, this section introduces Louvain algorithm for community detection and Fruchterman-Reingold algorithm for nodes layout covered in this paper.

2.1 Louvain Algorithm

The existing community detection algorithms for complex network are mainly divided into two categories. One is based on the graph theory, such as k-clique algorithm [17], Label propagation algorithm (LPA) [18] and so on. Another is hierarchy-clustering algorithm, such as Fast Newman algorithm (FN) [19], Louvain algorithm [20] and so on. Currently, researchers consider the Louvain algorithm the best non-overlapping community detection algorithm.

Girvan Newman [21] first proposed the concept of modularity Q in 2002. Then the modularity Q in formula (1) is commonly used to measure the strength of the network community structure. As the value of the modularity Q increases, the community structure is more robust and compact. The value of modularity Q is up to one.

$$\begin{aligned} Q &= \frac{1}{2m}\sum\nolimits_{i,j}[A_{ij} - \frac{K_i K_j}{2m}]\partial(c_i, c_j) \\ &= \frac{1}{2m}\left[\sum\nolimits_{i,j} A_{i,j} - \frac{\sum_i K_i \sum_j K_j}{2m}\right]\partial(c_i, c_j) \\ &= \frac{1}{2m}\sum\nolimits_c\left[\sum in - \frac{(\sum tot)^2}{2m}\right] \end{aligned} \tag{1}$$

In which, $\sum in$ is the sum of the weights of all the edges in community c. $\sum tot$ is the sum of the weights of the edges connected to all nodes in community c.

Louvain algorithm is based on modularity Q optimization. The change of the modularity increment ΔQ can be derived by formula (1)

$$\Delta Q = \frac{1}{2m}(k_{i,in} - \frac{\sum totk_i}{m}) \tag{2}$$

Where, $k_{i,in}$ is the sum of weight of edges which is connected to node n_i in community c. The use of greedy algorithm for large complex networks greatly improves computational efficiency.

Louvain algorithm's process is mainly divided into two steps:

The first step is to regard all nodes in the network as an independent community. Then we try to assign each node to another community which its neighbor node belongs to and calculate the change in modularity increment ΔQ. If ΔQ > 0, we choose the community which makes ΔQ the largest and then put this node into this community.

In the second step, we regard the nodes of the same community as a new node. The weights of the edges between communities are converted into the weight of edges between new nodes. Repeat step 1 until the modularity Q no longer changes.

2.2 Fruchterman-Reingold Algorithms

The most common graph drawing methods always rely in physical simulations, such as force-directed algorithm (FDA) [22], Kamada-Kawai algorithm (KK) [23], Fruchterman-Reingold algorithm (FR) [24] and so on. In this system, the edges between the nodes are equivalent to the spring or other physical connections, and the nodes are balanced by the interaction of the elastic force. Our research is based on FR algorithm. This method treats nodes as atoms in physical system and there is attractive force and repulsions force between each node. By calculating the total energy of the system, it can produce a beautiful and balance layout with a simple cooling table.

In order to make the nodes in graph well-distributed, FR algorithm thinks that nodes with edges connected should be as close as possible and nodes with no edges connected should be as far as possible. This method defines the concepts of attractive force (f_a) and repulsions force (f_r). There are attractive force among all nodes with edges connected and repulsions force among all nodes. K is used to control side length. The force can be calculated as following:

$$\begin{cases} f_a = d^2/k \\ f_r = -k^2/d \end{cases} \tag{3}$$

In which, $k = C\sqrt{\frac{S}{N}}$ is the balance coefficient. C is a constant. S is the layout area and N is the number of all nodes. Using FR algorithm, nodes are evenly distributed.

3 The Method of Two-Layer Network Topology Visualization

In our research, we just abstract the network and application as network control layer and application service layer. We focus on the topological structure of the network control layer as well as the relationships between each layer, so we use the 2.5D visualization method to design our two-layer model. This section introduces our work on network control layer topological visualization and the display algorithm of two-layer network model.

3.1 Visualization of Network Control Layer

Similar to social networks, there are communities in the real network. The AS nodes in the community interact closely and the relationships between communities are less interact. Traditional Louvain algorithm and FR algorithm have some defects in display and efficiency. In order to make the view structured and well-distributed, we modify Louvain algorithm via pruning the leaf nodes and add additional community attractive forces to our modified FR algorithm.

The Modified Louvain Algorithm

Since there are a large number of leaf nodes which are only connected to one node in real network, it would cause unnecessary loss of computational efficiency if we calculate modularity increment ΔQ for every node. As shown in Fig. 1, the black nodes have five leaf nodes. Because community detection will avoid individual nodes belonging to a community, the leaf nodes and the black node must be in the same community. To avoid unnecessary loss of computational efficiency, in the first step of the Louvain algorithm, we can assign the leaf nodes to its adjacent non-leaf nodes directly. With the increase of the ratio of leaf nodes in the network, the algorithm efficiency is obviously enhanced.

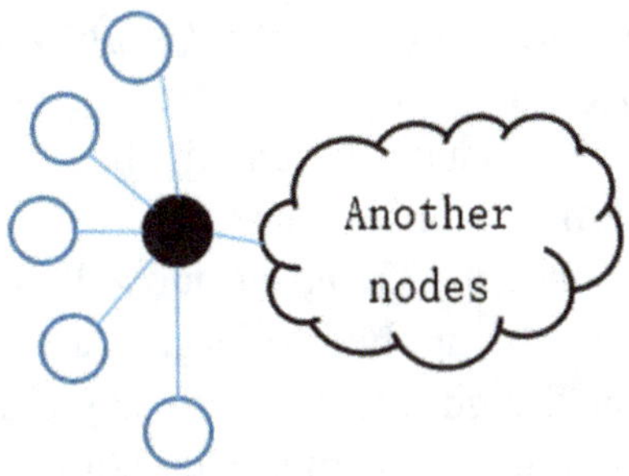

Fig. 1. Network with leaf nodes.

Our research obtains the routing data of the rrc00.ripe.net probe at 16:00 on May 7, 2018 from the RIPE Routing Information Service (RIS). We get the relationships between global AS nodes by Python processing. Since there are edges with higher repetition rate and edges with fewer paths in our routing data, we introduce the number of AS path as edge weights into the Louvain algorithm. Compared to the unweighted graph in real network, the nodes with high weight links are more likely in the same community.

We classify the nodes and edges by countries and select 338 nodes and 544 edges in China collection for experiment. We perform Louvain algorithm and modified Louvain one on this dataset. Compared with the Fast Newman algorithm (FN) and Label propagation algorithm (LPA), Table 1 shows the results of the experiment.

Table 1. Quantitative evaluation of FN algorithm, LPA algorithm, Louvain algorithm and modified Louvain one.

Algorithm	Time(s)	Number of community	Modularity Q
FN	0.9721	18	0.5620
LPA	0.0790	20	0.5469
Louvain	0.0870	15	0.6170
modified Louvain	0.0834	12	0.6231

As shown in Table 1, the Fast Newman algorithm performs worst. The Modularity Q is not bad but it takes too much time in iteration. The LPA algorithm is the fastest algorithm in those algorithms, but the Louvain algorithm performs much better in the modularity Q. Compared with the original Louvain algorithm, the modified one is better with 4.12% less time-consuming. At the same time, as the number of communities drops from 15 to 12, the modularity Q has also increased from 0.6137 to 0.6231. Therefore, this experiment proves the modified Louvain algorithm is the most suitable community detection for visualization of network control layer.

The Modified FR Algorithm

There are some issues on using FR algorithm to visualize large-scale data layout: (1) It is difficult for us to observe the community structure and the connection between communities when there are too many communities. (2) The time complexity of FR is $O(|E| + |V|^2)$. When using too many nodes, it will take a lot of time to calculate.

So, in our research, refer to FR algorithm, we redefine attractive forces (f_a) and repulsions forces (f_r), and add community force (f_{com}) to make the nodes in the same community more closely to each other while ensuring an evenly layout. In order to avoid the local optimum, we introduce the energy function into our method and use simulated annealing algorithm to approximate optimal solution. At the same time, Barnes-Hut force-calculation model [25] is introduced to reduce time complexity so that the modified algorithm can be applied to large-scale network layout.

Often, the nodes with high weight links should stay closer than other nodes, so we introduce the weight of each edges into the calculation of attractive forces (f_a). For another, the high-degree nodes usually belongs to different communities, so we hope these nodes father away from each other in order to display a better visualization of communities. Therefore, we also introduce the degrees of two nodes when we calculate the repulsive forces (f_r) between all nodes. The forces of every node in network are calculated as following:

$$\begin{cases} f_a = \frac{d^2(n_1,n_2)*w(n_1,n_2)}{\mathrm{k}} \\ f_r = -\frac{k^2}{d}\deg(n_1)*\deg(n_2) \end{cases} \quad (4)$$

For the nodes in the same community, we hope that edges with high weight connect nodes with each other tightly. Refer to the attractive force formula (3) defined in FR, we introduce the sum of edges weight in community (w_{com}) and define the formula for community forces as following:

$$f_{com} = \frac{d^2(n_1,n_2)}{k} * w(n_1,n_2) * \frac{w_{com}}{w_{all}} \quad (5)$$

In which $\mathrm{d}(n_1,n_2)$ is the distance between node 1 and node 2, $w(n_1,n_2)$ indicates the weight of edge (n_1n_2). $\deg(n_1)$ is the degree of node n_1. w_{com} is the sum of edge weight in a community. w_{all} is the sum of weight of all edges.

At the same time, in order to reduce the time complexity of the repulsion forces calculation, we introduce Barnes-Hut force-calculation model in the calculation of repulsive forces. In our modified FR algorithm, the time complexity of the repulsion calculation is reduced from $O(|V|^2)$ to $O(|V|\log|V|)$.

We use this modified FR algorithm and another classic layout algorithms for experiment in the public Dolphins data set (62 nodes, 159 sides) and Football Club data set (115 nodes, 613 sides). The results are as shown in Figs. 2 and 3.

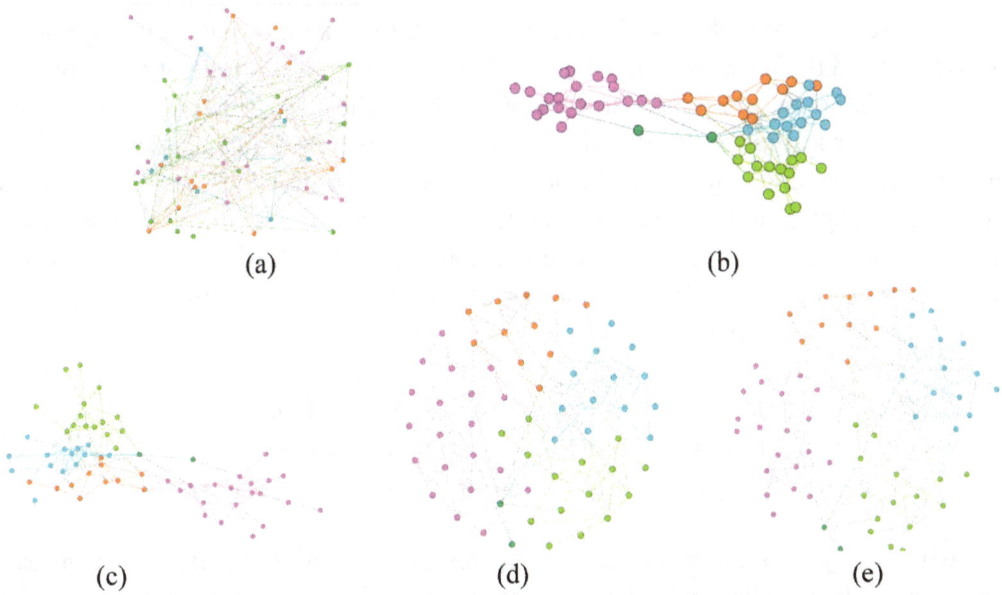

Fig. 2. Visualization of Dolphins Dataset (a. raw data without algorithm, b. Yifan Hu algorithm [26], c. ForceAlatas 2 algorithm [27], d. FR algorithm, e. modified FR algorithm).

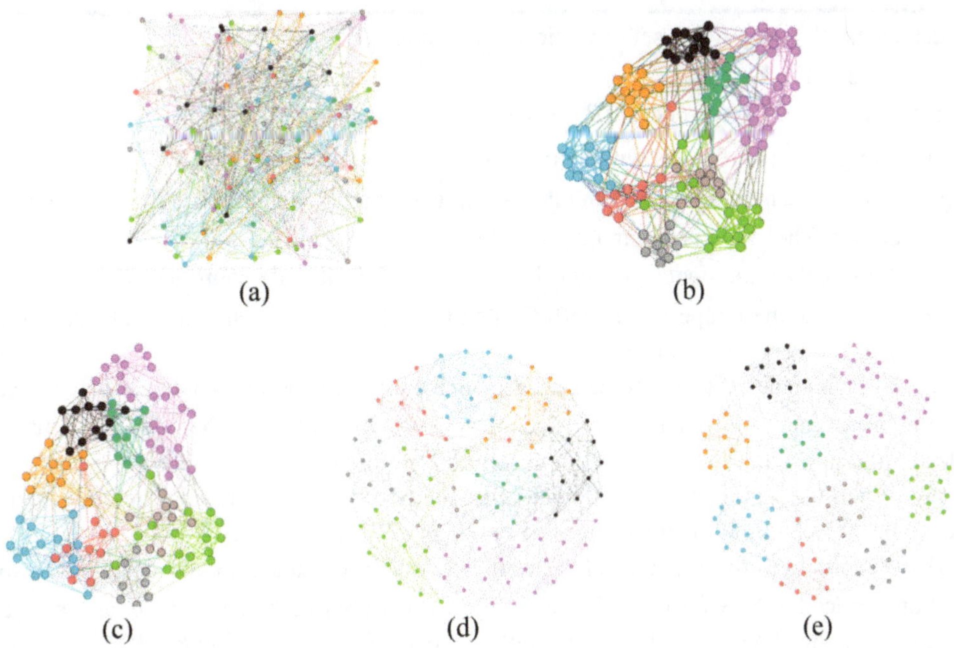

Fig. 3. Visualization of Football Club Dataset (a. raw data without algorithm, b. Yifan Hu algorithm, c. ForceAlatas 2 algorithm, d. FR algorithm, e. modified FR algorithm).

From the visualization of the two datasets in Figs. 2 and 3, it is easy to see that the modified FR algorithm shows the community relationships in network more clearly and structured than Yifan Hu and ForceAltas2 algorithm. We can easily distinguish community connections with greater connectivity in the current network state.

3.2 Establishment of Two-Layer Network Model

In our research, the real network is considered as a two-layer model of the application service layer and the network control layer. We find that the locations of the application service layer's nodes are related to the locations of the network control layer nodes closely. In order to reduce the visual confusion caused by the inter-layer crossing, we need to calculate and adjust the location of the application service layer's nodes. Generally, an application service corresponds to multiple nodes in the network control layer. So in our 2.5D model, it is assumed that the node coordinates of the network control layer are x_i, y_i, $z_i = 0$. Then the corresponding node coordinates in application service layer are as follows:

$$\begin{cases} x_j = (x_i + x_{i+1} + \cdots + x_{i+n-1})/n \\ y_j = (y_i + y_{i+1} + \cdots + y_{i+n-1})/n \\ z_j = 1 \end{cases} \tag{6}$$

In which, x_i, y_i, z_i represent node coordinates in the network control layer and x_i, y_i, z_i represent node coordinates in the application service layer. n is the number of nodes in network control layer corresponding to an application service.

The layout algorithm established by two-layer layout model can be described as following:

Input: Network $G(V_i, E)$: a set of vertices V and edges E
Nodes: $\{V_{j1}, V_{j2}, V_{j3} \dots\}$
Output: Location of every nodes :$\{P_{i1}, P_{i2}, P_{i3} \dots P_{j1}, P_{j2}, P_{j3} \dots\}$

Step1: Merging all leaf nodes with their adjacent non-leaf nodes in network G
Step2: Covert the network G into an undirected weight graph and execute the modified Louvain algorithm. The result is community partition C.
Step3: Randomly input nodes in network G and initialize all node coordinates $P_{i1}, P_{i2}, P_{i3}, \dots$
Step4: Initialize the temperature coefficient and build Barnes-Hut hierarchical space model according to the position of Step3
Step5: Calculate the attractive force between adjacent nodes and the repulsive force between all nodes according to formula (4) and alculate another attractive force between adjacent nodes in the same community according to formula (5), then update the node position.
Step6: When the temperature coefficient is gradually reduced to zero and the node position tends to be stable, output the node coordinates $P_{i1}, P_{i2}, P_{i3} \dots$
Step7: According to the positions of nodes in network G, calculate node coordinates in application service layer by formula (6). Take the z value of network control layer as 0 and the application service layer as 1, output the application server node position $P_{j1}, P_{j2}, P_{j3} \dots$

4 Visual Analysis

We select 338 nodes and 544 edges in China collection in network control layer and 13 website nodes in application service layer for experiment. Using IP mapping to connect two layers, the result is shown in Fig. 4. The black nodes represent 13 websites and the remaining colorful nodes are the AS nodes in network control layer. Different colors represent different communities.

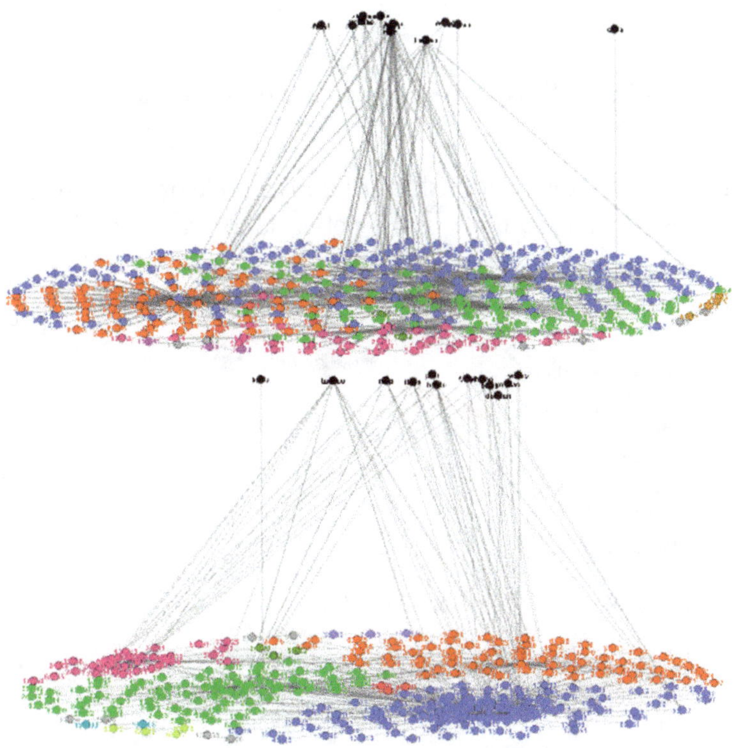

Fig. 4. Two-layer network topology for fault detection (FR algorithm and modified FR algorithm with community forces)

As shown in Fig. 4, compared the two-layer network model built by FR algorithm with two-layer network model built by modified algorithm, we can find that the community structure in our modified algorithm is more obvious and structured.

If you are interested in a website, you can select a node in the application service layer. Then, all business relationship related to it in network control layer are highlighted and we can get the AS node information from node labels. The result is shown in Fig. 5.

As shown in Fig. 5, we take the Baidu Fanyi node as an example, the AS nodes connect with it are AS4808, AS4847 AS9808, AS23724 and AS55967. Therefore, when these nodesare safe, we can ensure the proper operation of Baidu Fanyi.

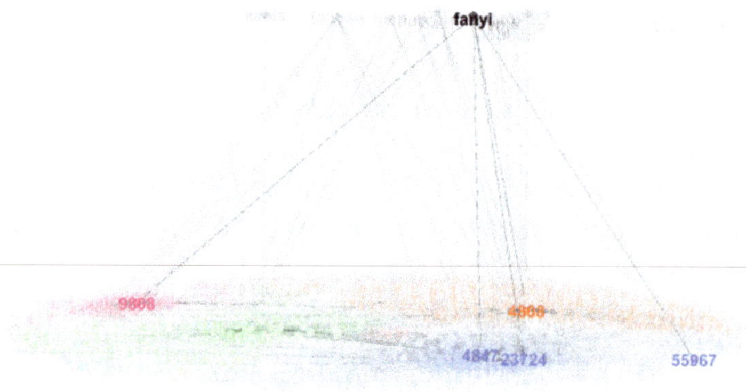

Fig. 5. Select a node in application service layer.

If you want to observe the relationships of an AS node or the business carried by an AS node, you can select an AS node in the network control layer. The result is shown in Fig. 6

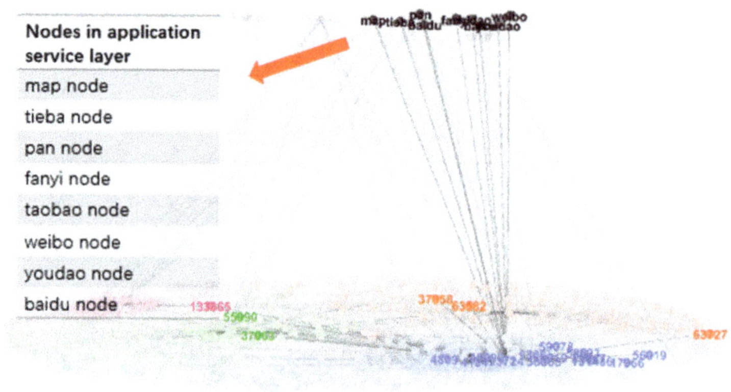

Fig. 6. Select an AS node (AS23724) in network control layer.

Figure 6 shows the result when we select an AS node (take AS23724 as an example) in network control layer. We can easily distinguish all nodes connected to AS23724 in network control layer and application service layer. If there is a problem with the AS23724 node, the nodes connected to it in network control layer and the website relied on it in application service layer may be also in trouble.

5 Conclusion

Currently, the visualization of real network mainly focused on the single-layer networks-based representation. Our research considered the application service layer and the network control layer with the IP mapping relationship between them. In network control layer, to avoid unnecessary loss of computational efficiency, we modified Louvain algorithm via pruning the leaf nodes to community detection. In order to make the view structured and well-distributed, we added additional community attractive forces to FR algorithm to make nodes in network control layer structured and well-distributed. Finally, we merged application service layer and the network control layer into a 2.5D visual model to facilitate the user's further analysis on observing the network trend, topology and incidence relation.

The future task of our multi-layer networks is to introduce a geographic location layer to show the IP location of each node in application service layer. From the future multi-layer visual model, the operating status of the network and topology can be observed in multiple dimensions.

Acknowledgement. This paper is supported by National Natural Science Foundation of China and Xinjiang under Project U1603261 and National Key R&D Program of China (2016YFE0133000): EU-China study on IoT and 5G(EXCITING) and Research Fund of Ministry of Education- China Mobile under Grant No. MCM20160304.

References

1. Kohlhammer, J., Keim, D., Pohl, M., et al.: Solving problems with visual analytics. Procedia Comput. Sci. **7**(29), 117–120 (2011)
2. Yin, X., Yurcik, W., Treaster, M., et al.: VisFlowConnect: netflow visualizations of link relationships for security situational awareness. In: Proceedings of the 2004 ACM Workshop on Visualization and Data Mining for Computer Security, pp. 26–34 (2004)
3. McPherson, J., Ma, K.L., Krystosk, P., et al.: Portvis: a tool for port-based detection of security events. In: Proceedings of the 2004 ACM Workshop on Visualization and Data Mining for Computer Security, pp. 73–81 (2004)
4. Abdullah, K., Lee, C., Conti, G., et al.: Ids rainstorm: visualizing ids alarms (2005)
5. Kan, Z., Hu, C., Wang, Z., et al.: NetVis: a network security management visualization tool based on treemap. In: 2010 2nd International Conference on Advanced Computer Control (ICACC), pp. 18–21. IEEE (2010)
6. Romero-Gomez, R., Nadji, Y., Antonakakis, M.: Towards designing effective visualizations for DNS-based network threat analysis. In: 2017 IEEE Symposium on Visualization for Cyber Security (VizSec), Phoenix, AZ, pp. 1–8 (2017)
7. Colitti, L., Di Battista, G., Mariani, F., et al.: Visualizing interdomain routing with BGPlay. J. Graph Algorithms Appl. **9**(1), 117–148 (2005)
8. Teoh, S.T., Ranjan, S., Nucci, A., et al.: BGP eye: a new visualization tool for real-time detection and analysis of BGP anomalies. In: Proceedings of the 3rd International Workshop on Visualization for Computer Security, pp. 81–90. ACM (2006)
9. Papadopoulos, S., Theodoridis, G., Tzovaras, D.: Bgpfuse: Using visual feature fusion for the detection and attribution of BGP anomalies. In: Proceedings of the Tenth Workshop on Visualization for Cyber Security, pp. 57–64. ACM (2013)
10. Alsaleh, M., Alqahtani, A., Alarifi, A., et al.: Visualizing PHPIDS log files for better understanding of web server attacks. In: Proceedings of the Tenth Workshop on Visualization for Cyber Security, pp. 1–8. ACM (2013)
11. ThousandEyes. https://www.thousandeyes.com/, last accessed 2018/7/21
12. RIPE NCC. https://atlas.ripe.net/landing/measurements-and-tools/. Accessed 21 July 2018
13. Xitao, Z., Lingda, W., Huaquan, H., Shaobo, Y.: Tasks for visual analytics in multilayer networks. In: 2017 IEEE Second International Conference on Data Science in Cyberspace (DSC), Shenzhen, pp. 368–371 (2017)

14. Katib, I., Medhi, D.: A study on layer correlation effects through a multilayer network optimization problem. In: Proceedings of the 23rd International Teletraffic Congress, pp. 31–38 (2011)
15. Wei, Y., Du, X.: Two-layer network visualization for comprehensive analysis. In: 2017 IEEE Second International Conference on Data Science in Cyberspace (DSC), pp. 363–367. IEEE (2017)
16. Dwyer, T.: Two-and-a-half-dimensional Visualisation of Relational Networks. School of Information Technologies, Faculty of Science, University of Sydney (2004)
17. Palla, G., Derényi, I., Farkas, I., Vicsek, T.: Uncovering the overlapping community structure of complex networks in nature and society. Nature **435**, 814–818 (2005)
18. Raghavan, U.N., Albert, R., Kumara, S.: Near linear time algorithm to detect community structures in large-scale networks. Phys. Rev. E **76**(3), 036106 (2007)
19. Newman, M.E.J.: Fast algorithm for detecting community structure in networks. Phys. Rev. E **69**(6), 066133 (2004)
20. Blondel, V.D., Guillaume, J.L., Lambiotte, R., et al.: Fast unfolding of communities in large networks. J. Stat. Mech: Theory Exp. **10**, 10008 (2008)
21. Girvan, M., Newman, M.E.J.: Community structure in social and biological networks. Proc. Natl. Acad. Sci. **99**(12), 7821–7826 (2002)
22. Eades, P.: A heuristics for graph drawing. Congressus Numerantium **42**, 149–160 (1984)
23. Kamada, T., Kawai, S.: An algorithm for drawing general undirected graphs. Inf. Process. Lett. **31**(1), 7–15 (1989)
24. Fruchterman, T.M.J., Reingold, E.M.: Graph drawing by force directed placement. Softw. Pract. Experience **21**(11), 1129–1164 (1991)
25. Barnes, J., Hut, P.: A hierarchical O(N log N) force-calculation algorithm. Nature **324**(6096), 446–449 (1986)
26. Hu, Y.: Efficient, high-quality force-directed graph drawing. Math. J. **10**(1), 37–71 (2005)
27. Jacomy, M., Venturini, T., Heymann, S., et al.: ForceAtlas2, a continuous graph layout algorithm for handy network visualization designed for the Gephi software. PLoS ONE **9**(6), e98679 (2014)

Trusted Secure Accessing Protection Framework Based on Cloud-Channel-Device Cooperation

Yexia Cheng[1,2,3(✉)], Yuejin Du[1,2,4(✉)], Jin Peng[3(✉)], Jun Fu[3], and Baoxu Liu[1,2]

[1] Institute of Information Engineering, Chinese Academy of Sciences, Beijing, China
chengyexia@iie.ac.cn
[2] School of Cyber Security, University of Chinese Academy of Sciences, Beijing, China
[3] Department of Security Technology, China Mobile Research Institute, Beijing, China
pengjin@chinamobile.com
[4] Security Department, Alibaba Group, Beijing, China
yuejin.dyj@alibaba-inc.com

Abstract. With the rapid development of network technologies, such as mobile Internet, Internet of Things (IoT), secure accessing is becoming an important issue. Security protection framework based on cloud-channel-device cooperation is proposed in this paper to solve the issue. The trust base is introduced to channel-end to improve trust of secure accessing device. Then, the trust and security module are designed in the cloud-end. Meanwhile, access control based on connection tracking is adopted to reduce access latency. The framework can be used to construct an open, trusted, resilient network for secure accessing and provide security solutions for mobile office, IoT security, information security management and control, etc. The effectiveness of the framework has been proved by its application to the market.

Keywords: Secure accessing · Cloud-channel-device cooperation · Trust base · Protection framework · Secure connecting · Access control

1 Introduction

With the rapid development of network technologies, such as mobile Internet, Internet of Things (IoT), etc., people's working and life patterns have been changed. The mobile smart terminals are becoming increasingly popular and the mobile offices have grown year by year. Security is critical to these services. The global Internet of Things business has developed rapidly. The Internet of Things has got the trillion-dollar market and is in the stage of large-scale explosive growth. It is estimated that by 2020, the scale of the Internet of Things market is expected to exceed US$1.7 trillion; by 2020, the number of IoT devices will reach 38.5 billion, an increase of 285% from 13.4 billion in 2015, and everything is becoming connected step by step. However, there are

X. Yun et al. (Eds.): CNCERT 2018, CCIS 970, pp. 165–176, 2019.
https://doi.org/10.1007/978-981-13-6621-5_14

a lot of security problems for IoT devices. For example, 80% IoT devices have the risk of disclosure and abuse of privacy. 80% IoT devices allow using weak password. 60% IoT devices have vulnerability problems with web page of device management. 60% IoT devices can download upgrade packages and upgrade without using any password. Due to a large number of the IoT devices accessing to Internet or Intranet, some other security problems have been brought. For example, some new attack patterns will be launched by these IoT devices and they will become new threat to the enterprise. Among these security problems, whether the accessing is secure or not is one of the most important. To solve the problem, the secure accessing protection should be taken.

When it comes to secure accessing, the researchers have already taken some studies on it. And their specific research directions of secure accessing have been changing with the time. Scarfo focus on analysis of security risks and security threats of accessing [1]. Peng et al. propose differential deployment algorithm [2]. Li et al. point out analysis of security policy [3]. Zahadat et al. and Yeboah-Boateng propose framework construction and security suggestion for secure accessing [4, 5]. Hovav et al. focus on strengthening network management and strategies for mobile applications and devices [6]. Hong et al. focuses on architecture design for secure accessing [7]. Kumar et al. propose anonymous secure framework in connected smart home environments [8]. Park et al. point out the lightweight access security for IoT and cloud convergence [9]. Ranjbar et al. discuss about the secure and persistent connectivity [10]. Zhao talks about the node capture attacks and Kim designs a secure digital recording protection System with network connected devices [11, 12]. The overall trend of secure accessing research is turned to the concrete architecture and methods.

The related researches are from different directions of secure accessing. The trusted secure accessing hasn't been proposed yet and especially the trusted secure accessing protection method based on cloud-channel-device cooperation hasn't been proposed until now.

Our Contributions. From the perspective of secure accessing, security protection framework based on cloud-channel-device cooperation is proposed in this paper to solve the issue. The trust base is introduced to channel-end to improve trust of secure accessing device. Then, the trust and security module are designed in the cloud-end. Meanwhile, access control based on connection tracking is adopted to reduce access latency. The framework can be used to construct an open, trusted, resilient network for secure accessing and provide security solutions for mobile office, IoT security, information security management and control, etc. The effectiveness of the framework has been proved by its application to the market. There are three innovations and contributions. The first is the cloud-channel-device cooperated protection framework. The second is the trust design of secure accessing devices. The third one is the connection tracking based access control of secure accessing devices and cloud platform.

The rest of this paper is organized as follows. Section 2 introduces the cloud-channel-device cooperated protection framework of secure accessing and for each part of protection framework, the function components of security and trust are designed. Section 3 presents the trust base of secure accessing devices. Section 4 proposes the trust of secure cloud platform. Section 5 mainly specifies the access control based on connection tracking for secure accessing. And in Sect. 6, the implementation and market application are introduced. Finally, in Sect. 7 we draw the conclusion of this paper.

2 Cloud-Channel-Device Cooperated Protection Framework

2.1 Secure Accessing Protection Framework Based on Cloud-Channel-Device Cooperation

As for secure accessing, especially with the development of mobile Internet, the mobility and boundary ambiguity is becoming much more obvious, as well as the openness of the various services and capabilities. So the security threats may be in any node and any different paths or links. Just relying on a single technology or a single protection device can no longer meet the demands. Therefore an integrated, coordinated, systematic security protection framework is a prerequisite for secure accessing.

Hence, in order to get the secure accessing, we propose a cloud-channel-device cooperated protection framework. The protection framework is shown in Fig. 1.

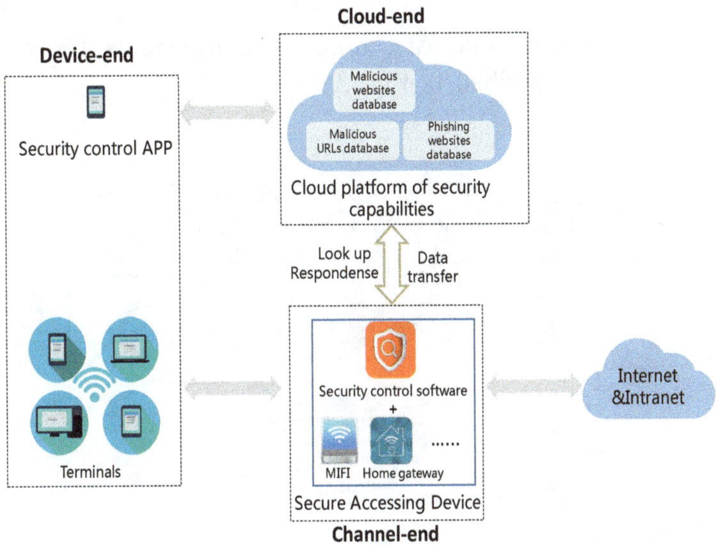

Fig. 1. Cloud-channel-device cooperated protection framework

We can see from Fig. 1 that there are three main parts of the protection framework, which are cloud-end, channel-end, device-end. As for cloud-end, it is the cloud platform of security capabilities. They can provide such realistic databases as malicious websites, malicious URLs, phishing websites, etc. As for channel-end, which is the channel between device to Internet or Intranet, there lies secure accessing devices. They can provide such functions as internet accessing, malicious website filtering, link selection, remote device monitoring, etc. The security control APP or software is used to manage the secure accessing device. As for device-end, it is terminal used by users, such as the smart phone, laptop and notebook. The security control APP will be installed in some terminals.

These three parts are cooperated with each other. The channel-end secure accessing device looks up the malicious websites, malicious URLs, phishing websites in the cloud-end. The cloud-end can transfer and exchange security data with the channel-end secure accessing device, by the operation of correspondence, etc. The channel-end secure accessing device also interacts with the device-end terminals. The websites data from device-end terminals can be extracted with the users' allowance and be compared with the data in the channel-end secure accessing device. The result will determine whether the access is secure or not. Besides, the device-end terminals with security control APP can also interact the control information with secure accessing device in channel-end.

Secure accessing protection framework based on cloud-channel-device cooperation can be used to construct an open, trusted, resilient network, which makes accessing secure and trusted. More specifically, the secure accessing protection framework can provide security solutions for information security management and control, mobile office and IoT security, etc.

2.2 Security and Trust Function Components for Secure Accessing Protection Framework

The architecture and security and trust function components for secure accessing protection framework are described in Fig. 2.

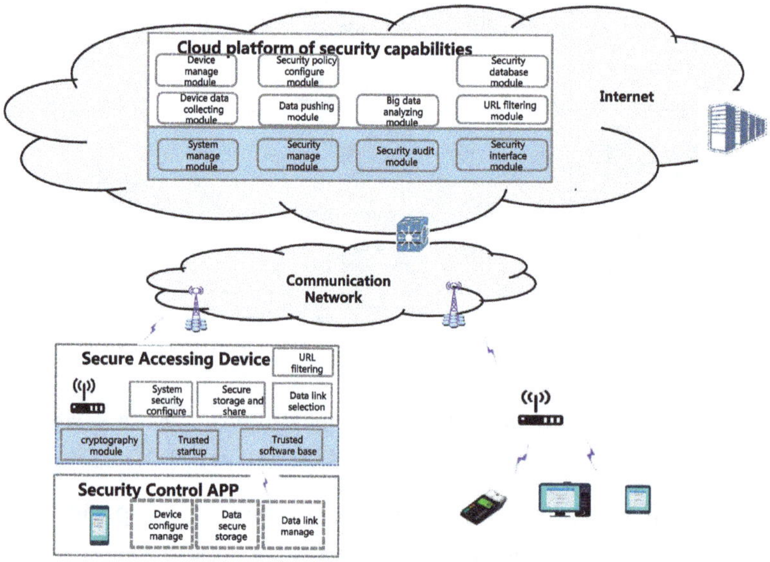

Fig. 2. Security and trust function components for secure accessing protection framework

According to the above Fig. 2, as for cloud-end, channel-end, device-end, we can get the components of security and trust for any one of the parts.

(1) **Cloud-end**
Cloud platform of security capabilities, it provides the security capabilities on the cloud and the ability of configuring the devices connected to the cloud platform of security capabilities, such as recognizing malicious websites and managing resources. The cloud platform of security capabilities can help secure connecting devices hold up the malicious URLs or phishing websites as well as real-time

querying the malicious URLs or phishing websites. The cloud platform of security capabilities provides the enterprise users with the user interface combining the functions of website blacklist configuring and user information maintenance, etc.
The security function components include device data collecting module, data pushing module, big data analyzing module, URL filtering module, device manage module, security policy configure module and security database module, etc.
The trust function components include system manage module, security manage module, security audit module and security interface module.

(2) **Channel-end**
Secure accessing device is a portable device with the security analysis and security filtering functions and meanwhile it is pre-configured with a SIM card. It is similar to the mobile WLAN hotspot device. The secure connecting device is used as a network access point for connecting to the Internet or the intranet of the enterprise. While accessing to the Internet, the secure accessing device will take advantage of various URL feature libraries on the cloud platform of security capabilities to check the user's accessing website or URL, and then hold up the malicious URL or phishing website. While connecting to the intranet of the enterprise, the secure connecting device will make use of various link selection modes to access to the intranet securely, such as APN, VPN, VPDN, etc.
The security function components include system security configure, secure storage and share, data link selection, URL filtering, etc.
The trust function components include cryptography module, trusted startup and trusted software base.

(3) **Device-end**
As for device-end, especially, the security control APP, users can easily manage security accessing devices through the security control APP. It can make sure the terminals are in secure environment to access.
The security function components include device configure manage, data secure storage, data link manage, etc.

3 Trust Base of Secure Accessing Devices

For the trusted base of secure accessing devices, we introduce Secure Element (SE) to support the establishment of trusted computing environment and provide the trusted base for secure services. Secure Element (SE) is described in detail as follows.

The Secure Element (SE) provides a miniature computing environment on a single chip, including CPU, ROM, EEPROM, RAM, and I/O interfaces, as well as cryptographic algorithm coprocessors and physical noise sources, etc. It can provide secure storage, secure computing, and cryptographic algorithm calculations for upper-layer software. Meanwhile, it provides with secure operating environment, random number generation capabilities, security protection and provides trusted computing capability as a trusted base.

The construction parts of the trusted base of secure accessing devices are shown in Fig. 3.

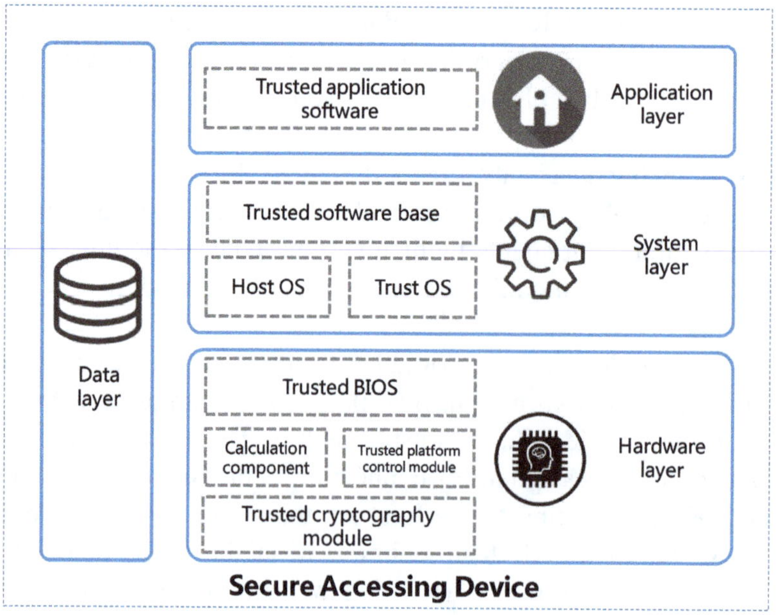

Fig. 3. Trusted base of secure accessing devices

In Fig. 3, the trusted base of secure accessing devices is constructed from four different layers, which are the hardware layer, system layer, application layer and data layer of the secure accessing devices. The specific construction parts are illustrated in below.

(1) **Hardware layer**
There are four trust modules in this layer, namely, trusted cryptography module, calculation component, trusted platform control module and trusted BIOS.
(2) **System layer**
In system layer, it is mainly based on Host OS, Trust OS, Trusted software base, etc.
(3) **Application layer**
The application layer is related to trusted application software.
(4) **Data layer**
The data layer is mainly about traditional security, which is the base insurance to trust part.

The secure accessing devices are designed with the strict security requirements of physical interface security, chip security, system privilege limitation, system update security, system security startup and system configuration security, etc. According to the requirements of different security level, the active trusted metrics and control of the equipment are introduced so as to ensure the security of the equipment fundamentally. Dived from the above four layers, the trust security requirements are listed as follows.

(1) **Hardware layer**
The trust security requirements of hardware layer include physical interface security and chip security. As for physical interface security, it includes debug interface security and peripheral interface security. As for chip security, it includes written protection security and trusted execution environment security.

(2) **System layer**
The trust security requirements of system layer include system authority restrictions, system update security, system configuration security, service configuration security and system security start. As for system authority restrictions, it includes multi-user authority control, remote connection authentication, application installation authorization and access control security. As for system update security, it includes OTA update security, firmware update security, version rollback mechanism and bug fixing ability. As for system configuration security, it includes important partition security, debug process authority restrictions and debug port control. As for service configuration security, it includes authorization minimization, application access control mechanism, data connection status and remote connection security. As for system security start, it includes integrity protection.

(3) **Application layer**
The trust security requirements of application layer include built-in application security, remote connection authentication, user's password security, multi-user access control, application update security, mobile client security, user's sensitive data security, data transmission security and login authentication mechanism.

(4) **Data layer**
The trust security requirements of data layer include data transmission, data storage, access control and log security. As for data transmission, it includes application and system sensitive data encryption. As for data storage, it includes user's privacy data encryption and application context sensitive data security. As for access control, it includes sensitive data isolation access control, third-party application access control and data isolation access control. As for log security, it includes web remote management, user's operation and alarm log management and log read authority control.

4 Trust of Secure Cloud Platform

The trust of secure cloud platform is constructed by deploying trusted computing platforms and establishing system-based platform protection measures. The following Fig. 4 shows the trust of secure cloud platform. All these designs guarantee the trust of secure cloud platform.

Accomplished with three layers' management, namely, system management, security management and audit management, we require the strict design of cloud platform of security capabilities, so as to build a trusted immune and active defense security protection.

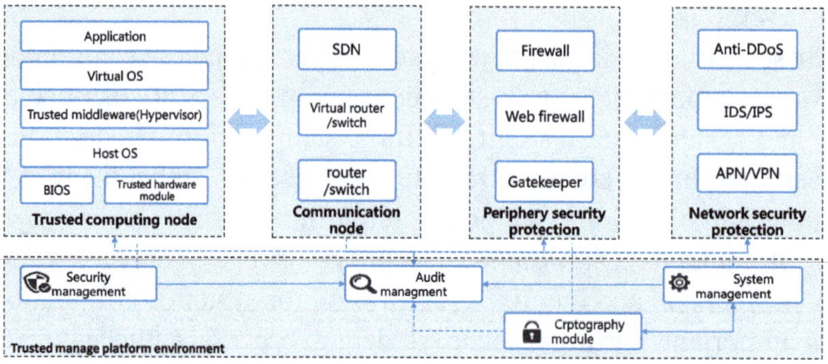

Fig. 4. Trust of secure cloud platform

5 Access Control Based on Connection Tracking for Secure Accessing

The access control based on connection tracking for secure accessing can realize application access and application queries in parallel and at the same time, it can reduce the access latency and user perception.

The method is as follows, which can also be seen in Fig. 5. Firstly, the application access traffic and extract the key feature information of the request message are analyzed. Secondly, the key feature information to query the security attributes of the traffic in the cloud platform of security capabilities is used while forwarding the request message. Thirdly, through connection tracking technology, the application access request and response message are associated. Finally, according to the lookup result from the cloud platform of security capabilities, the insecure response messages are intercepted.

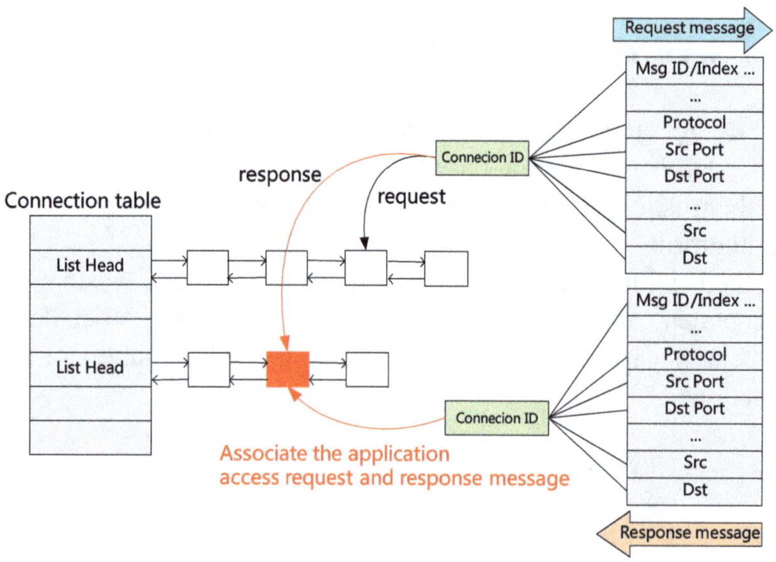

Fig. 5. Access control based on connection tracking for secure accessing

The comparison of our method based on connection tracking with other method is shown in Fig. 6. Our method can realize application access and application queries in parallel, while other methods are sequent, which is first making request, then accessing. The access latency of our method is much less than other methods.

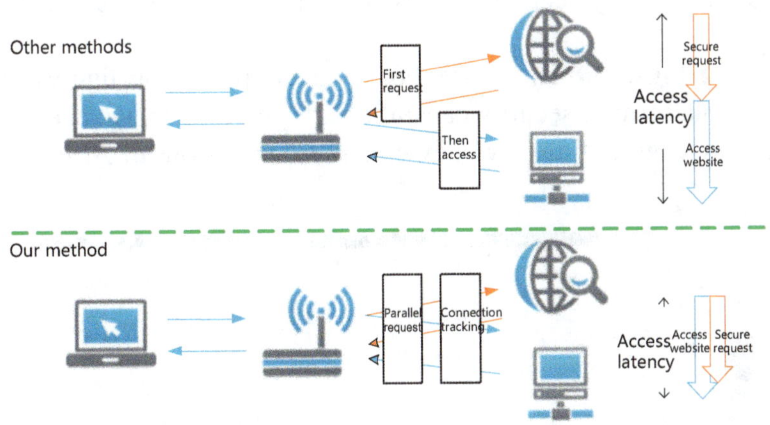

Fig. 6. Comparison of our method with other methods

6 Implementation and Market Application

The security protection framework proposed in this paper has been implemented and practically applied to the market.

What's more, the implemented system has already been tested by a third party testing agency, which showed a good test result. The query response time of the cloud platform of security capabilities is less than 200 ms. The accuracy is more than 99.9%. Concerning to the secure accessing device, when 30 terminals simultaneously access to Internet by the same secure accessing device, the latency is less than 500 ms and the system operates stably. The test results prove that the system meets the performance requirements of the existing network operation.

Compared with other relevant existing methods and systems, our framework and system has many more advantages in the analysis of performance indicators, function indicators and even in the scene parts. Specifically speaking, it is as follows.

From the perspective of performance indicators, compared with other methods and systems, our system can have more terminals involved in concurrent intervention, up to 30, while other systems can only reach up to 15. As for network latency, the network latency of our system is lower, less than 500 ms, while other systems reach up to 1000 ms. Concerning to the query response time of the cloud platform of security capabilities, our query response speed is faster, response time is shorter, less than 200 ms, while the query response time of other systems can generally reach up to 500 ms, sometimes even 1000 ms. For malicious URL detection accuracy, our system accuracy is greater than 99.9%, while the detection accuracy of other systems may only be 85–95%.

From the perspective of functional indicators, the functions of our system are more abundant than other methods and systems. In addition to network accessing and network routing functions of other systems, our system has link selection functions, security filtering functions, encrypted communication functions, and secure storage functions, etc.

From the perspective of scene, compared with other methods and systems, our system has mobile office security access, IoT security access, industry terminal security access, and home gateway security access scenarios, which is much more than other systems.

The following Figs. 7, 8 and 9 are the practical application figures. Figure 7 displays cloud-end platform of security capabilities. Figure 8 displays channel-end secure accessing devices. Figure 9 displays device-end security control APP.

Fig. 7. Display of cloud-end cloud platform of security capabilities

Fig. 8. Display of channel-end secure accessing devices

Fig. 9. Display of device-end security control APP

7 Conclusion

In this paper, security protection framework based on cloud-channel-device cooperation is proposed in this paper to solve the issue. The trust base is introduced to channel-end to improve trust of secure accessing device. Then, the trust and security module are designed in the cloud-end. Meanwhile, access control based on connection tracking is adopted to reduce access latency. The framework can be used to construct an open, trusted, resilient network for secure accessing and provide security solutions for mobile office, IoT security, information security management and control, etc. The security protection framework has been implemented and tested by a third party testing agency, the result shows that the proposed framework has better performance compared to other methods. At present, the framework has been practically applied to the market and the results show that it is useful and effective. It will be applied to operators, enterprises and government departments on a large scale.

Acknowledgement. This work is supported by the National Natural Science Foundation of China (No. 61702508 and No. 61602470) and Strategic Priority Research Program of Chinese Academy of Sciences. This work is also supported by Key Laboratory of Network Assessment Technology at Chinese Academy of Sciences and Beijing Key Laboratory of Network Security and Protection Technology.

References

1. Scarfo, A.: New security perspectives around BYOD. In: BWCCA 2012, pp. 446–451 (2012)
2. Peng, W., Li, F., Han, K.J., Zou, X., Wu, J.: T-dominance: prioritized defense deployment for BYOD security. In: CNS 2013, pp. 37–45 (2013)
3. Li, F., Huang, C.T., Huang, J., Peng, W.: Feedback-based smartphone strategic sampling for BYOD security. In: ICCCN 2014, pp. 1–8 (2014)
4. Zahadat, N., Blessner, P., Blackburn, T., Olson, B.A.: BYOD security engineering: a framework and its analysis. Comput. Secur. **55**, 81–99 (2015)

5. Yeboah-Boateng, E.O., Boaten, F.E.: Bring-Your-Own-Device (BYOD): an evaluation of associated risks to corporate information security. CoRR abs/1609.01821 (2016)
6. Hovav, A., Putri, F.F.: This is my device! Why should I follow your rules? Employees' compliance with BYOD security policy. Pervasive Mob. Comput. **32**, 35–49 (2016)
7. Hong, S., Baykov, R., Xu, L., Nadimpalli, S., Gu, G.: Towards SDN-defined programmable BYOD (Bring Your Own Device) security. In: NDSS (2016)
8. Kumar, P., Braeken, A., Gurtov, A., Iinatti, J., Ha, P.H.: Anonymous secure framework in connected smart home environments. IEEE Trans. Inf. Forensics Secur. **12**(4), 968–979 (2017)
9. Park, J., Kwon, H., Kang, N.: IoT-Cloud collaboration to establish a secure connection for lightweight devices. Wireless Netw. **23**(3), 681–692 (2017)
10. Ranjbar, A., Komu, M., Salmela, P., Aura, T.: SynAPTIC: Secure And Persistent connecTIvity for Containers. In: CCGrid 2017, pp. 262–267 (2017)
11. Zhao, J.: On resilience and connectivity of secure wireless sensor networks under node capture attacks. IEEE Trans. Inf. Forensics Secur. **12**(3), 557–571 (2017)
12. Kim, H.: Design of a secure digital recording protection system with network connected devices. In: AINA Workshops 2017, pp. 375–378 (2017)

Correction to: Automatic and Accurate Detection of Webshell Based on Convolutional Neural Network

Zhuo-Hang Lv, Han-Bing Yan, and Rui Mei

Correction to:
Chapter "Automatic and Accurate Detection of Webshell Based on Convolutional Neural Network"
in: X. Yun et al. (Eds.): *Cyber Security*, CCIS 970,
https://doi.org/10.1007/978-981-13-6621-5_6

In the version of this chapter that was originally published, the acknowledgment of the NSFC Foundation was missing. The chapter has been updated to include these corrections.

The updated version of this chapter can be found at
https://doi.org/10.1007/978-981-13-6621-5_6

X. Yun et al. (Eds.): CNCERT 2018, CCIS 970, pp. C1–C2, 2019.
https://doi.org/10.1007/978-981-13-6621-5_15

Author Index

www.ingramcontent.com/pod-product-compliance
Lightning Source LLC
LaVergne TN
LVHW082234200926
848484LV00008B/2355